Rubens to Picasso

Four Centuries of Master Drawings

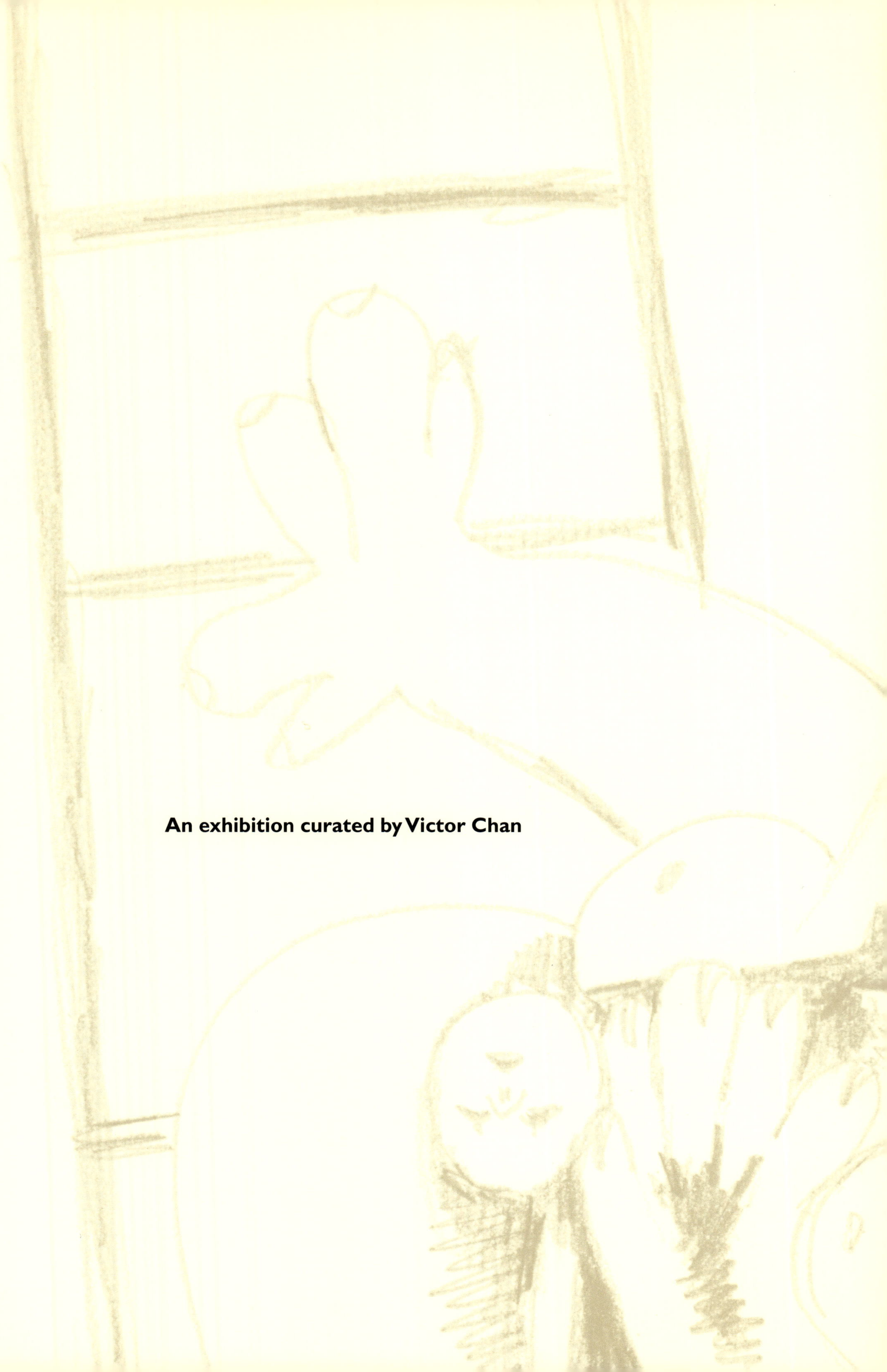

An exhibition curated by Victor Chan

Rubens to Picasso

Four Centuries of Master Drawings

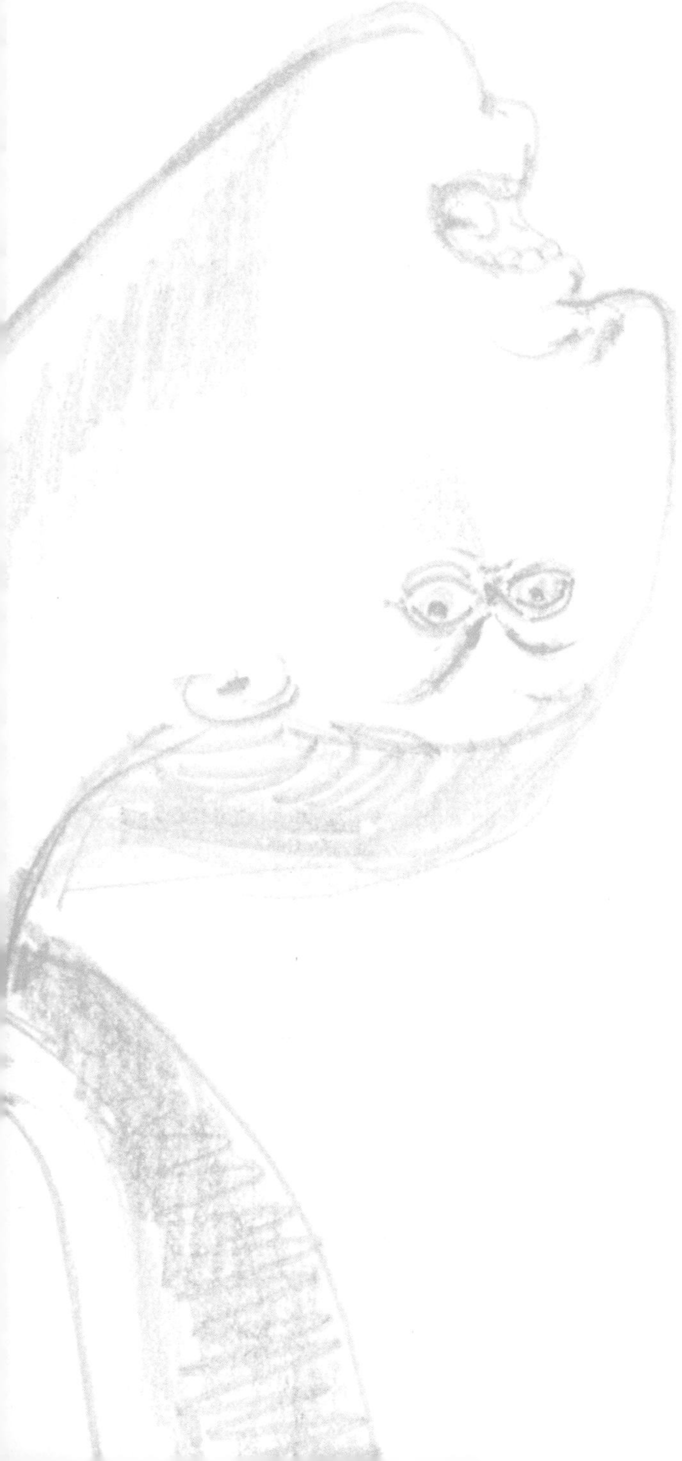

Department of Art and Design

University of Alberta

Canada 1995

Published by the Department of Art and Design, University of Alberta
in collaboration with The University of Alberta Press, Athabasca Hall,
Edmonton, Alberta, Canada T6G 2E8

Printed and bound in Canada 5 4 3 2 1

ISBN 0-88864-281-4

Book Credits

Graphic Designer | Susan Colberg
Photographer | Louise Asselstine
Editor | Shelley Wilson
Word Processer | Debbie Coulas
Film and Colour Separation | Screaming Colour, Edmonton, Canada
Printer | Quality Color Press, Edmonton, Canada

Exhibition Credits

Exhibition Curator | Victor Chan
Exhibition Director | Desmond Rochfort
Museums and Collections Services Director | Janine Andrews
Fine Arts Building Gallery Manager | Blair Brennan
Exhibition Designers | Bernd Hildebrandt and Jim Corrigan
Public Information Coordinator | Frannie Blondheim
Special Projects Coordinator | Anne Hayward
Exhibition Administrator | Tanya Harnett
Exhibition Assistants | Keith Rose, Dick Der, and Kyla Fischer

---

Canadian Cataloguing in Publication Data

Chan, Victor, 1947-
Rubens to Picasso

Catalog of an exhibition held at the Fine Arts Building Gallery
Sept. 16 - Oct. 30, 1995.
Includes bibliographical references.
ISBN 0-88864-281-4

1. Drawing--Exhibitions. I. University of Alberta. Dept. of
Art and Design. II. Title.
NC17.C2E34 1995 741.94'074'712334 C95-910873-4

Printed on acid free paper ∞

The University of Alberta Press would like to acknowledge, with gratitude,
the financial support provided by the Alberta Foundation for the Arts,
a beneficiary of the Lottery Fund of the Government of Alberta.

Contents

Acknowledgements

Rubens to Picasso: Four Centuries of Master Drawings is a unique cultural event in the life of this province and this university. Never before has an art exhibition that features the work of so many world-famous artists been shown in Alberta. That this exhibition is being presented exclusively in the University Department of Art and Design's Fine Arts Building Gallery makes it especially significant for us.

The exhibition *Rubens to Picasso: Four Centuries of Master Drawings* has come about as the result of the collaborative vision, hard work, commitment, planning, and most of all, the generosity of many people and organizations. The University of Alberta owes an enormous debt of gratitude to these people and organizations.

Above all, we owe the greatest debt to the owners of the drawings. The lending to the University of Alberta of these works — many of them are of great significance to the history of western art — is an act of extraordinary kindness and generosity. I wish therefore, on behalf of the University, to express a special thanks to the owners for giving us both the opportunity and the privilege of being able to present to the people of Alberta this unique exhibition.

All those in the business community and in the private sector whose generous contributions have helped make this exhibition possible also should be acknowledged. Their willingness to become partners in this important event is a testimony to the fact that the business community is not just the engine of our economic life, but, importantly, can also make crucial contributions to the realization and enhancement of the arts and culture in general.

Many members of the University community have helped, by their efforts and commitment, to make this exhibition possible. In particular I would like to thank my colleague, Dr. Victor Chan, Professor of Art History in the Department of Art and Design, and curator of *Rubens to Picasso: Four Centuries of Master Drawings*. It is through his vision and commitment that the exhibition has come about. His curating of the exhibit and his authorship of the accompanying catalogue are models of curatorial and scholarly achievement that will be remembered and referred to for many years to come. In the Department of Art and Design, several individuals have also played key roles in the team work for this project, most notably Susan Colberg, Graphic Designer; Blair Brennan, Manager of the Fine Arts Building Gallery and his assistant Shelley Wilson, editor of the catalogue; Dr. Jetske Sybesma, Professor of Art History; Stan Szynkowski, Administrative Professional Officer of the Department; Debbie Coulas, Chair's Secretary; Dick Der, Technician; Louise Asselstine, Photographer; Don Spence, Video Producer; Keith Rose, Technical Assistant and Kyla Fischer, Exhibition Assistant.

A very special thanks is due to the staff of the University of Alberta's Department of Museums and Collections Services. Their collaboration in and commitment to this event have been outstanding. Many of the most significant aspects of the planning and development of this exhibition could not have happened without the help and support of Janine Andrews, Director of Museums and Collections Services, and her staff: Bernd Hildebrandt, Exhibition Designer; Jim Corrigan, Exhibition Coordinator; Frannie Blondheim, Public Information Coordinator and Anne Hayward, Special Projects Coordinator.

In addition, the following persons in the University have made important contributions and given valuable assistance with the planning of this exhibition: Director of Campus Security Services Doug Langevin and Special Constable Dwight Bozak; Manager of Parking Services Allan Mah and Associate Director of Building Operations Kevin Moodie; Director of the Office of Public Affairs Tony Myers and Public Relations Officer Sandra Halme.

Thanks are also owed to Dr. Bill Bridger in the Office of the Vice President (Research), to former Acting President Dr. John McDonald and members of the President's Executive Committee for their imaginative and crucial initial support of this exhibition, and to the Faculty of Arts SAS Grants Committee for its support.

Finally, I would like to add my special thanks to University Chancellor Louis Hyndman; President Dr. Roderick Fraser; Board of Governors Chair John Ferguson; and Faculty of Arts Dean Dr. Patricia Clements; for all their support and assistance.

Dr. Desmond Rochfort
Chair, Department of Art and Design
Exhibition Director

Rubens to Picasso: Four Centuries of Master Drawings is presented by the Department of Art and Design, University of Alberta. The Department acknowledges with grateful thanks its private sector partners and sponsors, whose most generous support has helped to make this exhibition possible:

Sponsors

Syncrude Canada Limited
The Stanley Technology Group Incorporated
McLennan Ross Barristers and Solicitors
Canadian Utilities Limited
The Bank of Montreal
BML Security Incorporated
City Lumber and Millwork

Contributing Sponsors

AGT Mobility
Century Sales and Service Limited
Douglas Haynes
Ed Tel Mobility
KPMG Peat Marwick Thorne
Quality Color Press Incorporated
The Royal Bank
Studio Post and Transfer

Media and Promotion Sponsors

Canadian Broadcasting Corporation
The Edmonton Journal
Hook Outdoor Advertising

To FYC in fond memory
and MDS in gratitude

Introduction

Drawings are visually more veracious than paintings or sculptures. Often untouched by layers of textures and meanings, they are fresher, more vital, more spontaneous. As visual thoughts in progress, most drawings preserve and reveal the private and intimate struggles of artists coming to terms with their subjects at every stage of their careers. Drawings document the complicated process of learning, studying, experimenting, developing, mastering, transforming, and creating.

Although few drawings were exhibited publicly before the eighteenth century, the majority of artists stressed the importance of drawing. In the seventeenth century, Rubens specifically stated in his will that his own drawings were to be kept in the family for descendants who planned to go into his profession; only seventeen years after his death was the drawing collection dispersed. Picasso talked of his passion for drawing even during his teenage years in La Coruña, between 1892 and 1894:

> For being a bad student I was banished to the *calaboose* — a bare cell with whitewashed walls and a bench to sit on. I liked it there, because I took along a sketch pad and drew incessantly. . . . I think I provoked situations so that professors would punish me. I was isolated and no one bothered me — drawing, drawing, drawing. I could have stayed there forever drawing without a stop. True, all my life I've been in the habit of drawing, but in that cell it was a special pleasure — difficult to explain. It's not that I wanted to excel, rather to work — that's what one must always do.[1]

Perhaps few artists would emphasize so frequently and so eloquently the intellectual and practical significance of drawing as Ingres, one of the greatest draughtsmen of all times. He said, "Drawing is the probity of art" and insisted that "one must always draw, draw with your eyes if you cannot draw with a pencil." In his estimation, "drawing includes three-quarters and a half of what constitutes painting. If I had to put a sign over my door, I should inscribe it *School for Drawing*, and I am sure that I should produce painters."[2]

At least since the fourteenth century, drawing has been considered the basic training in art. Cennini advised students that they must study drawing for at least one year. Likewise, Leonardo repeated the primacy of drawing. Vasari recorded that in Bertoldo's sculpture school, which Michelangelo attended in 1490, drawings by Donatello, Brunelleschi, Masaccio, Uccello, Fra Angelico and Filippo Lippi were used, along with antique sculptures, as models for students. In 1563 Cosimo de Medici established the Accademia del Disegno (Academy of Drawing), a prototype for similar institutions not just in Italy, but also for those official art academies founded throughout Europe since the eighteenth century, and to a large extent, the art schools and programs of our own time. The curriculum in these institutions begins with drawing after the Old Masters and antique sculptures and then proceeds to life models. The examples of Rubens, Carracci, Fragonard, David, Ingres, Courbet, Degas, and Picasso in this exhibition will attest to this familiar pattern of artistic education well into this century. These copies — many of which were creative rather than merely imitative — allowed young artists to interpret and synthesize their sources, developing dialogues that would foster new solutions to future problems. Ingres' advise to the young Degas in 1855 was: "Make copies, young man, make copies. You can only become a good artist by copying the masters."[3] Degas went further: he suggested that the secret "is to follow the advice the masters give you in their works while doing something different from them."[4] But Degas was not the only one who drew after the masters. So did many nineteenth- and twentieth-century artists whom we consider radically independent, including Goya, Géricault, Delacroix, Manet, Courbet, van Gogh, Seurat, Cézanne, Matisse, and Picasso. Since drawings possess the quality of immediacy and informality, they have become the preferred medium for creative copies. The curriculum of drawing after the antique and the Old Masters thus forms part of the traditional "scientific" foundation of art education, considered to be as essential as the studies of anatomy, geometry, and perspective. To copy has been viewed as the embodiment of a rational approach to knowledge. Conservative academic training has always insisted that such practical knowledge is not merely a means, but an end.

Yet to provide a convincing naturalistic representation is to understand the world only in its external, physical appearance. Essentially, the practice is passive. Rodin suggested that "it is a false idea that drawing itself can be beautiful. It is only beautiful through the truths and the feelings that it translates."[5] As early as the seventeenth century, the *capriccio* drawings of Callot, and later those of Piazetta and Tiepolo, introduced an unconventional element. Since the late eighteenth century, when the entrenched art academies were facing critical challenges to their rigid routines, a notable change occurred in drawings. Beginning with the Romantics, greater emphasis is placed on individuality and the creation of new moods and symbols. Friedrich stated that "the artist's feeling is his law. Pure sensibility can never be unnatural; it is always in harmony with nature. But the feelings of another must never be imposed on us as our law." For Friedrich, "a painter should not merely paint what he sees in front of him, he ought to paint what he sees in himself."[6] So, for example, Romney's *Howard* drawings are intended to capture a sense of doom and despair. Géricault's drawings for *The Raft of the Medusa*, while resembling traditional anatomical studies, are meant to convey the horror and suffering of the passengers on the raft. This passion for dramatic effects would explain why he also did sketches of the severed heads and dissected limbs. By the late nineteenth century, many drawings were more often personal expressions than mere realistic depictions. The works of Seurat, Redon, Munch, Ensor, Gauguin, Hugo, Khnopff, Rodin, and van Gogh point in a new direction. The process of external representation has been modified to reveal the inner structure of reality and to suggest the psychological complexity of human emotions. But the growing anti-naturalism was not just a matter of visual stylistic changes. It underlines major ideological shifts. Traditional realism and naturalism in art had been associated with an established order — from the instructions of academies to the tastes and outlook of the bourgeoisie; parallels can be drawn in contemporary literature, science, and politics. Increasingly, realistic images have come to stand for conservative and anti-modern values. Thus the deliberate aversion to sensuous surface realism in the late nineteenth century reflects a broad spectrum of political and social ideologies ranging from anti-bourgeois attitudes to anarchism.

The accelerated momentum of industrialization and advances in science and technology, combined with a new political awareness, clearly intensified the opposition to naturalism in this century. No longer willing to remain merely observers, artists demanded their license and liberation — the right to transform, to distort, to invent. The Cubist revolution of Picasso and Braque launched the intellectual debate and presented the visual challenge. Drawings such as Braque's *Guitarist* of 1911 and Picasso's *Woman with a Dead Child* of 1937 consciously violate traditional canons of aesthetics, forcing the viewer to confront a new reality. Artists and viewers no longer deal with a continuous renewal of the familiar. Instead, their mental and visual perceptions are probed, questioned, and restructured. When facing the works of Picasso, Braque, Modigliani, Matisse, or Klee, we experience an increasingly subjective, inner inquiry about art. For these artists performed a challenging and daring act. But such an act encompasses more than artistic freedom. The complex process of dissecting, analysing, and reconstituting — resulting in a new way of seeing — goes beyond re-creation. It is creation. The process is about artistic empowerment. And it begins with drawing.

Footnotes

1 **Antonio D. Olano**, Interview with Picasso, quoted in Antonio L. Marino, "Los cuatro años de Picasso en La Coruña," in *Picasso La Coruña*, La Coruña, 1982, page 7.

2 **Henri Delaborde**, *Ingres, sa vie, ses travaux, ses doctrines*, Paris, 1870. Quoted and translated in Lorenz Eitner, *Neoclassicism and Romanticism 1750-1850: Sources and Documents*, Englewood Cliffs, 1970, Volume II, page 136.

3 **A. Vollard**, *Souvenirs d'un marchand de tableaux*, Paris, 1937, page 207.

4 **P.A. Lemoisne**, *Degas et son oeuvre*, Paris, 1946-49, Volume I, page 4.

5 **Auguste Rodin**, *On Art and Artists*, Introduction by Alfred Werner, New York, 1957, page 109.

6 **Lorenz Eitner**, *Neoclassicism and Romanticism 1750-1850: Sources and Documents*, Englewood Cliffs, 1970, Volume II, pages 54-55.

Balthasar van der Ast

1593/4 – 1657 | Dutch

Seashells

circa 1645-50
pen and wash in brown ink
131 x 226 mm
inscription:
B. van der Ast fec.

Balthasar van der Ast was the brother-in-law of Ambrosius Bosschaert the Elder, the founder of a dynasty of fruit and flower painters in Middelburg at the beginning of the seventeenth century. In 1609, following the death of his father, van der Ast moved in with the Bosschaerts and began his training as a floral artist in Bosschaert's studio. In 1613, he followed Bosschaert to Bergen op Zoom and then to Utrecht in 1619. After Bosschaert's death in The Hague in 1621, he stayed in Utrecht until 1632, then moved to Delft, where he died in 1657.

Although most of his early works strongly resemble his brother-in-law's, van der Ast's compositions show a greater variety and suppler brushwork. As well, his floral representations often include insects, snails, lizards, toads, and salamanders. His speciality, however, is compositions consisting entirely of seashells, as represented in this drawing. Almost certainly these still-life works of seashells were commissioned by shell collectors. Like the flowers and other objects depicted in the seventeenth-century Dutch *pronk Stilleven* (show-off still-lifes), these representations reveal not merely the artist's dazzling skills, but frequently were intended to convey symbolic meanings. Impressive floral pieces, sumptuous banquets, luxurious household items and equipment, and rare and expensive objects such as wines, animals, or shells mark the conspicuous display of wealth, power, and discernment. In seventeenth-century Holland, tropical seashells were rarities, highly prized objects for collectors' "curiosity cabinets." Geographically and economically, these exotic specimens underline the prowess of the seventeenth-century Dutch traders, explorers, collectors, and lords of the sea. But in addition, the seashell, as a symbol of eternity, would subtly suggest religious and philosophical meditation on the consequences of a conspicuously acquisitive society. An awareness of transience and advocacy of temperance are often evoked in such works. Paradoxically, while *pronks* blew the horn for those who owned them, they also signalled the arrival of the Day of Wrath. These representations of the Dutch Golden Age thus reveal the inherent tension of the era, the precarious balance between extravagant consumption and Calvinist morality.

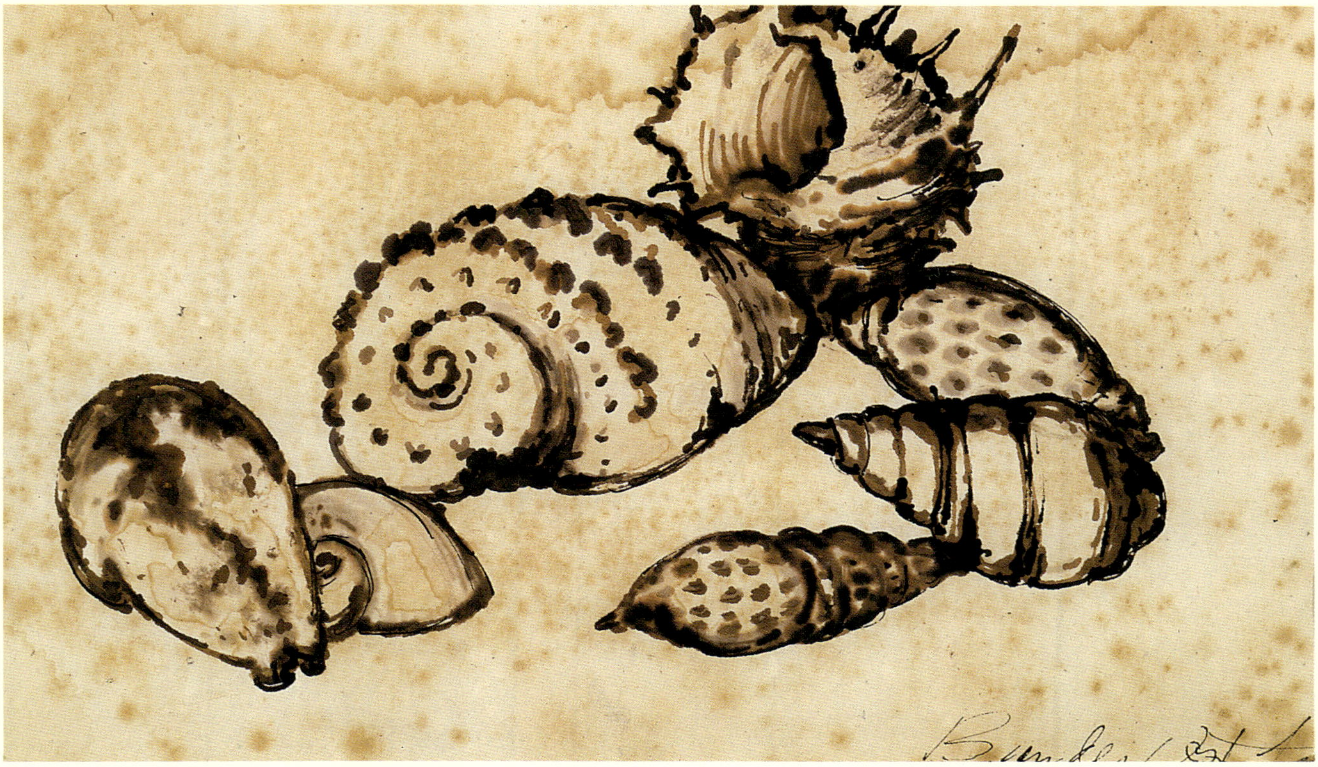

Seashells

circa 1645-50

pen and wash in

brown ink

131 x 226 mm

inscription:

B. van der Ast fec.

Georges Braque

1882 – 1963 | French

The Guitarist

circa 1911
black chalk and
sepia wash
322 x 245 mm
inscription:
signed *G. Braque*

Born in Argenteuil-sur-Seine, Braque moved with his family to Le Havre in 1890. There Braque attended evening classes at the École des Beaux-Arts in 1897. Two years later he apprenticed to a painter-decorator, M. Roney. He went to Paris in 1900 to continue his craftsman's training at the Cours Municipal of Batignolles. Between 1902 and 1904, he studied at the free Académie Humbert, and also briefly at the École des Beaux-Arts under Léon Bonnat. In the galleries of Durand-Ruel and Vollard and in the Louvre, he studied works ranging from Egyptian and Greek sculpture to Poussin and Corot. By 1905, through his friendship with Raoul Dufy and Othon Friesz, he was drawn into the Fauve circle and met Matisse, Derain, and Vlaminck; he also began to examine the works of Cézanne. In 1907, he exhibited in the Salon des Indépendants and the Salon d'Automne, and through Guillaume Apollinaire, went to Picasso's studio and saw *Les Demoiselles d'Avignon*. By 1909, he had formed a close friendship with Picasso and began his great Analytic and Synthetic Cubist periods. In 1911-12, he lettered his paintings and made the first *papier collé*. But his career was interrupted by the First World War. Wounded in the head at Carency, he recovered slowly, not painting again until 1917; Léonce Rosenberg became his dealer then. In the 1920s, he did a number of *décor* for the ballets of Diaghilev and Comte Etienne de Beaumont: *Les Fachaux* (1923-24), *Salade* (1924), and *Zéphyre et Flore* (1925). His first important retrospective was held in the Kunsthalle, Basle, in 1933, followed by others in London and Brussels in 1934 and 1936. The Carnegie Institute in Pittsburgh awarded his *Yellow Tablecloth* first prize at the International Exhibition in 1937, while 1939-40 saw a number of retrospectives, in Chicago, Washington, and San Francisco. In 1946, with Rouault, he exhibited his war time paintings at the Tate Gallery in London. At the Venice Biennale in 1948, he was awarded first prize for *The Billiard Table*. That year he began the series, *Studios*, *Birds*, and *Terraces*. In 1952-53, he worked on three ceiling paintings of *Birds* for the Etruscan Gallery in the Louvre and completed designs for three stained-glass windows for a chapel at Varengeville. His health had begun to decline by the time he finished the *Studios* and *Birds* series in 1956, and he died seven years later.

Between 1909 and 1912, Braque and Picasso, via different artistic routes and checking their competitive personalities, worked closely, equally, and wholeheartedly to create the new pictorial language of Cubism. Joined by Louis Marcoussis, Roger de la Fresnaye, Marcel Duchamp, Fernand Léger, Juan Gris, Albert Gleizes, Francis Picabia, and Robert Delaunay, Braque and Picasso began the Cubist fragmentation of the object, its multiple or simultaneous views, and its tactile representation of space. During the spring and summer of 1911, when he was staying and working with Picasso at Céret in the Pyrenees, Braque further dissected the solid structure of objects and figures into looser configurations of overlapping opaque, transparent, and refractive planes with superimposed scaffolding lines, as demonstrated in this drawing. Inspired perhaps by inscriptions in Gothic paintings and signs on café windows, he also introduced stencilled or commercial lettering into his works as a means of psychological surprise and dislocation. In the case of this drawing, "GB" may refer to his initials. The subject — a favourite Cubist urban theme of sidewalk cafés and street musicians — might have been derived from the important pioneer exhibition of Corot's figurative paintings of pensive women with musical instruments (circa 1860s-70s) organized in Paris in 1909. Braque produced at least three monumental figure paintings on this subject in 1911; the present drawing is closest to the painting called *The Portuguese* (Kunstmuseum, Basel.)

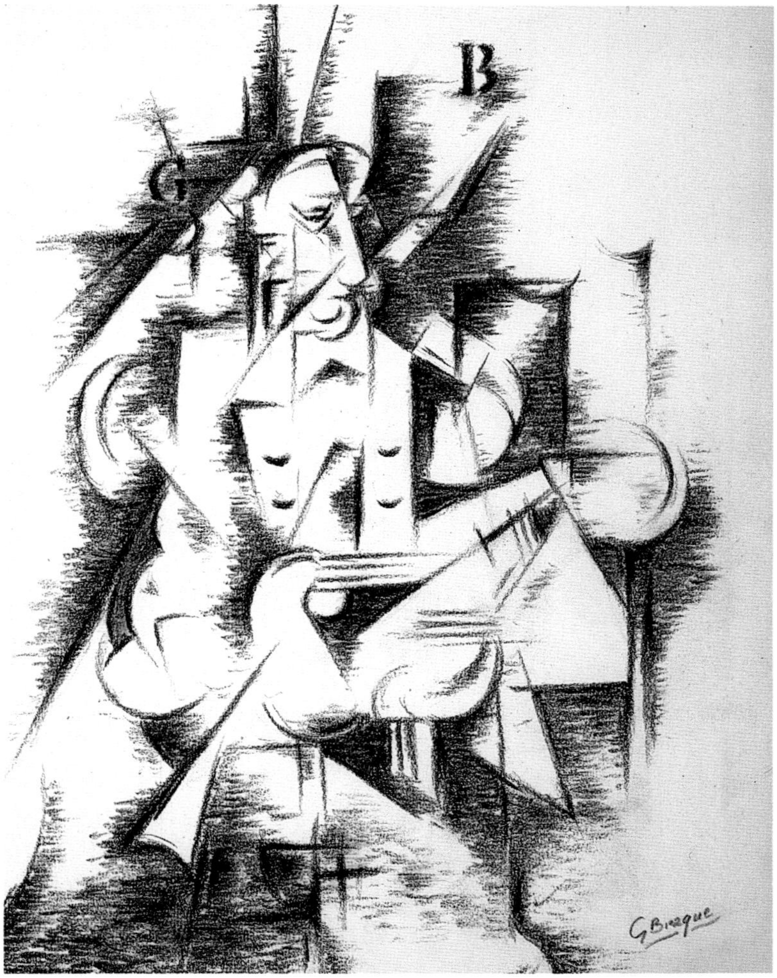

The Guitarist

circa 1911

black chalk and

sepia wash

322 x 245 mm

inscription:

signed *G. Braque*

Sir Edward Burne-Jones

1833 – 1898 | British

Study for "Le Chant d'Amour"

1865

graphite

206 x 122 mm

Born in Birmingham, Burne-Jones began taking evening courses at the Government School of Design in 1848. In 1853, intending to take holy orders, he enrolled at Exeter College, Oxford, where he met and formed close ties with William Morris. After encountering Pre-Raphaelite paintings in 1854-55 — Millais' *Return of the Dove* at Oxford, Holman Hunt's *Awakening Conscience* and *Light of the World* at the Royal Academy, and especially the works of Rossetti — and meeting with Thomas Combe, director of the Clarendon Press in Oxford, both Burne-Jones and William Morris decided to abandon theology in favour of painting. In 1856, Burne-Jones met Rossetti and the art critic John Ruskin. Giving up his studies at Oxford, he moved to London and became Rossetti's student. During 1857-58, he assisted Rossetti on the mural decoration in the Oxford Union. Between 1859 and 1873, he repeatedly visited Italy, where he came under the influence of Mantegna, Botticelli, and Michelangelo. In 1861, with Philip Webb, Rossetti, and Morris, he became a founder member of the famous Morris, Marshall, Faulkner & Co.; the London firm sold furniture, stained-glass windows, ceramics, furnishing fabrics, and *objets d'art*. His teaching career began at the Working Men's College (1859-61). In 1864, he was elected associate of the Old Water-Colour Society. His first exhibition at the Grosvenor Gallery in 1877 caused a great sensation. Subsequently, he participated in every showing there for the next ten years. In 1878, he visited Paris, where his *Beguiling of Merlin* was shown at the World's Fair. That year he also gave evidence for Ruskin in the notorious Ruskin vs. Whistler libel trial. He was honoured with degrees from Oxford in 1881 and 1883. In 1885 he became president of the Birmingham Society of Artists and an associate of the Royal Academy. In the 1880s he began exhibiting in the Royal Academy and the New Gallery in Regent Street. After the exhibition of his *King Cophetua and the Beggar Maid* at the Paris World's Fair of 1889, he received the French Legion of Honour. In 1894, he was created a baronet by Queen Victoria. Like Richard Wagner, Burne-Jones was adored by other late nineteenth-century artists; he was the idol of the "Temple of Aesthetes."

Among the artists of his time, Burne-Jones was perhaps the most literarily inspired: almost all his works were derived from written texts and legends. *Le Chant d'Amour*, for which this drawing is a study of the central music-playing female figure, was based on an old Breton song: "Hélas! je sais un chant d'amour,/ Triste ou gai, tour à tour." Typical of his works in the early 1860s in its Chaucerian spirit and Giorgionesque representation, this picture captures the essence of Pre-Raphaelitism, its poetic symbolism, languid unearthiness, and subdued sensuality. A finished watercolour version of *Le Chant d'Amour*, dated 1865, is in the Museum of Fine Arts, Boston. A gouache version, dated 1866, is in a private collection, and the large oil version, exhibited in the Grosvenor Gallery in 1878, is in the Metropolitan Museum, New York.

Study of a King from "The Wheel of Fortune"

circa 1871 graphite 260 x 190 mm

inscription: signed *E.B-J*

The idea of *The Wheel of Fortune* was developed independently from a triptych illustrating the story of Troy that Burne-Jones conceived in 1870. He made at least six versions of this subject between 1871 and 1885; the largest and best-known version, shown in the Grosvenor Gallery in 1883, is in the collection of Vicomtesse de Noailles in Paris.

This study of one of the kings on Fortune's Wheel, with his massive torso and languishing pose and expression, was derived from a number of Italian sources: Michelangelo's *Dying Slave* in the Louvre; his *Captives* in the Accademia, Florence, as well as his

Deposition in the National Gallery, London; a king figure in Annibale Carracci's *Christ in Glory* in the Galleria Pitti, Florence; and the works of Leonardo da Vinci. Burne-Jones copied these works in an Italian sketchbook dated 1871 (Mary Chamot collection); he also owned a small plaster version of Michelangelo's *Dying Slave*. A number of related graphite studies for this figure are in the Fitzwilliam Museum, Cambridge, and the Birmingham Museum and Art Gallery.

Study of the Head of "Nimuë"

circa 1872-73 red chalk and graphite 215 x 170 mm

inscription: signed *E.B-J*

This study of Nimuë's head is for the painting called *Beguiling of Merlin*, commissioned by Frederick Leyland for his Prince's Gate residence in 1872 (now in the Lady Lever Art Gallery, Port Sunlight), and exhibited in the Paris World's Fair of 1878. The subject is based on the medieval legend of Merlin, lulled by Nimuë to sleep in a hawthorne tree in the Forest of Broceliande. The model for Nimuë was Maria Zambaco, a Greek beauty having glorious red hair and almost phosphorescent white skin with whom Burne-Jones was deeply in love. Maria Zambaco, was born Maria Cassavetti in Athens in 1843; her grandfather founded a prosperous cotton import business in London. She married a Greek doctor, Demetrius Zambaco, in Paris in 1861 but left him to return to London in 1864. Burne-Jones met her soon after and their relationship caused a great stir in the late 1860s. (Burne-Jones had married Georgiana MacDonald in 1860.) She was an important influence on Burne-Jones, who drew and painted her many times in the late 1860s and 1870s. As well as the intimate relationship, Maria Zambaco might have embodied the Greek ideal Burne-Jones sought in his works.

Other studies of Nimuë are in the Fitzwilliam Museum, Cambridge. A large gouache hangs in the Delaware Art Museum, Wilmington.

Study of Andromeda

1887 graphite 320 x 229 mm

inscription: signed and dated *E.B-J 1877*

This Andromeda drawing is related to the painting *The Doom Fulfilled* from the Perseus series, representing Perseus slaying the sea monster to which Andromeda was to have been sacrificed. The Perseus series was commissioned in 1875 by Arthur Balfour, a statesman and philosopher, for the music room in his London house. Burne-Jones's choice of the Perseus subject was undoubtedly influenced by William Morris's earlier treatment of the same theme in *The Doom of King Acrisius* in *The Earthly Paradise*. The Perseus series, consisting of four large oils, was completed in 1892 (Stuttgart Stattsgalerie). Numerous drawings, gouache panels, and full-scale cartoons are now in the Southampton Art Gallery, the Huntington Hartford of New York, the Tate Gallery, the Victoria and Albert Museum, the Fitzwilliam Museum, and private collections. A similar graphite drawing of *Andromeda*, dated 1885, is in the British Museum.

Study of the Head of "Nimuë"

circa 1872-73

red chalk and graphite

215 x 170 mm

inscription: signed *E.B-J*

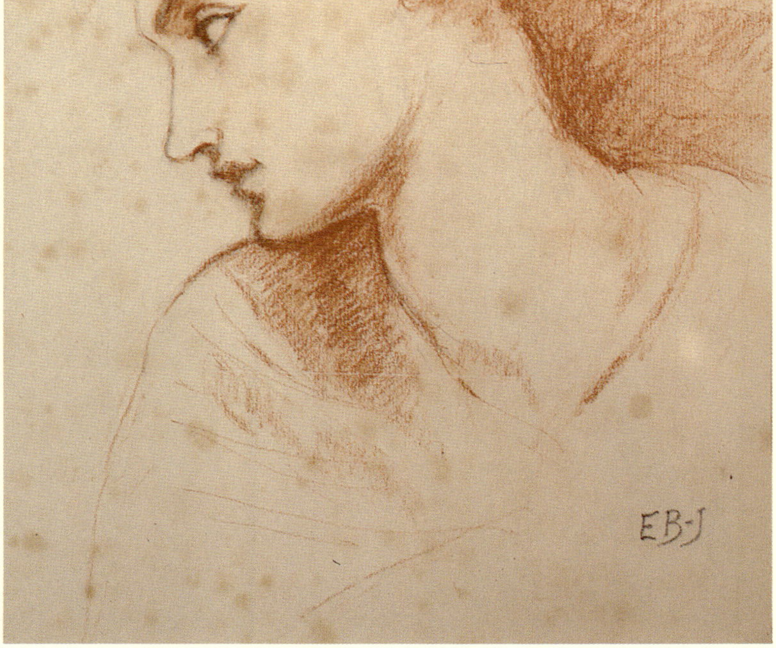
EB-J

Gustave Caillebotte

1848 – 1894 | French

Woman Reading

circa 1875
black chalk
highlighted
with white
310 x 208 mm
inscription:
signed on verso
G. Caillebotte

Born in Paris, Caillebotte was the son of prosperous parents, originally from Normandy, who ran a successful textile business and owned considerable real-estate in Paris. In 1868, Caillebotte was in the army briefly, but he purchased a replacement in 1869-70 in order to pursue legal studies. However, during the Franco-Prussian War, he was in active service again. In 1872, he began art studies with the popular Salon artist, Léon Bonnat, through whose sponsorship he was admitted to the École des Beaux-Arts in 1873. He met Degas and the other Impressionists in 1874, when they were holding their first group exhibition. That year was indeed the turning point for Caillebotte: he committed himself to the Impressionist cause, undoubtedly aided by a substantial inheritance from his father, who died that same year. After his rejection by the official Salon in 1875, he was invited to join the second Impressionist exhibition in 1876. His eight works there, with their curious perspective and proletarian realism created a stir. But his presence in the Impressionist group was more than that of a participant, he was also an essential financial supporter: he purchased his colleagues' works at generous prices. In addition, he funded the Impressionist exhibitions of 1877 and 1878. His will, drafted in 1876, guaranteed continued support of the Impressionist cause and declared the posthumous gift of his Impressionist collection to the state, on the condition that it would eventually be placed in the Louvre. He was especially committed to the Impressionist painters; he was often in their company, meeting in cafés and boating at Argenteuil. By 1877, his works, in style and subject, were becoming more Impressionist — in line with Monet, Renoir, and Sisley — looser in structure and brushwork. Themes like boaters and bathers reflect the open-air aspect of Impressionism. In the early 1880s, his compositions became bolder and more innovative; they were praised by the critic and novelist, J.K. Huysmans. Yet, at the same time, the Impressionist group was fast disintegrating, owing to internal dissension. Caillebotte finally abdicated all responsibility for organizing the 1882 Impressionist exhibition after failing to unite all the factions. By 1882, the artists he advocated and supported — Monet, Renoir, and others — began to seek out their own dealers and collectors. At this point Caillebotte retreated from the Parisian scene to his home in Petit-Gennevilliers, near Argenteuil, but he remained close to Renoir and continued to correspond with Monet. Among his new circle of friends were the younger Neo-Impressionists, Paul Signac and George Seurat. In 1888, he was invited to exhibit with Les XX in Brussels. His works in the 1880s are dominated by pure landscapes, marine views, and still-lifes. The Durand-Ruel Gallery organized a retrospective of his works a few months after his death in 1894. And after some difficult negotiations, a portion of his Impressionist collection was accepted by the government; although many important works by Manet, Monet, Renoir, and Pissarro were rejected.

Caillebotte's works, in his formative years from the middle to late 1870s, were mostly based on themes from his family life. After his father's death in 1874, he continued to live with his widowed mother, his brothers and sisters, and painted in a studio in the family home on the rue de Miromesnil. The family also owned a summer property at Yerres, near Paris. Not surprisingly, many of his early works represent the surrounding in Yerres — the river, the woods, the farm, and boating. In addition, he often painted his mother and sisters sewing, reading, and embroidering, in the Dutch genre tradition. In the second Impressionist exhibition, in 1876, he showed *Portraits à la campagne*, painted the previous year, which depicts his mother and sisters reading and sewing in the garden of their home at Yerres. The present drawing is probably related to this group of images, the figure representing one of Caillebotte's sisters.

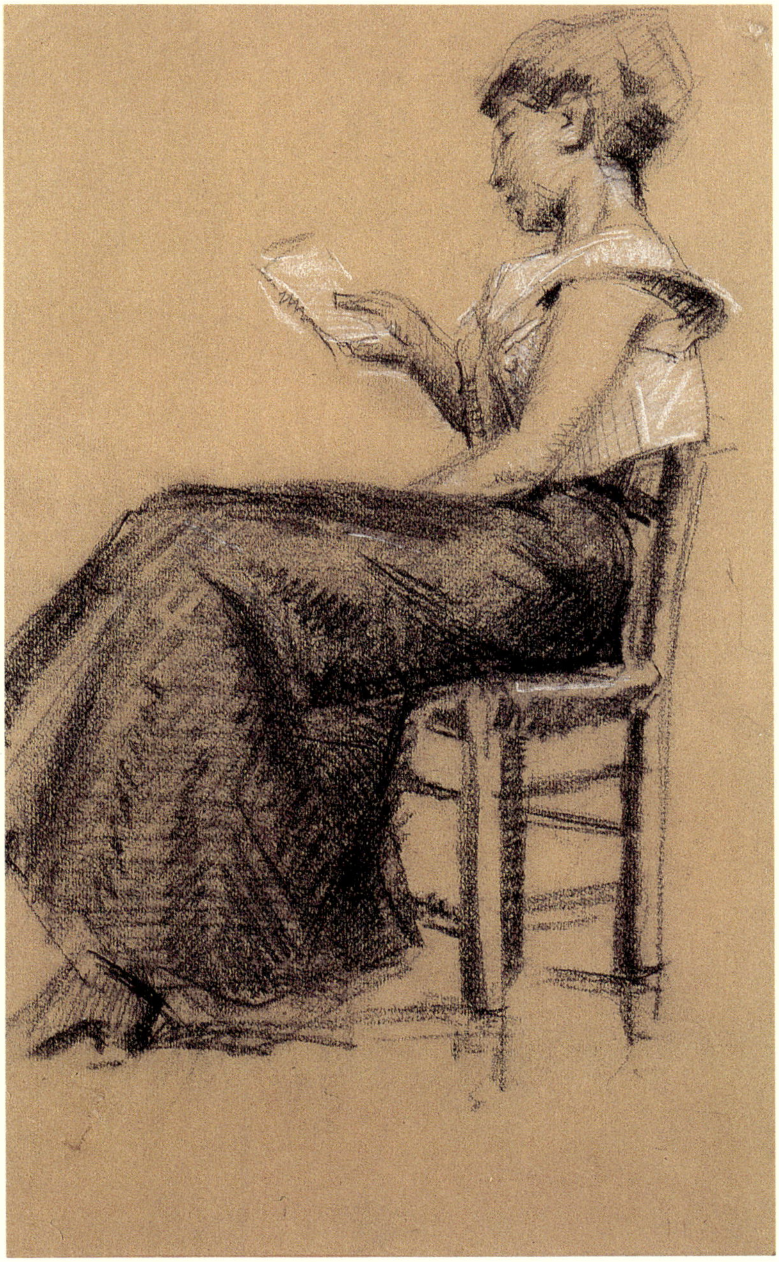

Woman Reading

circa 1875
black chalk
highlighted
with white
310 x 208 mm
inscription:
signed on verso
G. Caillebotte

Jacques Callot

1592/3 – 1635 | French

Figure Studies for the "Balli di Sfessania": Fritellino, Cap. Bombardon and Metzetin

circa 1620 graphite 225 x 280 mm

inscription: *Jac Callot Fec.*

Figure Studies for the "Balli di Sfessania": Smaraolo Cornuto and Ratsa di Boio (?)

circa 1620 red chalk 110 x 180 mm

Figure Study for the "Balli di Sfessania": Coviello (?)

circa 1620 red chalk 120 x 80 mm

One of the greatest printmakers, Callot was born in Lorraine, at Nancy. In 1607, he apprenticed to the Nancy goldsmith, Demange Crocq. Between 1608 and 1611, he lived in Rome, where he shared the studio of his compatriot, the engraver Philippe Thomassin, and began engraving works by Flemish artists and late Mannerist works in Roman churches. His career began in 1611 when he moved to Florence, where he joined the Medici court of the grand duke, Cosimo II, an art patron and a lover of festivals and celebrations. In 1621, he returned to Nancy. His works became increasingly serious, culminating in his most famous series of etchings, the *Grandes Miseres de la Guerre* in 1633 — a horrifying record of the Thirty Years War.

It was during his Florentine period in the service of the Medicis that Callot produced most of his theatrical works. His Medici commissions consisted of illustrations for the published descriptions and the dramatic text of spectacles organized by the court: *The War of Love* and *The War of Beauty* in 1616, the *Intermezzi* in 1617, *Solimano* in 1619-20 and *The Combat at the Barrier* in 1627. In addition, Callot began producing images representing the *commedia dell' arte* in about 1616-17. His fascination with the Italian comedians continued even after his return to Nancy in 1621, where he etched the *Balli di Sfessania*, an extensive series of prints on the *commedia dell'arte*. All three of the present drawings are directly related to this project. (Most drawings for this series are now in the Hermitage and the British Museum; the complete set of *Balli di Sfessania* etchings can be found in the Rosenwald and Baumfeld Collections in the National Gallery, Washington D.C.)

The *Balli di Sfessania* representations, while resembling pure artistic fantasies, were inspired by the impromptu street entertainment that flourished in Italian cities, especially during carnivals. As such, Callot's series forms a visual document of early seventeenth-century theatrical history and performances. Throughout the twenty-four small plates in the series, Callot arranged the comedians in pairs, many of them masked; they are shown interacting with each other in rapid movements and bodily contortions. In some plates the figures are engaged in acrobatic dancing or playing musical instruments. The drawings, perhaps more than the etchings, capture these improvised gestures, attitudes, and movements in the most imaginative and convincing way.

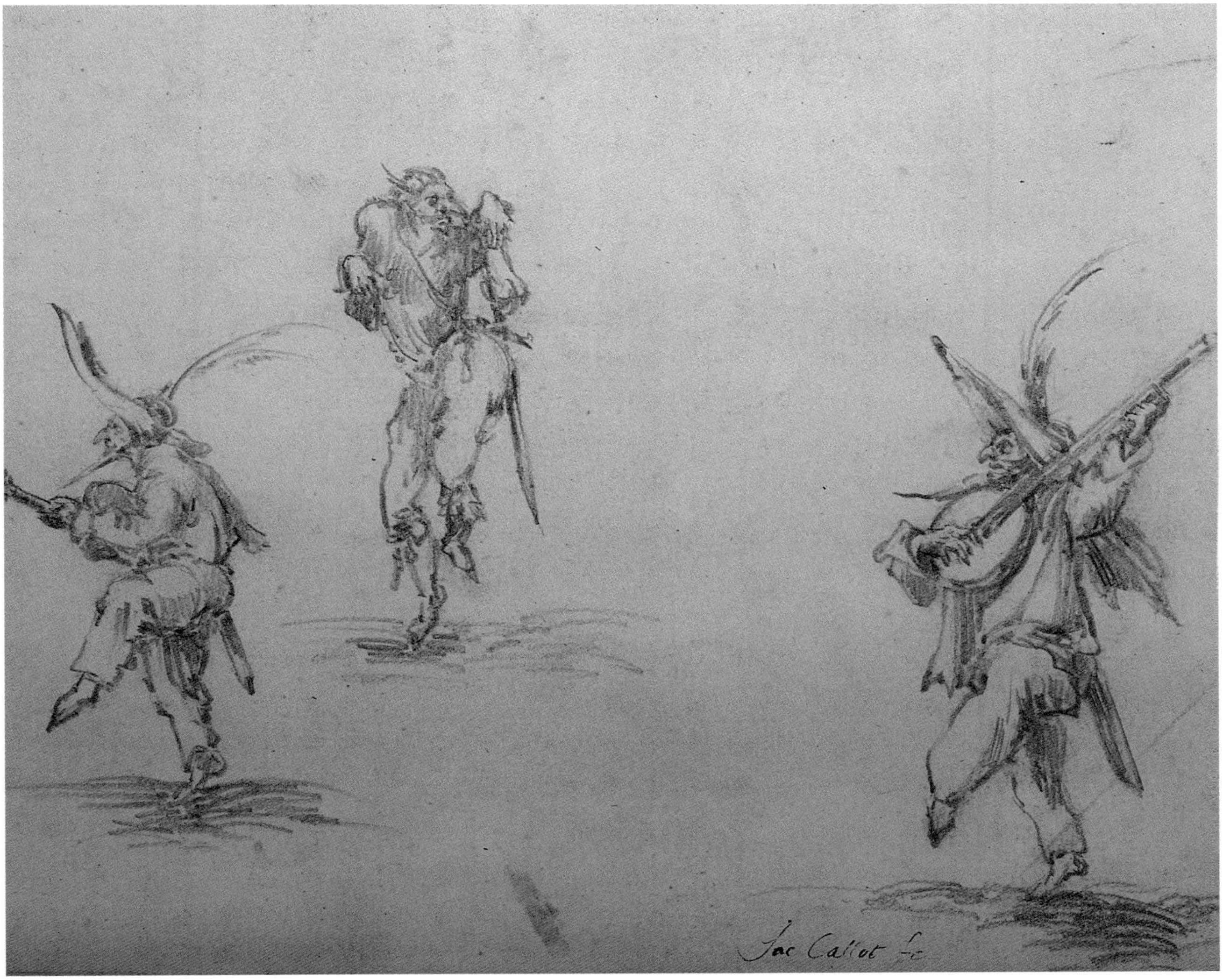

Figure Studies for the "Balli di Sfessania": Fritellino, Cap. Bombardon and Metzetin

circa 1620 graphite 225 x 280 mm

inscription: *Jac Callot Fec.*

Giovanni Antonio Canal (Canaletto)

1697 – 1768 | Italian

Three Figure Studies

circa 1728-30
black chalk, pen and brown ink
131 x 72 mm
102 x 61 mm
131 x 63 mm
inscription:
signed *Canaletto*

Canaletto was born at S. Lio, in Venice, where his father was a highly respected painter of theatrical scenery for Baroque operas. In 1719, Canaletto was his father's assistant in Rome, but he returned to Venice the following year. From 1720 to 1767, he was listed in the Venetian guild. As a Venetian *vedutista* ("painter of views"), his early works were influenced by Carlevaris, the founder of the Venetian school of *vedute*, as well as Marco and Sebastiano Ricci. His early patrons included Stefano Conti, a Luccan textile merchant, and Zaccari Sagredo. In 1726, Owen McSwiney, an Irishman living in Italy, recommended Canaletto to the duke of Richmond to collaborate with other artists on a series of paintings of English historical figures; Canaletto painted the "perspectives and landscapes." With the promotion of McSwiney and Joseph Smith, an art dealer and later British consul to Venice (1744), he began to paint sunny views of piazzas, piazettas, and the Grand Canal for various clients, especially English aristocratic patrons. During the 1730s and 1740s, Smith even produced various editions of his paintings, titled *Prospectus*, to further his reputation and popularity in England. The duke of Bedford and the second earl of Normanton, among many others, eagerly collected his Venetian topographical paintings. But in the early 1740s, Canaletto's career suffered a setback, due partly to the War of the Austrian Succession in 1741 and partly to the new competition posed by Michele Marieschi, whose Venetian view album was published in 1741. Smith now encouraged him to devote more time to etchings and drawings and continued to provide commissions. In 1746, Canaletto went to England, where he stayed until about 1755, painting English views and *capricci* for Sir Hugh Smithson (later earl of Somerset), the duke of Richmond, and the duke of Beaufort. Returning to Italy, he was elected to the Venetian academy in 1763, five years before his death.

Although many of Canaletto's early works were painted on the spot, his later paintings were nearly all based on drawings, some of which were probably made with the use of a *camera obscura*. However, regardless of his working methods, Canaletto consciously constructed his views of cities with firmness, precision, and order. Apart from the brilliant use of light and colour and the diminishing perspective, his *vedute* of Venice, London, and Rome sensitively combine a collection of urban buildings and the activities of the local communities. His urban views are always animated with lively and engaging vignettes of figures — individuals — in various attitudes and poses. As these three small fragments indicate, his figures are also rich in character, costume, and social variety — Jews, Turks, noblemen, workers, women, and children. They do not merely enhance, but enliven and form an essential and inseparable part of the elaborate architectural framework of every composition. The civic vitality and the theatre of life Canaletto captured in his works are totally dependent on these human accents.

Most likely these three fragments originally belonged to the same sheet and might have come from one of Canaletto's sketchbooks. The figures are related to the painting *Piazza S. Marco: Looking East Along the Central Line* (circa 1730), now in the Metropolitan Museum, New York.

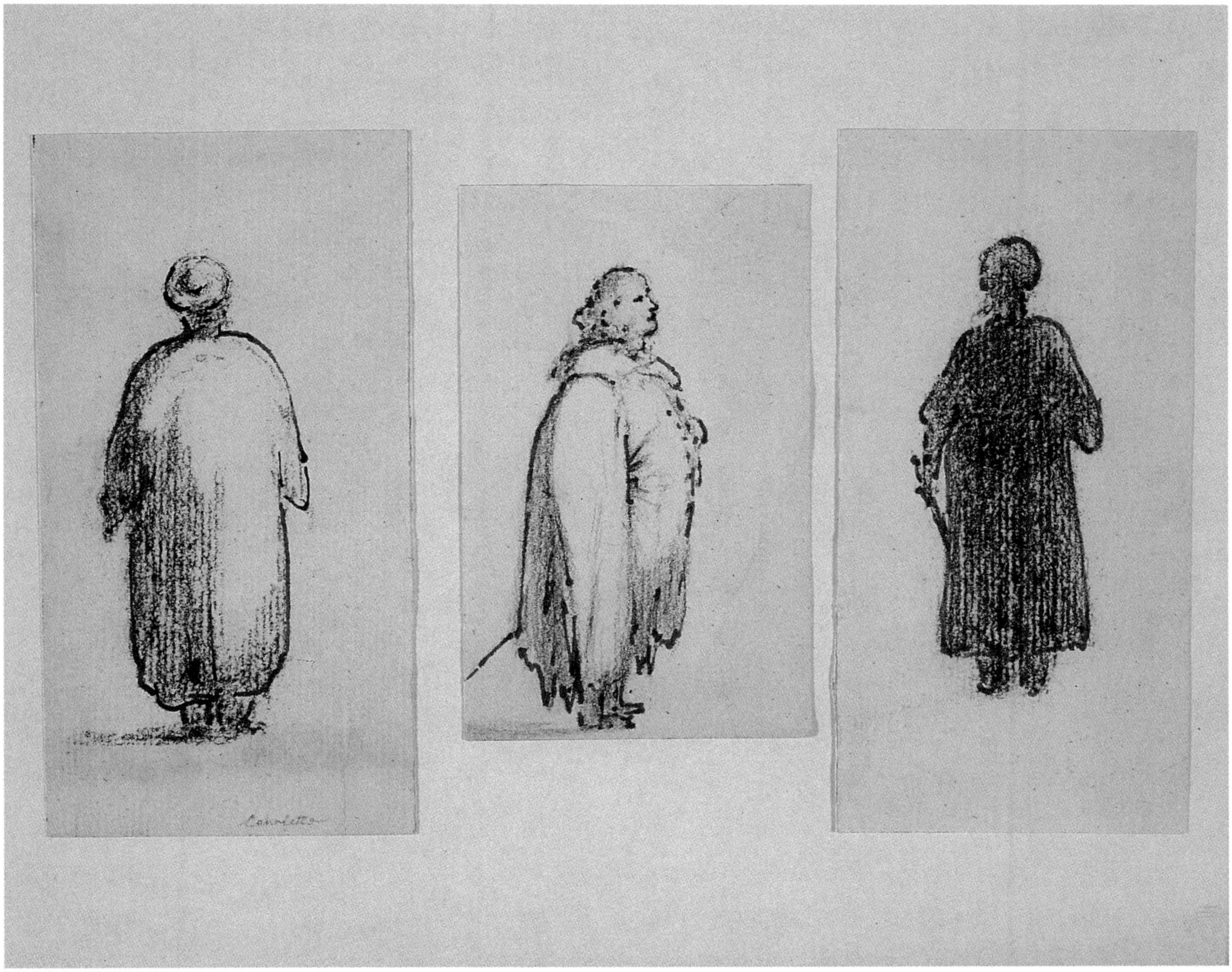

Three Figure Studies

circa 1728-30
black chalk, pen
and brown ink
131 x 72 mm
102 x 61 mm
131 x 63 mm
inscription:
signed *Canaletto*

Ludovico Carracci

1555 – 1619 | Italian

Study of a Hand and Legs

circa 1592
pen and brown ink
350 x 205 mm
inscription:
par Louis Carrache

At the dawn of the seventeenth century, three Carraccis — Ludovico and his two cousins, Agosinto and Annibale — were responsible for revitalizing the grand classical tradition in Italian art in spite of the prevailing artificiality and complexity of Bolognese Mannerism. In 1585-86, they founded a teaching academy in Bologna, the Accademia degli Incamminato, which was to become the most celebrated of its kind. It educated a whole generation of major Bolognese painters including Domenichino, Albani, Guido Reni, and Guercino. One of the founding principles of this private art academy was a special emphasis on life drawing and draughtsmanship. In 1595, however, the Carraccis broke up. Annibale left for Rome; Agostino followed two years later. Ludovico remained in Bologna to run the academy.

Ludovico, who had studied with Prospero Fontana and Camillo Procaccini and travelled throughout Italy, was the most traditional of the three Carraccis. While it is often difficult to distinguish the works of the three Carraccis before the early 1580s, since they shared many of their projects from a common studio, Ludovico's development became increasingly separated from his cousins' from the mid-1580s onwards. Ludovico's compositions are characterized by their conventional restraint and aloofness. Great stress is placed on the gestures and glances of the figures and on colouristic principles. His art represents a form of studied, superficial classicism, with a veneer of elegant sweetness and a sense of decorative patterns.

Compared to the classicism of his cousin Annibale, Ludovico appears far more Baroque, painterly, and emotional, especially in the handling of light and colour. This is borne out by some works of the 1590s such as *The Preaching of St. John* of 1592 (Pinacotecca, Bologna), for which the present drawing was produced as a study for the figure of the boatman. The painting, whose qualities to some extent are reflected in the drawing, shows the strong influence of the Venetians Correggio, Veronese, and Tintoretto. As Rudolf Wittkower has perceptive-ly remarked: "Ludovico's whole trend in these years [was] towards the colossal, the passionate, dramatic and heroic, towards rich movement and surprising and capricious light effects."

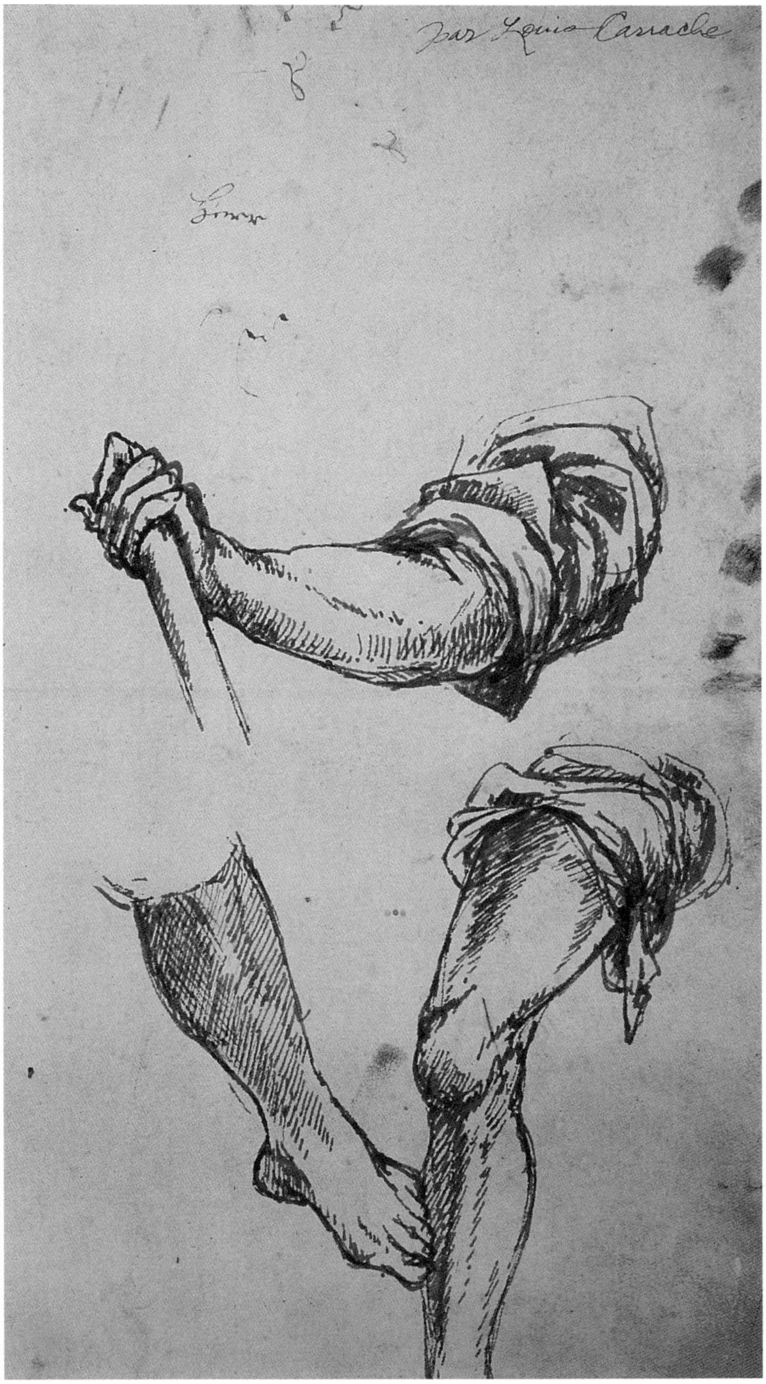

Study of a Hand and Legs

circa 1592

pen and brown ink

350 x 205 mm

inscription:

par Louis Carrache

Paul Cézanne

1839 – 1906 | French

Portrait of Madame Cézanne

1877
black-gray wash over graphite
245 x 150 mm
inscription: signed *P. Cézanne*

Cézanne was born in Aix-en-Provence, the son of a wealthy banker, who wanted him to study the law. In 1861, he abandoned his legal studies and attended the Académie Suisse in Paris. He befriended Pissarro, Guillemet, Bazille, Monet, Renoir, and Sisley and began to study the works of Poussin, Delacroix, and Courbet. Between 1864 and 1870, he lived alternately in Aix and Paris. His works were repeatedly rejected by the Salon. In 1874, he participated in the first Impressionist exhibition, on the insistence of Pissarro and despite the opposition of the other exhibitors. He refused to join the second Impressionist exhibition in 1876, but was back at the third in 1877, where he encountered great public hostility. Shortly after, he began to break away from Impressionism. In the early 1880s, he worked at Médan, Aix, L'Estagne, Paris, and La Roche-Guyon, occasionally in the company of Zola, Pissarro, or Renoir. In 1889, he exhibited with Les XX in Brussels and was included in the Paris World's Fair that year. The early 1890s was an extremely fertile period: he produced different versions of *The Card Players*, the series of *Baigneuses* and that of *Montagne Sainte-Victoire*. By 1900, his reputation began to spread. By 1904, at the Salon d'Automne, an entire room was devoted to his work, and the Galerie Cassirer in Berlin gave him a one-man exhibition. Earlier in 1901, he had purchased a property on the Chemin des Lauves, on a hill overlooking Aix, where he continued to work until his death in 1906.

Cézanne met his future wife, Hortense Fiquet (b. 1850) in 1869 in Paris, and the following year the two were together in L'Estaque, where Cézanne was staying to avoid the draft for the Franco-Prussian War. Cézanne kept the liaison from his father, fearing a reduction of his allowance. In 1872, Hortense gave birth to a son. Cézanne's father discovered the secret two years later. Although Cézanne denied the relationship and the existence of his child, his father did reduce his allowance. Thus when he painted *Madame Cézanne in a Red Chair* (Museum of Fine Arts, Boston), for which this drawing is a study, he was in financial straits and under considerable stress. In the end, his friend Emile Zola promised and provided generous financial support. The final reconciliation with his father was probably brought about by Cézanne's mother, and the artist and Hortense were married in 1886, months before his father's death. By then, the marriage was in name only, perhaps undertaken to legitimize their son. Cézanne continued to work and live in Aix while Hortense stayed in Paris with the boy. Ironically, Cézanne rarely painted any other woman from life and Hortense continued to pose for him into the 1890s.

Montagne Sainte-Victoire

circa 1904-06 graphite 310 x 260 mm
inscription: signed *P. Cézanne*

Although Cézanne's *Montagne Sainte-Victoire* series was begun in the 1890s, it was not until 1901, after Cézanne built his studio in the hills of Les Lauves, to the north of Aix and overlooking the town, that he discovered a new panoramic view of the mountain. Seen from above his studio, Mont Sainte-Victoire, remote but imposing, is an irregular triangle, with its long back rising gently to the abrupt cliff front; below lies a vast undulating plain of fields and clusters of trees. Floating ethereally in the southern light, Sainte-Victoire is the symbol of Provence. Here in the turbulent, densely textured surroundings, the mountain remains immobile, static, and timeless, a balance of energy and repose. As Cézanne said: "The landscape thinks itself in me and I am its conscience."

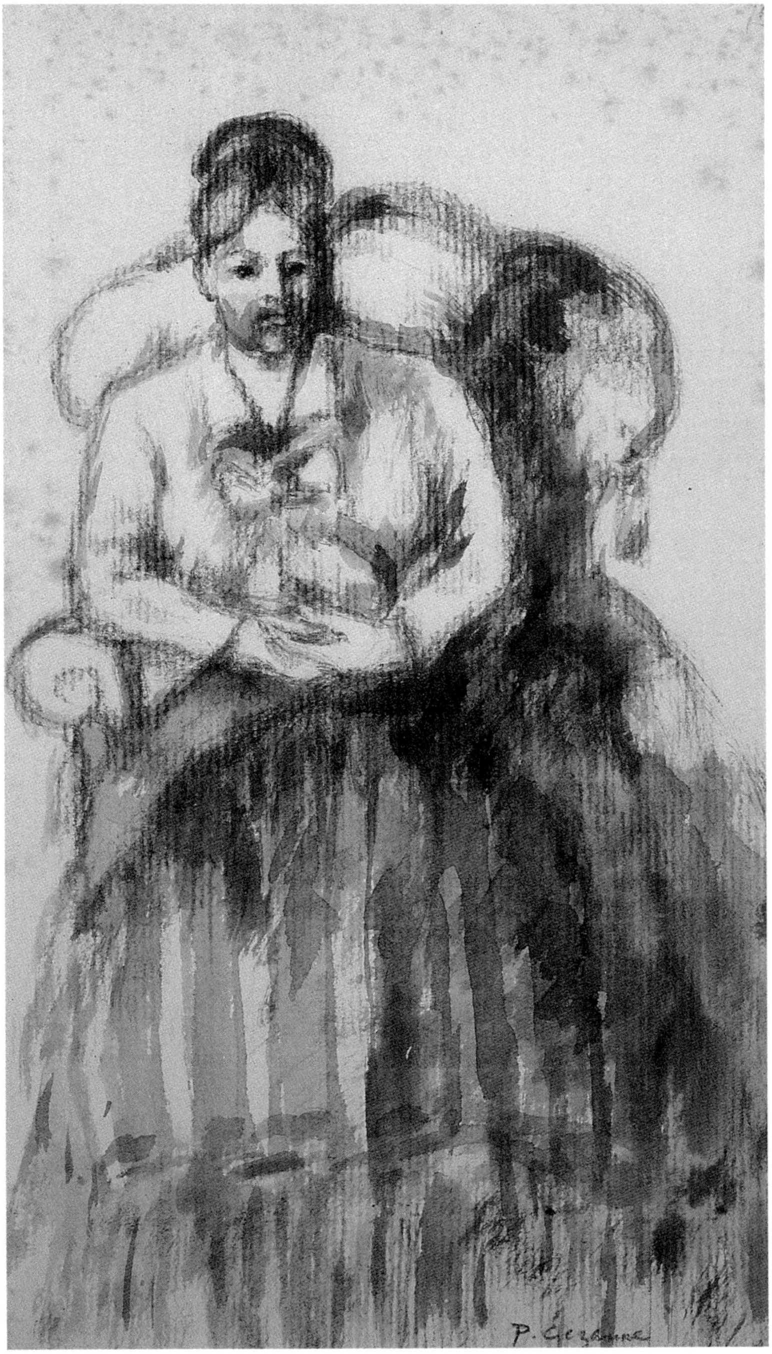

Portrait of Madame Cézanne

1877

black-gray wash over graphite

245 x 150 mm

inscription: signed *P. Cézanne*

Jean Baptiste Siméon Chardin

1699 – 1779 | French

Three-Cornered Hat

circa 1738
red chalk
90 x 140 mm
inscription:
J.B.S. Chardin F.

Probably the finest eighteenth-century French painter of still-life and genre, Chardin was the student of Pierre-Jacques Cazes and Noël-Nicolas Coypel, and a member of the Académie de Saint-Luc. In 1728, at the Salon de la Jeunesse, an open-air exhibition at the Place Dauphine, his two still-lifes, *La raie* and *Le buffet*, attracted the attention of the painter Largillierre, who immediately invited him to enter the French Royal Academy as "peintre des fleurs, fruits et sujets de caractere." During the 1730s and 1740s, Chardin produced still-lifes and intimate domestic genres that were eagerly collected by patrons and highly esteemed by fellow artists. From 1755 on, he had the very delicate and important position of official *tapissier* ("placer of pictures") in the academy Salons, attesting to his "good sense and good judgment." The encyclopedist and art critic Denis Diderot, beginning with his Salon review of 1761, became Chardin's spokesman. Diderot praised Chardin, saying: "Welcome back, great magician, with your mute compositions! How eloquently they speak to the artist! How much they tell him about the representation of nature, the science of colour and harmony! How freely the air flows around these objects." Indeed, Chardin hides his painstaking effort under the guise of ease. Created patiently and slowly, Chardin's works are richly textured and intensely concentrated; he is the consummate disciplined creator. Both his style and subject emphasize a sense of gravity, an immutable work ethic, and a world of honesty, understanding, and reassuring dependability. Chardin's objects are like "familiar old friends." Their convincing modesty, tenderness, and human warmth often conceal eye-deceiving technical effects.

Among Chardin's great gifts is his profound feeling for childhood and its pastimes. His portraits of children are especially moving and intelligent. Often in these pictures, subtle, small human dramas unfold themselves in such good-mannered gestures that many spectators would feel, as one visitor to the Salon of 1741 suggested, "Not one woman of the Third Estate goes there [to the Salon] who does not think she sees an image of her gestures, her family life, her straightforward manners, her bearing, her daily occupations, her moral code, the moods of her children, her furniture, her wardrobe." One of Chardin's most important domestic genres is *The Governess* (National Gallery of Canada, Ottawa), exhibited in the Salon of 1739. In the nineteenth-century, the Goncourt brothers first saw in this painting's portrayal of a serious governess reproaching a young boy for excessive play a truthful representation of the hard-working bourgeoisie. This drawing may be a study of the three-cornered hat that the governess is brushing in that painting.

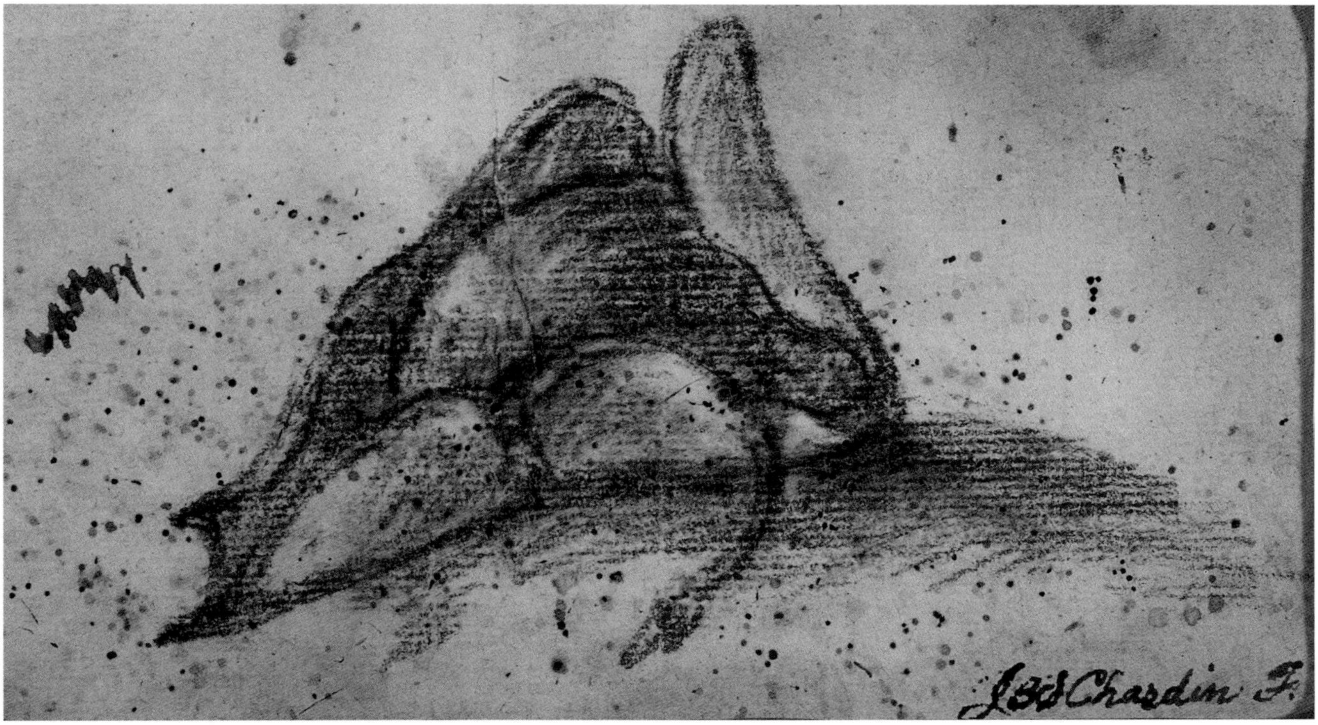

Three-
Cornered Hat

circa 1738

red chalk

90 x 140 mm

inscription:

J.B.S. Chardin F.

John Constable

1776 – 1837 | British

View of Hampstead

circa 1819

pen and brown ink

140 x 240 mm

Born in East Bergholt, Suffolk, Constable entered the Royal Academy in London in 1799. Advised by Joseph Farington and Benjamin West, he copied after Claude, Poussin, Ruysdael, and Girtin. In 1802, he exhibited for the first time in the Royal Academy. From 1814 onwards, he produced several notable series of landscapes: *Dedham* (circa 1814), *Boatbuilding near Flatford Mill* (1815), *Weymouth Bay* (1816), and *Wivenhoe Park* (1816). In 1819, he was elected associate of the Royal Academy. In 1821, he exhibited at the Royal Academy *The Hay Wain*, which went on to create a great sensation in the Paris Salon of 1824. At the beginning of the 1820s, he made many studies of sky and clouds, based on his own precise observations of time, weather, and temperature, and influenced by contemporary scientific writings on meteorology. About this time he also began painting several important views of Salisbury Cathedral, expressing the effects of the transient states of nature on the architectural monument. Although he was elected a royal academician in 1829, his later years were burdened by personal tragedies and recurring rheumatism. His late landscapes show unmistakable elements of stress and drama in their forceful execution and symbolic suggestions.

In 1819, the year he was elected associate of the Royal Academy, Constable first rented a house — Albion Cottage — on Upper Heath, Hampstead, for his family. His wife, Maria Bickwell, whom he married in 1816, had just given birth to a daughter, but she had been unwell and a change of air was suggested. Maria and her two children were sent to stay in Hampstead. During his visits, Constable often sketched and painted outdoors nearby. This drawing was probably made on the spot, perhaps for future reference. From this period onwards, Hampstead was added to East Bergholt and Salisbury in his repertoire of favourite subjects. His *View of Hampstead* was first exhibited in the Paris Salon of 1824, together with *The Hay Wain*. In 1820, his family moved permanently to Hampstead, living at various addresses. Both Constable and his wife are buried in the Hampstead parish church.

Stonehenge

1820 graphite 180 x 270 mm

inscription: dated *1820*

One of Constable's best-known late watercolours is the powerful and awesomely turbulent rendering of England's foremost pre-Roman monument, Stonehenge. Dating from 1835, the picture was shown in the Royal Academy in 1836 (Victoria and Albert Museum, London). Constable described the work in the Academy catalogue: "The mysterious monument of Stonehenge standing remote on a bare and boundless heath, as much unconnected with the events of past ages as it is with the uses of the present, carries you back beyond all historical record into the obscurity of a totally unknown period." Constable paid his only recorded visit to Stonehenge on 15 July 1820 when he was staying with Archdeacon Fisher in Salisbury. He made a number of studies, including this one, of distant and near views of the monument. Unlike most of the others, this drawing introduced an overpowering skyscape, anticipating the dynamic and stormy composition of the 1835 watercolour. Constable's early interest in Stonehenge was most likely influenced by Fisher, who was a friend of two of the most reputable authorities on Stonehenge at that time, Sir Richard Hoare and John Britton. Constable himself knew these two antiquarians. His library contained Britton's *Wiltshire* (1814), which includes an account of Stonehenge. In 1811, he had gone to Stourhead to visit Hoare when the author was working on his *Ancient History of South Wiltshire* (1812).

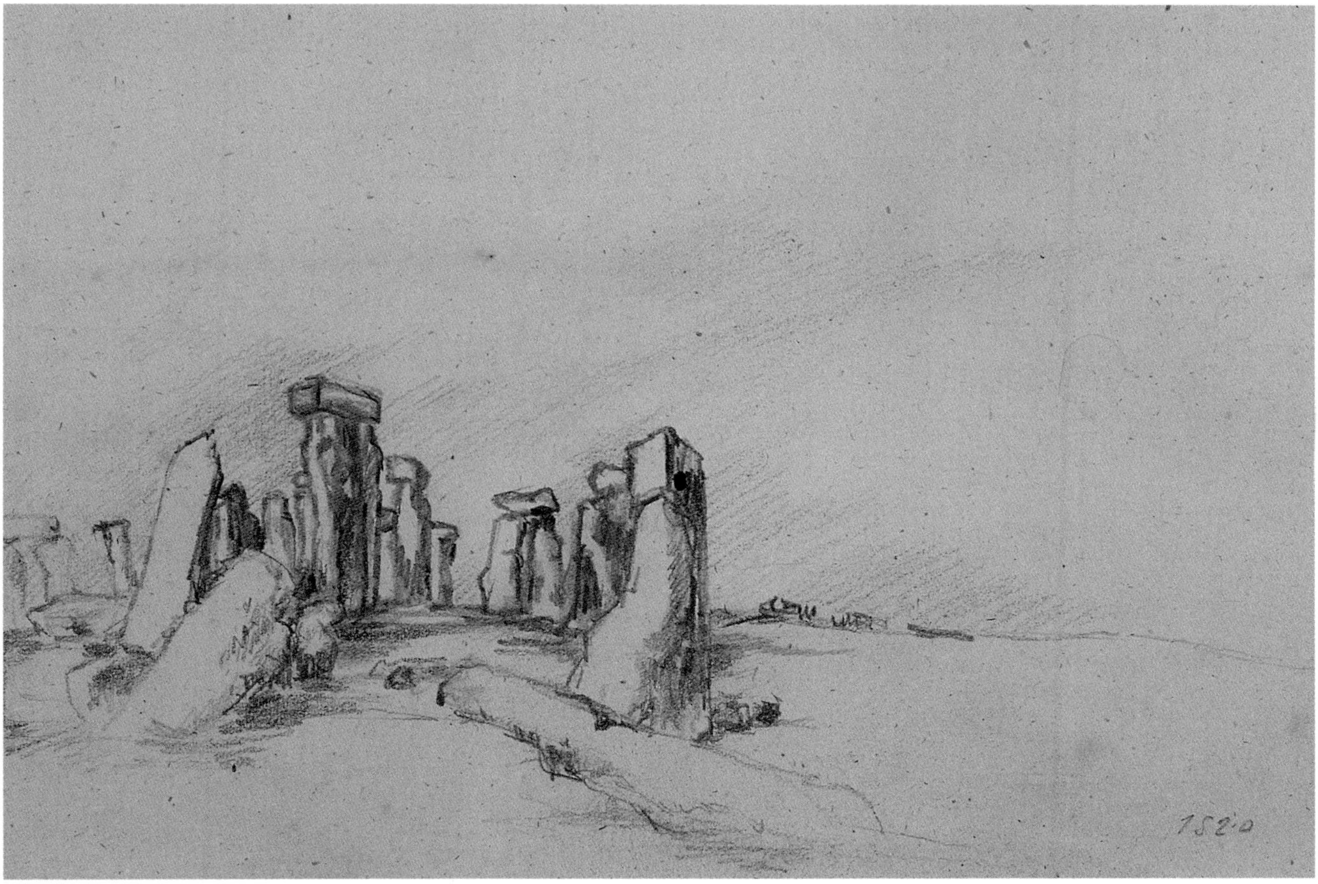

Stonehenge

1820

graphite

180 x 270 mm

inscription:

dated *1820*

Gustave Courbet

1819 – 1877 | French

Copy of Rembrandt's "Self-portrait of 1669"

circa 1840-47
brush and black ink
inscription:
Rembrandt 1669

Courbet came from a family of prosperous landowners from Ornans in the French Jura. He went to Paris in 1839 and, after abandoning the law, he studied briefly with two academic artists, Steuben and Hesse. Soon he launched himself in a program of self-training. At the free studios of the Académie Suisse and in the Louvre galleries, he carefully absorbed the works of the great Spaniards, the Venetians, and the Dutch as well as those modern artists like Géricault and Delacroix. Around this time he met regularly with artists, writers, and philosophers, including Bovin, Champfleury, Baudelaire, Duranty, Silvestre, and Proudhon. Beginning with the Salon of 1850-51, his social and political messages in paintings such as *The Stone-breakers*, *The Peasants of Flagey Returning from the Fair,* and *The Funeral at Ornans* placed him in the centre of the Realist controversy. In the Salon of 1853, another of his notorious paintings, *The Bather* — which Louis Napoleon hit with his riding crop because of the figure's offensive non-ideality — was purchased by his life-long patron, Alfred Bruyas of Montpellier. With Bruyas' financial backing he created the pavilion of Realism in 1855 as an artistic manifesto and a protest against the rejection of his paintings by the 1855 Paris World's Fair. The programmatic centrepiece of this private exhibition is *The Artist's Studio: A Realist Allegory*, which amounts to Courbet's declaration of artistic independence. His unyielding stand remained strong throughout his life. After the Franco-Prussian War, he became the president of the federal commission of artists, but following the collapse of the Paris Commune, he was imprisoned briefly for the politically inspired destruction of the Vendome Column. Fearing further imprisonment, he went into voluntary exile in 1873 in Switzerland, where he remained for the last four years of his life.

Contemptuous of taste and unafraid of modernity, Courbet aimed to cleanse painting of its traditional artifice and time-worn clichés. It was his new Realist attitude towards subject-matter and style that allowed the next generation, the Impressionists, to concentrate on problems of direct visual experience.

Because of the growing Realist interest in direct recording of visual fact on canvas, Courbet's drawings are fairly rare and only a small number exists, most of them dating to the beginning of his career. The *Copy of Rembrandt's Self-portrait of 1669* (Rembrandt's painting is in the National Gallery, London) is a work of the 1840s — perhaps as late as 1847 when he visited Holland — when Courbet concentrated on studying and copying the great masters. Jules-Antoine Castagnary, his friend and early biographer, described Courbet's activity at this time: "The great Venetians, Flemish, Dutch and Spanish colourists monopolized almost all his attention. He passed whole days in front of their works, looking, comparing, thinking, trying, 'by reasoning,' to understand their technique. When he did not understand it, he copied the part that puzzled him, and he copied it over and over again until he had penetrated the secret of execution." Among the Dutch masters, Rembrandt was one of his favourites, and his early compositions owed much to the seventeenth-century artist. Even in his mature years, Courbet continued to make copies of the past masters; in the summer of 1869 while visiting Munich, he made copies of three Old Masters in the World's Fair exhibition, and one of them is another *Rembrandt Self-Portrait* (Courbet's painting is now in the Musée de Besançon).

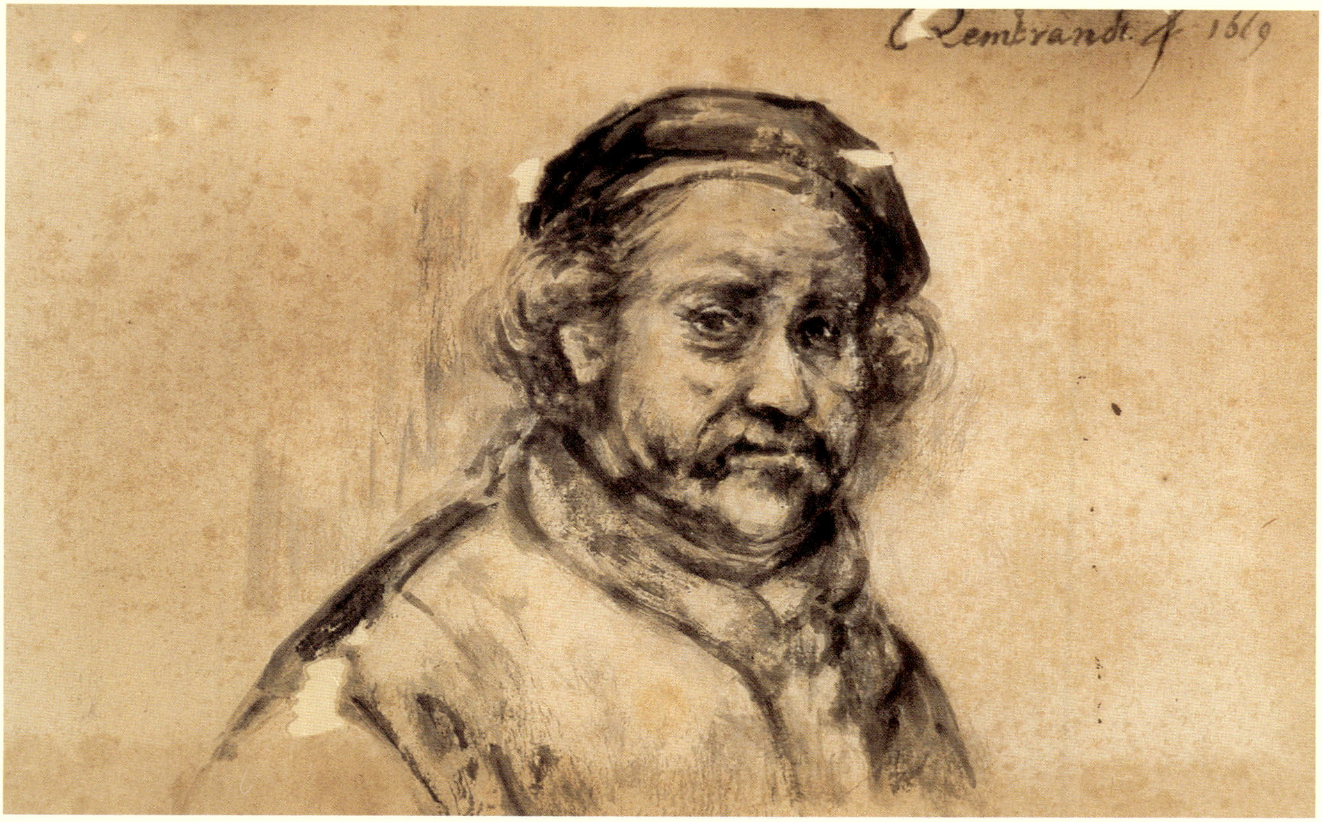

Copy of Rembrandt's "Self-portrait of 1669"

circa 1840-47

brush and black ink

inscription:

Rembrandt 1669

Nathaniel Dance or George Dance

1734 – 1811 | 1741 – 1825 | British

Whimsical Grotesques

circa 1800-15
pen and brown ink
with gray wash
230 x 190 mm

Nathaniel and George Dance were sons of George Dance, Sr., the architect to the corporation of the City of London. Both Nathaniel and George studied in Italy in the late 1750s and early 1760s. Nathaniel was well known as a history and landscape painter and very successful as a portraitist. In 1790, he resigned from the Royal Academy in London, of which he was a founding member, added the name of Holland to his own and became a member of Parliament. He was created a baronet in 1800. George Dance succeeded his father as architect to the City of London in 1768 and subsequently designed his most famous building, Newgate Prison, and also the façade of London's Guildhall. Like his brother, George Dance was a founding member of the Royal Academy and a professor of architecture; one of his gifted pupils was Sir John Soane.

Both Nathaniel and George produced profile portraits (usually in graphite and red chalk) of their distinguished contemporaries. But they also made many satirical drawings and humorous grotesques, including this sheet, which, like many other drawings of similar subjects, has been attributed to both brothers. (A large scrap-book is in the library of the Royal Academy.) Many of these humorous drawings were given to friends. The Goyaesque character of many of these compositions might well have been inspired by Goya's *Los Caprichos* (published in 1799); these George's son, Charles, might have collected, since he was in Wellington's army during the Spanish Peninsular Wars and entered Madrid in 1812.

In any case, grotesque studies of this kind were very much in the popular eighteenth- and nineteenth-century tradition of political caricatures and social satires, especially in England. Two of the most virulent satirists that England ever produced, Thomas Rowlandson and James Gillray, were the Dance brothers' well-known contemporaries, while comic and satiric routines in the theatre, and the contemporary interest in physiognomy, also helped to whet the public appetite for such representations.

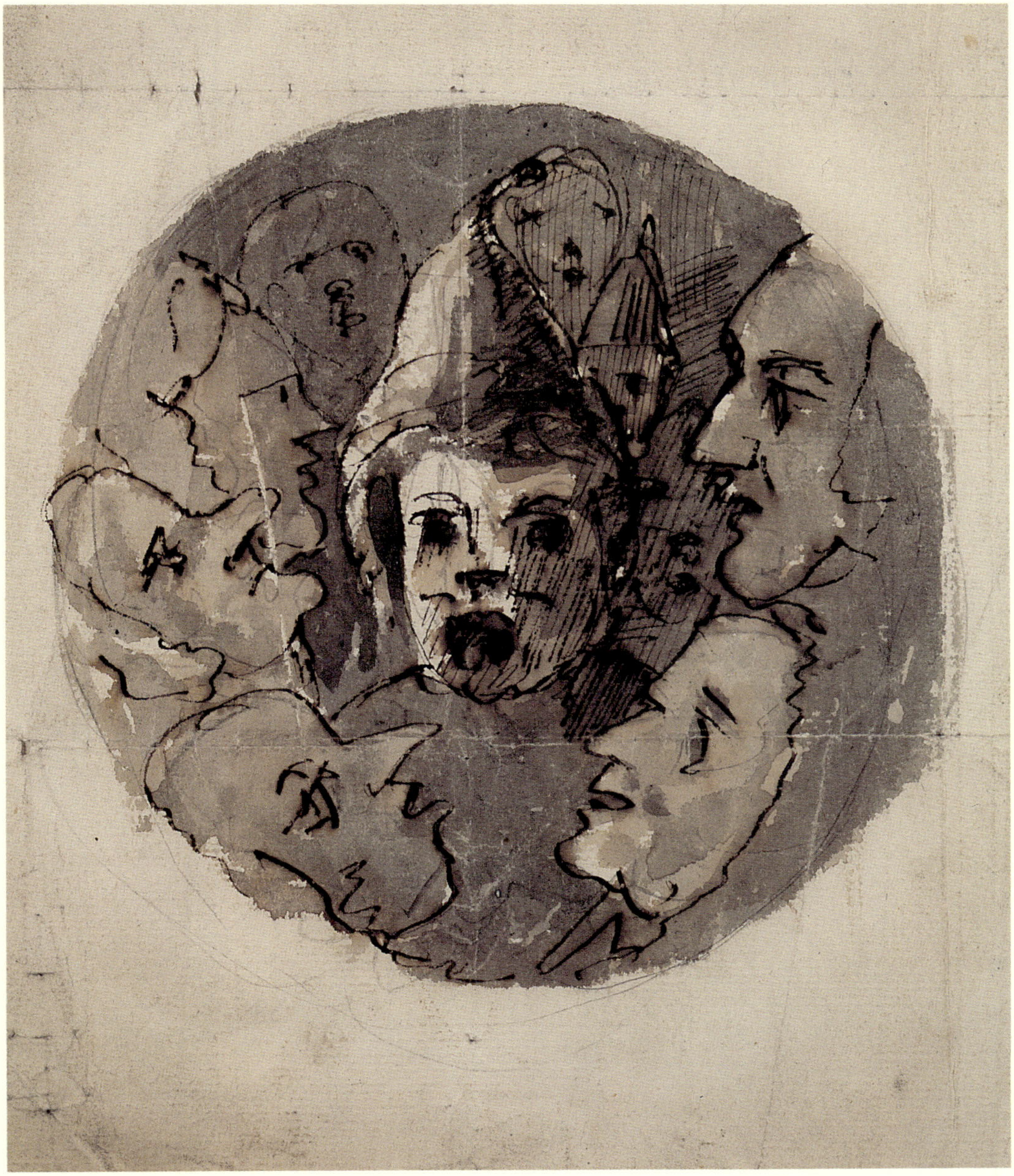

Whimsical Grotesques

circa 1800-15

pen and brown ink with gray wash

230 x 190 mm

Honoré Daumier

1808 – 1879 | French

Saltimbanque Playing the Drum

circa 1865
conté crayon
258 x 204 mm
inscription: signed *h.D.*

Daumier's family came originally from Marseilles and moved to Paris in 1816. Although his father was a minor poet, Daumier did not receive any formal education. At an early age he worked as a notary errand boy. In 1822, he was employed briefly in Delaunay's bookstore in the Palais-Royal. Soon he began art lessons with Alexandre Lenoir, an art collector, archaeologist, and director of the royal museum of French monuments. Lenoir sent his students to copy classical models in the Louvre. There the works of Michelangelo, Rubens, Tintoretto, and Rembrandt became Daumier's major influences. During his student years he also learned the art of lithography, the new medium that was to be of crucial importance for the development of an illustrated, democratic, cheap press. His career began in 1831 when he joined the successful weekly created by Charles Philipon, *La Caricature*. In 1832, both Philipon and Daumier were imprisoned briefly for depicting the king, Louis Philippe, as a "simpleton/pear" and Gargantua. *La Caricature* was wiped out by the new censorship law of 1835, but Daumier immediately joined Philipon's other paper, the daily *Le Charivari*, for which he worked until his retirement in 1872. Between 1831 and 1872, Daumier produced over 4,000 lithographs, commenting on the governments of Louis Philippe and Louis Napoleon, the legal profession, the feminist movement, and even his artist-friends, alternating indignation with good-natured humour. Indeed, his lithographs have become an indispensable source for the examination of nineteenth-century French society, history, politics, culture, and literature.

Besides prints, Daumier also produced a sizable number of paintings, watercolours, and drawings. But this group of works, seldom seen by the public in Daumier's lifetime, represents a private and philosophical undertaking almost entirely separate from his outspoken public prints. One subject dominating much of his private works in the 1850s-60s is the sad clown, of which the present drawing is representative. Thematically, the series of clowns is linked with his other serial works of this period — *The Fugitives, The Third-Class Carriage* and *Don Quixote* — in the representation of modern, transient society and the daily struggles of many of its neglected and anonymous citizens.

The only true portrait Daumier ever painted is that of Charles Deburau in his most famous role as the sad clown, Pierrot. But besides their relation to the performances of Deburau, Daumier's clowns and saltimbanques are also connected to contemporary literary works such as Champfleury's pantomime, *Pierrot, valet de la Mort*, Verlaine's *Jadis et Naguere* and Baudelaire's *Vieux Saltimbanque*. In these literary depictions, as well as the visual ones of Daumier, Degas, Rouault, Cézanne, and Picasso, the popular genre of the sad clown underlines the artist's sense of drift and plight, his homelessness, and his metaphysical sadness in the face of an unappreciative public. In this drawing and a number of others (in the Victoria and Albert Museum, the Metropolitan Museum, and the Wadsworth Atheneum in Hartford), Daumier shows the same saltimbanque failing to attract an audience. Poignantly, Baudelaire has described the clown's situation: "la misère absolue, la misère affublèe, pour comble d'horreur, de haillons comiques, où la nécessité, bien plus que l'art, avait introduit le contraste."

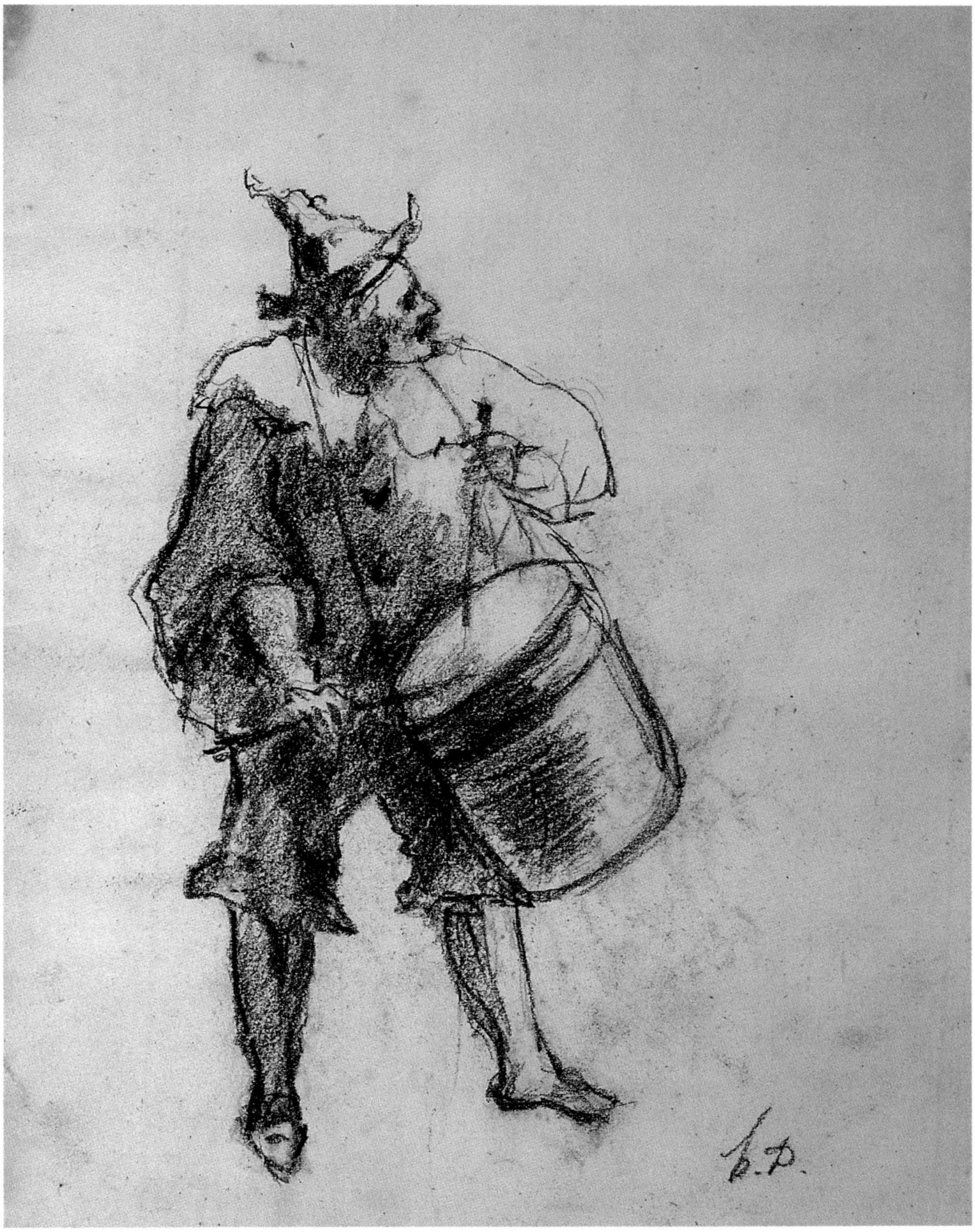

Saltimbanque Playing the Drum

circa 1865

conté crayon

258 x 204 mm

inscription: signed *h.D.*

Jacques-Louis David

1748 – 1825 | French

Dionysos (Bacchus Richelieu)

circa 1775-80
black chalk
372 x 242 mm
inscription:
signed on verso *L.D.*

Study of a Leg

circa 1775-80
black chalk and graphite
168 x 106 mm
inscription:
signed on verso *L.D.*

David was born in Paris, into a family with members in the arts and architecture. On the advice of painter François Boucher, David began studying with Joseph-Marie Vien, the Neoclassicist, in l'Académie française. He won the Prix de Rome in 1774. During his Italian stay (1775-80), David gradually transformed himself from a Baroque-Rococo artist into a true Neoclassicist. Upon returning to Paris, he was invited to join the Académie in 1783. In 1784-85, he returned to Rome, where he painted *The Oath of the Horatii*. The work, inspired by Corneille's stage drama, was a great success in the Paris Salon of 1785. From the outbreak of the French Revolution in 1789, David played an important political role. Briefly imprisoned after the collapse of the Terror in 1794, he returned to centre-stage with the rise of Napoleon. From 1797 until Napoleon's final abdication in 1815, he was the premier painter to the government. A series of state commissions glorifying the triumphs of Napoleon occupied him during those years — *Napoleon at St. Bernard* (1800), *Coronation of Josephine* (1805-07), *Presentation of the Eagles* (1808-10), and *Napoleon Received at the Hôtel de Ville* (unfinished). Following the defeat of Napoleon, David settled in Brussels, where he remained for the last nine years of his life.

A national ideology in the 1780s, antiquity was already a Paris fashion in the 1760s, stimulated by archaeological excavations and the writings of Johann Winckelmann. David had stated in 1774 that "the Antique will not seduce me," but he certainly underestimated the artistic and intellectual change he was to go through under the spell of Italy. From the time he arrived in Rome in 1775, his sketchbooks are filled with copies of antique sculptures and medals. As a pensioner of the Académie, he had access to the great Roman collections in the Palazzi Giustiniani, Mattei, Spada, Farnese, and Rospigliosi; the Villas Albani and Medici; and the Vatican Library. While these studies — including the two drawings *Dionysos* and *Study of a Leg* — did not directly translate into any painted works, they were a necessary means of discipline, formal exercises in realism and classical aesthetics.

Portrait of Napoleon

circa 1804 graphite 147 x 85 mm
inscription: signed *J.D.*

This life study is one of the preparatory drawings for the monumental painting, *The Coronation of Josephine* (Louvre) that David executed between 1805 and 1807. Shown in the Salon of 1808, the painting was one of the commissions given to David to commemorate the ceremonies that marked Napoleon's assumption of the title of hereditary emperor of the French. To achieve the vigorous realism needed to record this august contemporary event in the chancel of Paris's Notre-Dame, David made a large number of life-studies during the dress rehearsal of the coronation. The best are preserved in the sketchbook now in the Fogg Art Museum, Cambridge, Massachusetts. The present drawing illustrates Napoleon's decision to have himself portrayed already crowned and preparing to crown Josephine. (Originally David had intended to show Napoleon crowning himself with the intimidated Pope looking on, in accordance with historical fact.)

Napoleon followed the progress of the painting closely. Upon its completion in 1808, he came to David's studio and said, "This is not painting; one can walk around in this picture, life is everywhere. . . . I am grateful to you for recording for posterity the proof of affection I wished to give to the woman who shares with me the burden of office. . . . David, I compliment you." To which David replied: "Sire, I receive your compliment on behalf of all artists, and am happy to be the one to whom you deign to offer it."

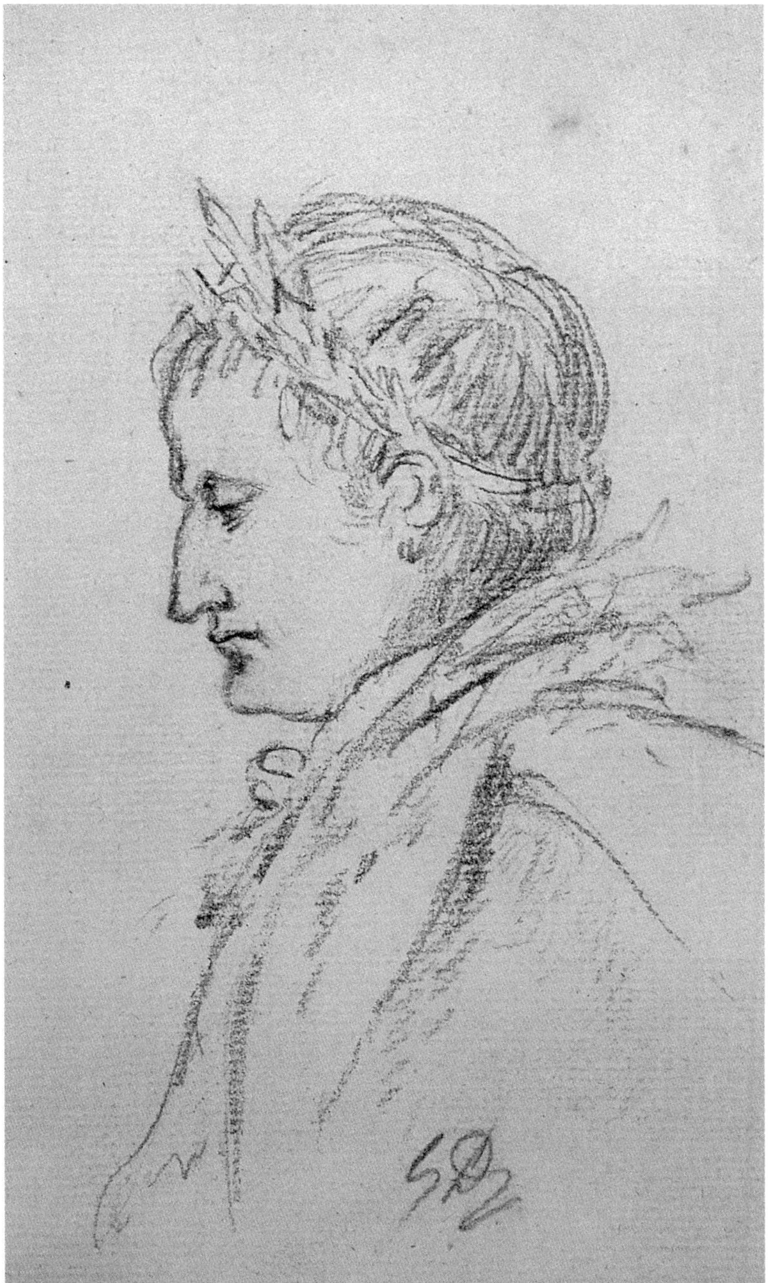

Portrait of Napoleon

circa 1804

graphite

147 x 85 mm

inscription:

signed *J.D.*

Edgar Degas

1834 – 1917 | French

Copy After Pontormo's "Madonna and Child"

circa 1857-59

red chalk

330 x 245 mm

inscription:

signed *Degas*

Copy After Pontormo's "Deposition of Christ"

1857

red chalk

340 x 280 mm

inscription:

signed and dated

Degas 1857

Copy After Raphael's "Venus"

circa 1857-59

red chalk

280 x 220 mm

inscription:

signed *Degas*

Born in Paris, Degas came from a family with ramified connections with the financial and aristocratic elites of France, Italy, and the United States. While Degas was acquiring a classical education between 1845 and 1853, his uncle, Léon Cogniet, gave him drawing lessons. In 1853, he studied art with Félix Barrias and registered as a copyist at the Louvre and the Bibliothèque Impériale. Two years later, he enrolled at the École des Beaux-Arts as a student of Louis Lamoth, a former pupil of Ingres; there he met Fantin-Latour and Léon Bonnat. In 1855 he studied Ingres' works at the Paris World's Fair and was advised by Ingres on drawing. Between 1856 and 1860, he repeatedly visited Italy, sitting in life classes at the official French school in the Villa Medici and studying antique sculptures and the works of medieval and Renaissance artists in Orvieto, Arrezzo, Florence, Naples, Rome, Pisa, and Genoa. Degas' early works are mostly self-portraits and portraits of his family, observed with penetrating psychological insight. By 1860, he had set up a private studio in the rue Madame, and for a number of years devoted himself to history painting on themes from antiquity, the Bible, and medieval history, conceived in a modern spirit. In this period, he met Manet and became a member of the circle at the Café Guerbois. Throughout the 1860s, he exhibited regularly in the official Salon; he also began exploring the themes of landscape, laundresses, and the stage, and pioneered the "modern" genre of horse racing and the turf. From the early 1870s onwards, he suffered from worsening eyesight. He visited London, New Orleans, and Italy in the early 1870s and began to engage in an intensive study of dancers, often visiting the rehearsal rooms of the Opéra ballet in the rue le Pelletier. Between 1874 and 1886, he participated in seven of the eight Impressionist group exhibitions, abstaining only in the seventh in 1882. In the late 1870s he experimented with monotypes and sculptures in wax or clay as well as photography, and was fascinated by Muybridge's photographs of animals in motion. He also amassed a large collection of Old Master paintings and important works by Delacroix, Ingres, Daumier, Corot, Manet, Pissarro, Cézanne, Gauguin, and van Gogh. In spite of his scornful wit and aloofness, he was far more tolerant and broader in outlook than his Impressionist colleagues, and he continued to encourage younger artists, including Toulouse-Lautrec and Suzanne Valadon. In his later years, half-blind, he compensated for his handicap with technical and stylistic ingenuity, often replacing oil with pastel as his chief medium. The *Bathers* series is among the most powerful works of his old age.

Degas' study of the great masters covered his entire career. His copies number more than 500. He said: "No art was ever less spontaneous than mine. What I do is the result of reflection and study of the great masters; of inspiration, spontaneity, temperament . . . I know nothing." During the 1850s and 1860s he produced many copies after the great masters, including these two drawings after Pontormo's works in Florence and the one after Raphael's *Venus* in the Villa Farnesina in Rome. The initiative for such copies came not just from the academic tradition, but also from Degas' own father, Auguste, who wrote to him in 1858: "One must detect and capture the artifices of the great masters, but shrug off all restraint in front of nature and represent it solely by one's own inspiration." Degas was to repeat his father's saying many times later in life: "One must copy and recopy the masters, and it is only having given every proof of being a good copyist that permission could reasonably be given to paint a radish from life." For Degas, these copies were used partly to instill in himself a way of seeing through the eyes of the masters and partly as a benchmark for continual measurement of his own art. Furthermore, he was following the examples of the two contemporary artists he admired: Ingres was copying Giotto at the age of eighty-seven, and Delacroix, in 1839, travelled to Belgium solely to study Rubens.

RUBENS TO PICASSO

Four Centuries of Master Drawings

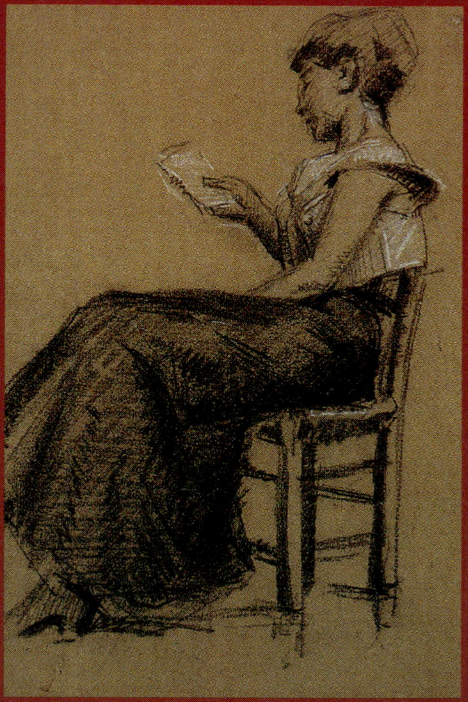

WHERE Edmonton **Takes You On A Tour of a Major Art Exhibition At The University of Alberta's Fine Arts Building Gallery**

WHERE
EDMONTON

RUBENS TO PICASSO

Four Centuries of Master Drawings

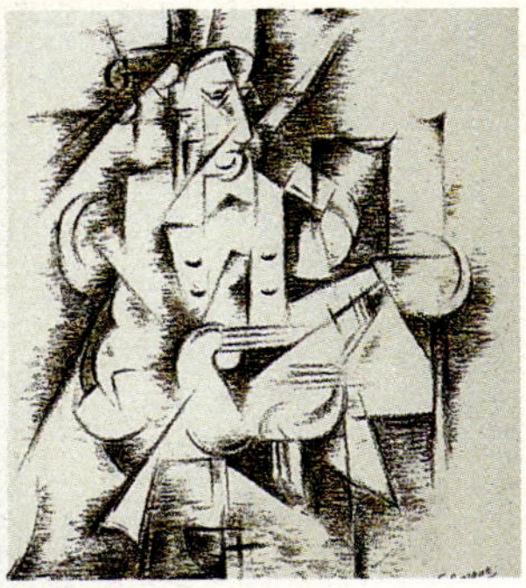
PHOTO BY LOUISE ASSELSTINE

RP4
STROKES OF GENIUS

Edmonton residents and visitors have a unique opportunity to view works by some of the greatest artists of all time in **Rubens to Picasso: Four Centuries of Master Drawings** September 16 through October 29 at the University of Alberta's Fine Arts Building Gallery.

RP5
MICHELANGELO'S MASTERPIECE UNVEILED

Dr. Walter Persegati, former Secretary General and Treasurer of the Vatican Museums, entertains and awes his audiences with the slide-illustrated story of the recent unveiling of Michelangelo's *Last Judgement* from its blanket of soot in the Sistine Chapel. Dr. Persegati performs at the Jubilee Auditorium October 3.

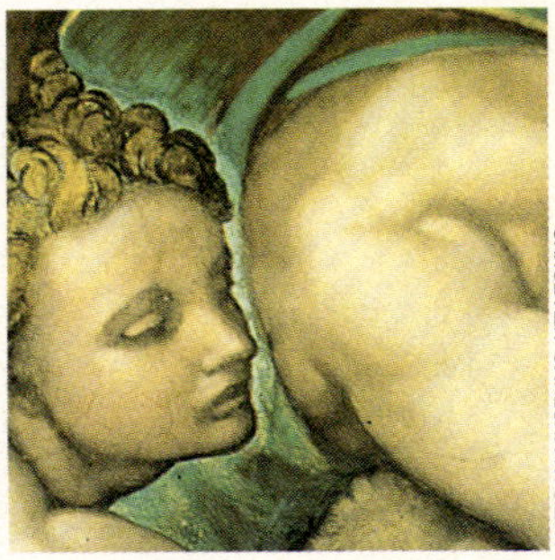
VATICAN MUSEUMS–NTV TOKYO

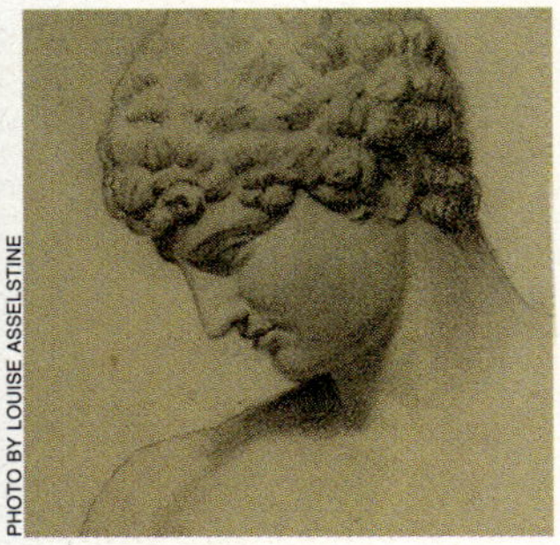
PHOTO BY LOUISE ASSELSTINE

RP6
PICASSO IN PERSPECTIVE

"Picasso was a consummate draughtsman from an early age." So notes Dr. Desmond Rochfort, Professor and Chair of the University of Alberta's Department of Art and Design. **Rubens to Picasso: Four Centuries of Master Drawings** exhibits 10 drawings by Picasso, showing his work from the age of 12 to maturity.

RP7
ART BEAT

Edmonton's art galleries offer a wide range of works by local, Canadian and international artists. Take a look at the fall lineup and then take a tour of one of our many gallery-rich neighborhoods.

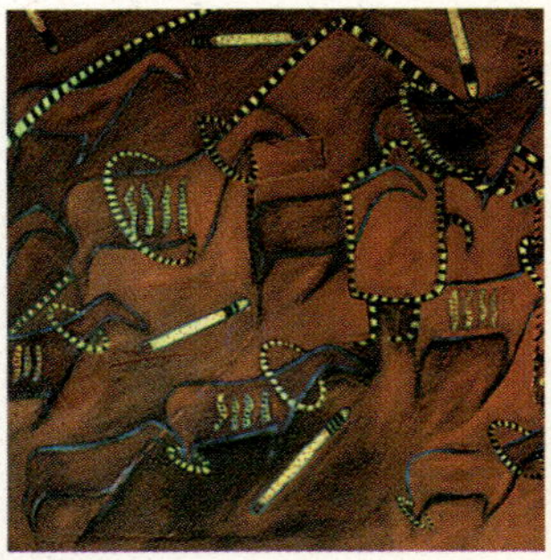

THE COVER

Gustave Caillebotte (1848-1894, French) Woman Reading, *circa 1875, black and white chalk.*

THIS PAGE (Top to Bottom)

Georges Braque (1882-1963, French) *The Guitarist,* circa 1911, black chalk and sepia wash; Michelangelo's, *Last Judgement restored*; Pablo Ruiz y Picasso (1881-1973, Spanish) detail of *Study After a Plaster Cast: "Antinous,"* 1893-94, black chalk; Joane Cardinal-Schubert, *Hoop Dance,* 1994, acrylic on canvas showing at Bugera/Kmet Gallery.

WHERE
EDMONTON

Editor **Deborah Witwicki**
Art Director **Kevin Nienhuis**

Publisher/President **R.H. (Rob) Tanner**

Sales Manager **Rick Davidson**
Account Executives **Ken Wells, Gerry Leibel, Doug Stirrett, Maureen Manning Michelle Martin**

Office Manager **Marie Tanner**
Administrative Assistant **Dawn Osborne**
Graphic Artist **Carolyn Mock**

TANNER PUBLISHING

WHERE Edmonton offers essential reading for visitors through Edmonton hotel rooms and is published quarterly by
Tanner Publishing Ltd.
#4 Parkwood Office Centre
9343 - 50 Street, Edmonton, Alberta, Canada T6B 2L5
TEL (403) 465-3362 • FAX (403) 448-0424

Rubens to Picasso
Four Centuries of Master Drawings

Rubens to Picasso: Four Centuries of Master Drawings
is made possible through the sponsorship of the business community, private donations and the University of Alberta.

Sponsors
The Bank of Montreal, Syncrude Canada Ltd., Stanley Technology Group Inc., Canadian Utilities Limited, McLennan Ross Barristers and Solicitors, City Lumber and Millwork, BML Security Inc.

Contributing Sponsors
AGT Mobility, The Royal Bank, Quality Colour Press Inc., Century Sales and Services Ltd., Professor Douglas Haynes, Studio Post and Transfer, KPMG Management Consulting

Media and Promotion Sponsors
The Edmonton Journal, Canadian Broadcasting Corporation, Hook Outdoor Advertising

University of Alberta
University of Alberta President's Fund, Office of the Vice President (Research and External Affairs), Parking Services

Members of the Rubens to Picasso Team
Department of Art and Design
Dr. Victor Chan, Professor of Art History, Department of Art and Design, Dr. Desmond Rochfort, Professor and Chair, Department of Art and Design,

Dr. Jetske Sybesma, Stan Szynkowski, Deb Coulas, Sue Colberg, Blair Brennan, Tanya Harnett, Kyla Fischer, Louise Asselstine, Dick Der, Keith Rose, Shelley Wilson.

Museums and Collection Services
Janine Andrews, Director, Bernd Hildebrandt, Jim Corrigan, Anne Hayward, Frannie Blondheim, Christina Johanssen

Other University Participants
Dr. Bill Bridger, Office of the Vice-President (Research and External Affairs), Chancellor Louis Hyndman, President John Ferguson, Dr. Patricia Clements, Dean of the Faculty of Arts, Dr. John McDonald, Doug Langevin, Director of Campus Security, Dwight Bozak, Allan Mah, Kevin Moodie, Tony Myers, Sandra Halme

Printed in Canada

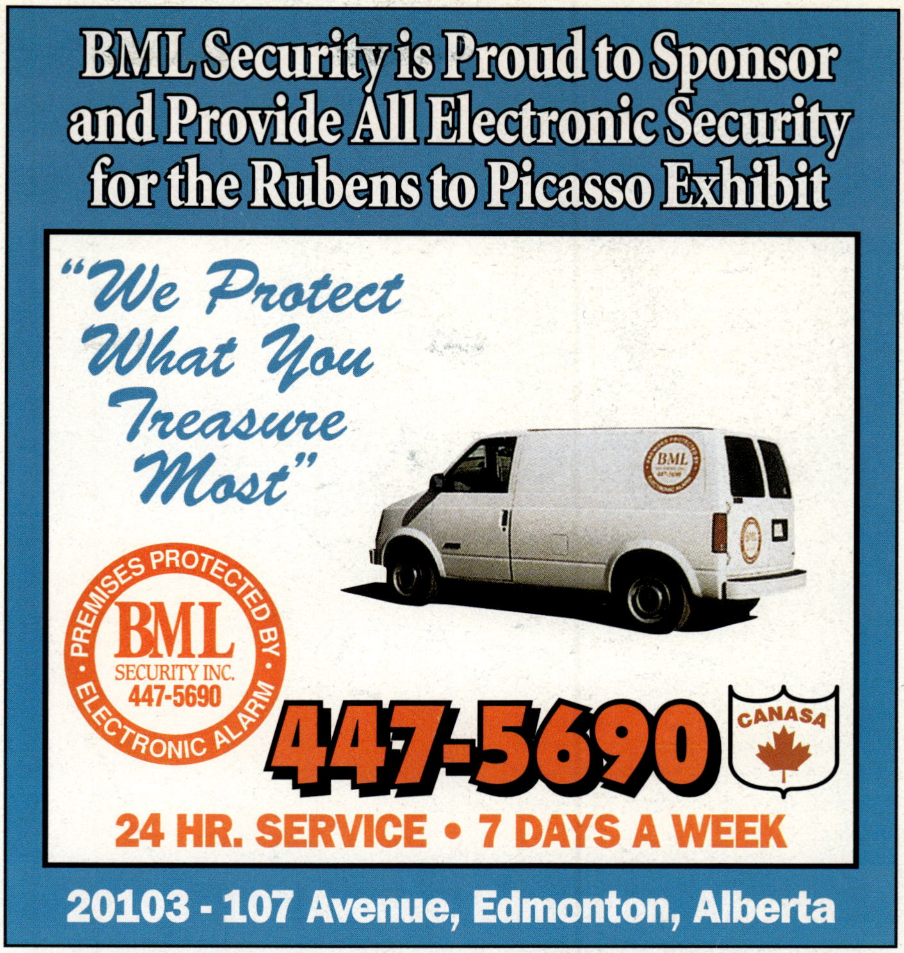

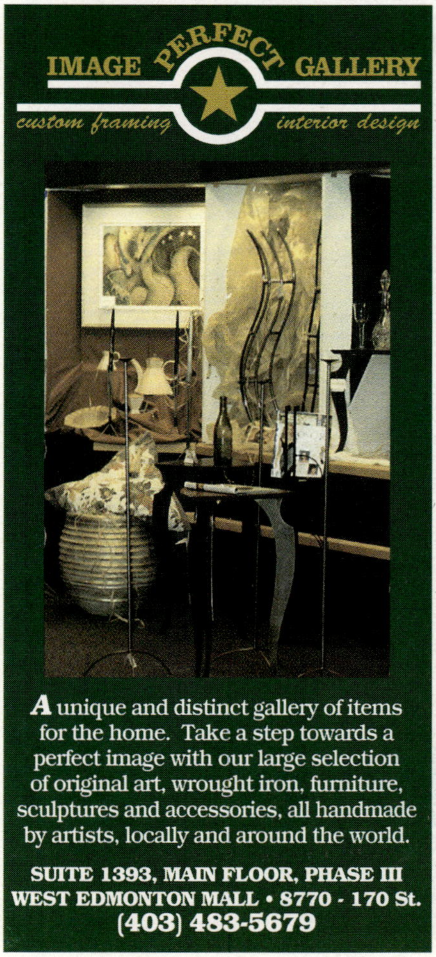

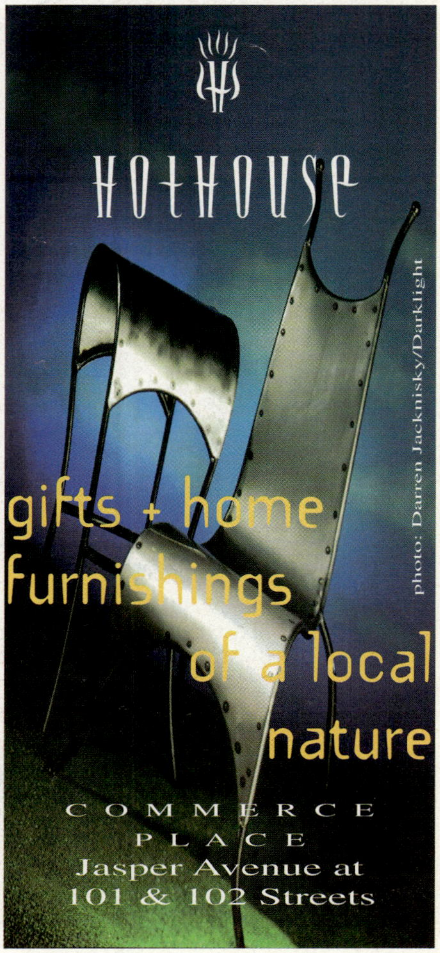

STROKES OF GENIUS

The University of Alberta Department of Art & Design presents Four Centuries of Master Drawings

BY DEBORAH WITWICKI

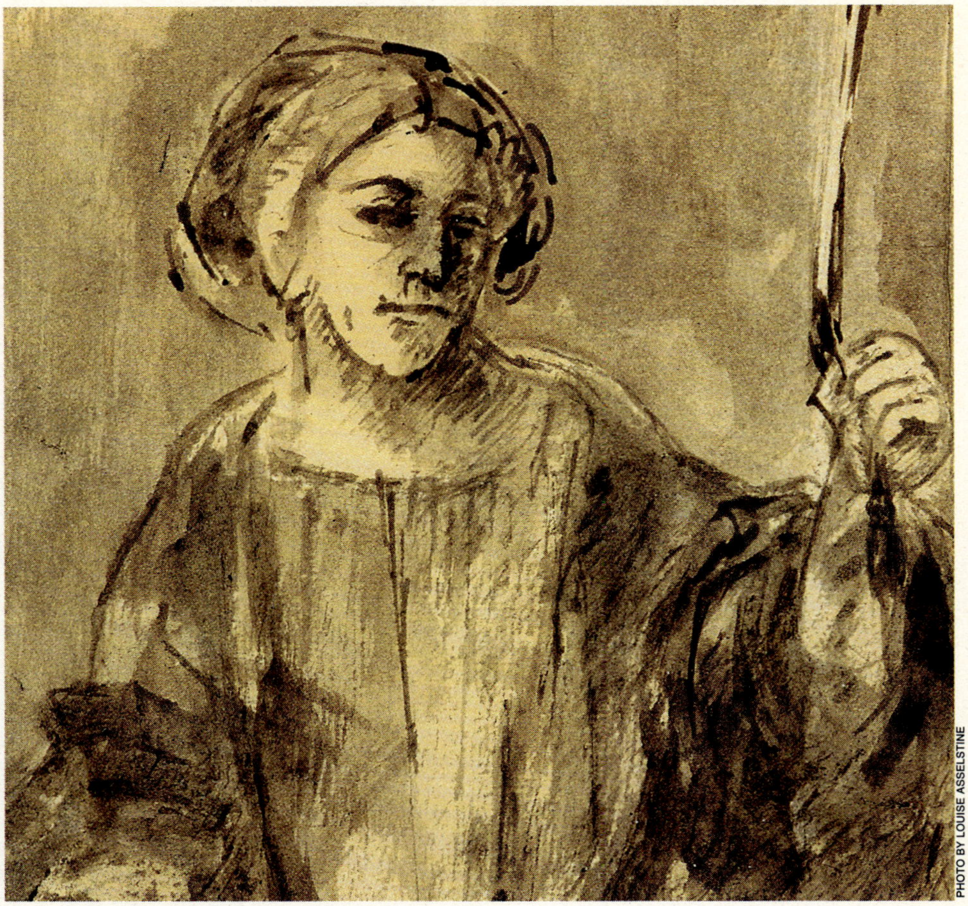

PHOTO BY LOUISE ASSELSTINE

Edmonton residents and visitors have an exclusive opportunity this Fall to see works by some of the greatest artists of the past 400 years. Undoubtedly one of the most important art exhibitions ever mounted in Edmonton, **Rubens to Picasso: Four Centuries of Master Drawings** is showing exclusively at the Fine Arts Building of the University of Alberta September 16 through October 29. Over 150 drawings by 64 outstanding artists are in the exhibition. **Rubens to Picasso** is a unique, one-time-only event, allowing art fans to get closer to some of the most accomplished and influential artists of all time.

The list of artists in **Rubens to Picasso** reads like a compendium of art history. The exhibition includes such seminal artists as Peter Paul Rubens, Francisco Goya, John Constable, Paul Cezanne, Edgar Degas, Claude Monet, Pierre Auguste Renoir, Vincent Van Gogh, Henri Matisse and Pablo Picasso, among more than 50 others. The drawings in the exhibition represent a wide range of styles and techniques which the artists employed to achieve various goals, making the exhibition an interesting way to learn about art history and the roles of individual artists.

The master drawings are on loan to the University from private collectors in Great Britain and North America. The exhibition is curated by Victor Chan, Professor of Art History in the University's Department of Art and Design, and author of the exhibition's lavish 160-page, illustrated catalogue. For Professor and Department Chair Desmond Rochfort, the exhibition's director, and the many other university representatives who have committed extensive time and energy to organize this major event, **Rubens to Picasso** is a chance to reach out to the community in and beyond the University and to offer everyone in Edmonton a unique opportunity to see art by the masters. (New York, London or Paris is much more likely than any place in western Canada to host an exhibition of this size, significance and variety.)

Master drawing exhibitions themselves tend to be a rarity. As Rochfort explains, "These works, particularly the earliest ones, are very vulnerable to light and damp. Paintings are more often exhibited. What is especially rare, however, is to have the opportunity to see the works of so many major artists in one exhibition." The private collectors who are generously lending their treasured works of art, notes Rochfort, demonstrate faith in the University's expertise in appropriately and safely exhibiting the drawings. They are also showing their support for the educational and community outreach goals of the University.

This gathering of 64 artists represents a wide range of work. **Rubens to Picasso** includes everything from spontaneous notations of ideas, to sketches of people and places, to studied drawings.

"Artists have always drawn," says Professor Rochfort. "Drawing is an artist's primary tool in the visual investigation of the world. It's like jotting down ideas; a means to conjure up images." In drawings, we have the intimacy of a diary in visual form.

It is this quality of intimacy–an intimacy with greatness–that is among the most enticing aspects of the exhibition. In fact, the Fine Arts Building Gallery is being transformed for the exhibition to enhance this quality. Walls are rich reds and warm greys; lights are low. The effect is reminiscent of the salons of homes or the smaller rooms in traditional museums which are designed for the visitor to contemplate the

Attributed to Rembrandt van Rijn (1606-1669, Dutch) Lucretia, *circa 1666, pen and wash in brown ink.*

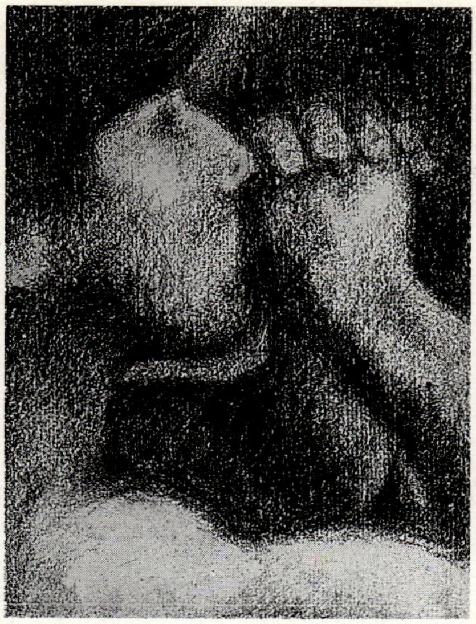

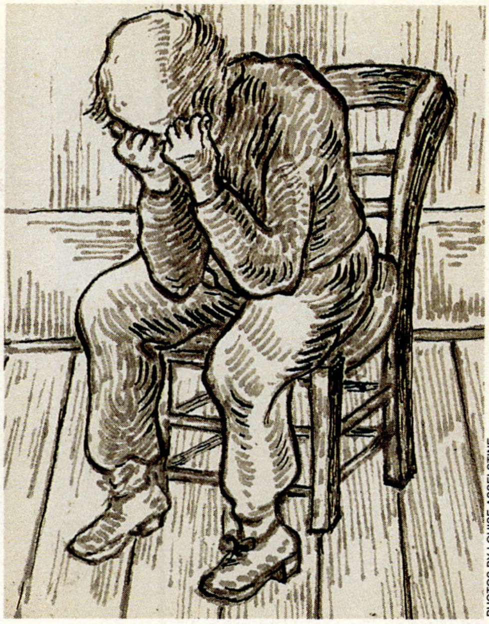

PHOTOS BY LOUISE ASSELSTINE

Left: Georges Seurat (1859-1891, French) The Echo: Study for "Une Baignade, Asnières," *1883, conte crayon; Right: Vincent van Gogh (1853-1890, Dutch)* Worn Out At Eternity's Gate, *1890, pen and gray-black ink.*

works of art in a more intimate and personal setting. This concept, as well as the exhibition's overall design and construction, was developed by Professor Chan together with the staff of the Department of Museums and Collections Services at the University, under the direction of Janine Andrews.

Among the highlights of **Rubens to Picasso** are 10 drawings by Picasso. As a youth, Picasso studied art in the traditional way: by copying the masters. Several of his drawings in the exhibition show just what an astonishing prodigy he was, for as he says, as a youth he could already "draw like Raphael." From Picasso's mature years, a study for one of his most famous paintings–*Guernica*–suggests how enormously inventive he became. Picasso remains the greatest single influence on the art of our century. Many people are aware of the amazing ways in which he distorts and reforms the figures in his art, and of his limitless energy and creativity. But fewer may realize that, as Professor Rochfort says, "Picasso was a consummate draughtsman from an early age. This is a side of the artist of which many familiar with his Cubist paintings have not seen. Such insights, which the exhibition offers in abundance, enhance our understanding and appreciation of the creative genius of these artists."

Besides Picasso's drawing for *Guernica,* the exhibition shows a large number of other artists' drawings that are studies for paintings, some of them for paintings held in the British National Gallery in London, the Louvre in Paris, the Art Institute of Chicago and other great museums. There are several exquisite drawings by Seurat, for example, for his large and innovative paintings, *The Bathers, Asnieres* and *Sunday Afternoon on the Grande-Jatte.* These are among the best-loved masterpieces of the 19th Century. Visitors to the exhibition will also find drawings characteristic of many of the artists– Renoir's young female bathers, Degas' ballet dancers, Constable's landscapes and Gauguin's Polynesian women, to name but a few examples.

As Degas said, in a sentiment, echoed by many visual artists, "Above all, I was born to draw." Drawing is a way of learning from other artists, by copying the masters who came before; a way of learning from nature, by sketching in the open air. It is a way of measuring oneself against the best and a way of challenging them. A way of improvising, of stimulating the imagination and a way of recording its "secrets", as Gauguin called his own drawings.

For those who are intrigued by **Rubens to Picasso** and want more information, Professor Chan has written a detailed catalogue that is extensively illustrated. In it, each artist in the exhibition is represented by at least one illustration, along with personal and historical information. Both the catalogue and exhibition design give visitors a rare glimpse of a private side of these famous artists.

Rubens to Picasso: Four Centuries of Master Drawings is the most exciting art exhibition to occur in Edmonton and a superb way to learn about some of the greatest artists in a great tradition of western art. It is a unique opportunity to share in that tradition, and to get to know the more private sides of these masters of the visual.

MICHELANGELO'S MASTERPIECE UNVEILED

Dr. Walter Persegati, former Secretary General and Treasurer of the Vatican Museums, reviews the fourteen years of delicate, painstaking work by the Vatican Conservation Laboratory to restore Michelangelo's *Last Judgment.* This fascinating illustrated lecture is 7 pm, October 3 at the Jubilee Auditorium. Tickets, $6 ($3 for students and people under age 18) are available at TicketMaster, 451-8000 (agency fees apply). The lecture is sponsored by the University of Alberta Department of Art and Design and Grant MacEwan Community College, Department of Art.

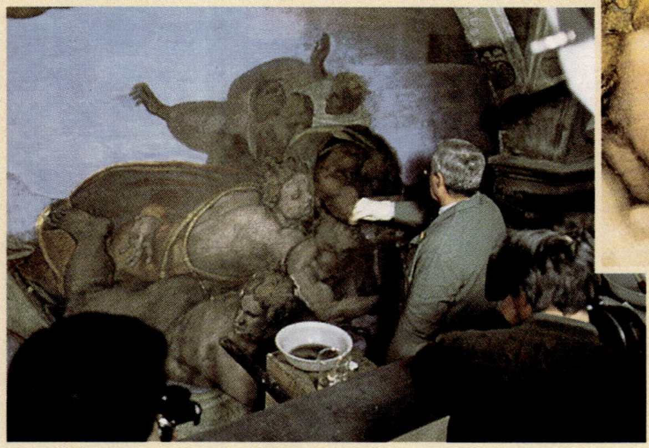

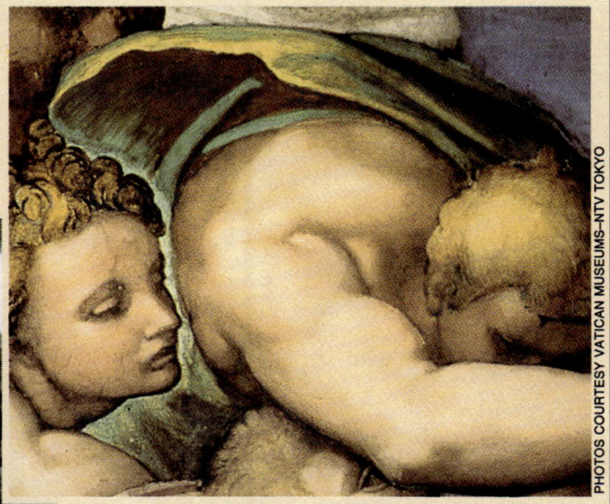

PHOTOS COURTESY VATICAN MUSEUMS–NTV TOKYO

These photos show Michelangelo's The Last Judgement *before (left) and after (right) restoration.*

PICASSO IN PERSPECTIVE

Rubens to Picasso: Four Centuries of Master Drawings

includes 10 drawings by Pablo Picasso, showing his

Doubtless the best-known artist of this century, Picasso was as diverse and influential a creator as Matisse, but more flamboyant and less traditional. Picasso was, in a sense, the first art "star." As his acclaim grew, he gathered the trappings of stardom: an entourage of admirers and protectors, fancy cars, a chateau. Photographers, reporters and fans hounded him. The artist was not shy about promoting himself either; he once said that "at the age of 12 he could draw like Raphael." In the **Rubens to Picasso** exhibition are some remarkable drawings from his early youth which testify to the prodigy-genius image of Picasso.

Cezanne was the artist Picasso named as his greatest influence but many other names (and the art from many other cultures) could also be cited. Picasso never lost the capacity to be influenced by what he saw. His memory and imitative abilities were uncanny–as was his inventiveness. He is regarded as the artist who could make art out of anything (his sculpture of a bull's head made from a bicycle seat and handlebars is a famous example). One of his most revealing character traits was a desire to surprise himself in all that he did. It is what makes his art so adventurous and what led to his exploration and creation of so many different styles throughout his lengthy creative life.

Picasso was Spanish by birth and although he lived in France for most of his adult life, he remained a loyal and proud Spaniard. During the Spanish Civil War he was deeply angered by the destruction of the innocent *pueblo* by Fascist General Franco's bombings. He expressed his horror in a monumental painting named *Guernica* which depicts the bombing of innocent people in the town of that name. The drawing in the exhibition, shown here on the right, illustrates two figures used in the painting, a mother holding her dead child. Picasso drew the classical drawing on the left when he was only 12 years old. These two examples give indication of the tremendous range in this seminal artist's work.

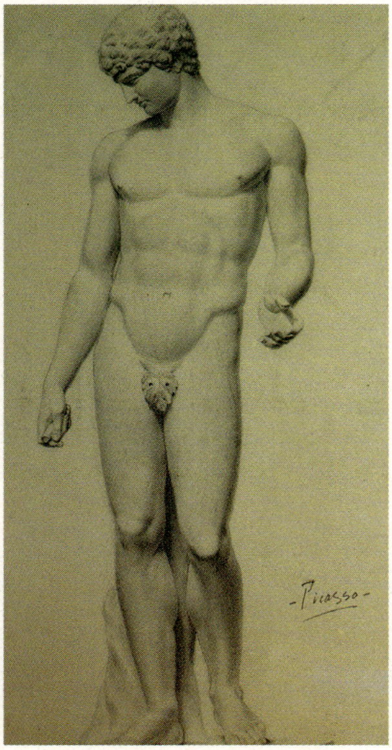

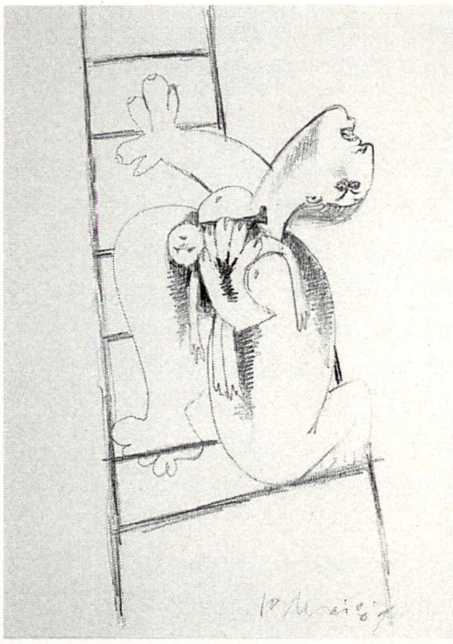

PHOTOS BY LOUISE ASSELSTINE

Pablo Ruiz y Picasso (1881-1973, Spanish) Left: *Study After a Plaster Cast: "Antinous,"* 1893-94, black chalk. Right: *Mother with Dead Child on a Ladder*, 1937, graphite.

FALL SHOWS AT EDMONTON GALLERIES

Art lovers will find a rich variety of art at local commercial galleries.

HIGH STREET/124 STREET AREA

The eight galleries in this area present the Gallery Walk, featuring tours with complimentary shuttle bus service and refreshments. The next Gallery Walk is September 21 from 5 pm to 9 pm.

Bugera/Kmet Galleries (10114 - 123 Street, 482-2854) specializes in Canadian contemporary art and offers an eclectic mix of figurative, landscape and abstract works. This fall, Bugera/Kmet presents *Exploring the Figure:* an exhibition of drawings, monoprints and paintings September 21 to October 5 and an exhibition of works by Joane Cardinal-Schubert October 21 to November 2. **West End Gallery** (12308 Jasper Avenue, 488-4892) specializes in paintings, original prints and sculpture by prominent Canadian artists. Fall exhibitions include new paintings of the West Coast by Robert Genn October 5 to 17 and *French Canadian Collection:* New Works by Bruno Côté, Louise Martineau and Del Signore October 19 to 31. **Front Gallery** (12312 Jasper Avenue, 488-2952) focuses on contemporary art and craft by Alberta artists. Fall highlights include *Totally Bear Rugs* by Lynn Malin and Elizabeth Beauchamp October 13 and 14 and *First Nations: Painted Visions* October 21 to November 1. The newest addition to the neighborhood is **Alberta Craft Council Presents... Gallery and Craft Shop** (10106 - 124 Street, 488-6611) which represents Canadian and Alberta artists and crafts people.

In tribute to the Rubens to Picasso exhibition, **Douglas Udell Gallery** (10332 - 124 Street, 488-4445) opens a contemporary drawing show September 18. Also this fall is *Black Sea Blue,* paintings by Natalka Husar October 7 to 21. **Bearclaw Gallery** (10403 - 124 Street, 482-1204) specializes in First Nations art and features paintings and soapstone carvings by many well-known artists as well as Navajo jewelry and jade carvings. **Kathleen Laverty Gallery** (10411 - 124 Street, 488-3619) represents a wide variety of Albertan and Canadian artists. Fall exhibitions include the watercolors of Edmonton artist Robert Sinclair September 16 to October 7, three Edmonton abstractionists: Dick Der, Greig Rasmussen and Barbara Akins October 14 to October 28, and paintings by Leslie Poole opening November 4. **Electrum Design Studios** (12419 Stony Plain Road, 482-1402) offers one-of-a-kind jewelry by Wayne MacKenzie and a variety of guest artist exhibitions.

WEST EDMONTON MALL

Northern Images (#2864 - 8770 - 170 Street, 444-1995) features stone sculpture and original graphics from Arctic Canada. Among the artists represented are Kenojuak, Nuna Parr, Judas Ooloola and Oviloo Tunnillie. Jade sculptures by Lyle Sopel and sterling silver and gold jewelry are also sold in this fascinating shop. **Snowbird Gallery** (8770 - 170 Street, 444-1024) features First Nations arts and crafts, from original painting and pottery to dream catchers.

DOWNTOWN

Rowles and Parham Design Galleries (10130 - 103 Street, 426-4035) is presenting the *Canadian Glass Show* September 14 to November 30, featuring up to 300 pieces of glass by some 40 artists from across Canada. Corporate gifts and art are the specialties of this gallery which represents 200 artists.

SOUTH SIDE

Imagination, originality and a sense of fun characterize the south side shopping scene. **Serendipity Gallery & Frame Shop** (9860 - 90 Avenue, 433-0388) is set in an historic building and specializes in works by western Canadian artists such as Nathalie Shewchuk-Pare, Paul Jelley, Predrag Rajkovic and Mahara Sinclaire. There's a wide variety of art and crafts by local artists available at **Scona Clayworks** (8103 - 104 Street, 433-8866), including pottery, metal work, wood carving, glass work and jewelry. Scona has a bridal registry. **Off the Wall!** (8111 - 104 Street, 433-9825) bills itself as a mixed bag gallery offering "art with a sense of humor". Located in the handsome Strathcona Shoppes on 4th, this funky gallery showcases a wide range of works by local, regional and national artists. With two locations (7111 - 85 Street, 465-6171 and 11817 - 80 Street, 479-8424), **Johnson Art Gallery** specializes in works by Alberta artists, including Susan Gardiner, Joe Haire, Peggy Heer, Marion Barker, Myrna Wilkinson, Jim Brager and Wendy Risdale. Artist prints, book marks and cards are also sold here.

Copy After Ingres' "Venus Anadyomene"

1861 graphite 245 x 200 mm

inscription: signed and dated *Degas 1861*

Degas' admiration for Ingres was unmistakable: he owned thirty-seven drawings and twenty paintings by Ingres. As early as 1854, he began copying Ingres' works in the Louvre; and as late as 1897 he visited Montauban, Ingres' birthplace, to study Ingres' drawings in his museum. After all, his teacher at the École des Beaux-Arts, Louis Lamoth, was a former pupil of Ingres. Degas first met Ingres, then seventy-five, in 1855; Ingres advised him: "Make copies, young man, many copies. You can only become a good artist by copying the masters." At the heart of his love for Ingres was the science of design and selection, deeply rooted in the classical tradition.

Ingres' sinuous *Venus Anadyomene* (completed in 1848; Musée Condé, Chantilly) — the new-born Venus emerging from the sea — was inspired by Botticelli's *Birth of Venus* (circa 1485) in the Uffizi, Florence. Two years before he copied Ingres' *Venus*, in 1859, Degas had made a copy of Botticelli's *Birth of Venus* (collection of Marianne Feilchenfeldt, Zurich).

Study of Dancers at the Barre

circa 1875-76 graphite 346 X 255 mm

inscription: signed *Degas*

Degas' lifelong passion for the theatre and its contrived artifice can be traced to his childhood education, supervised by his father. Beginning in the 1870s, when he was experimenting with various subjects of the modern genre, he began to focus on the dance as a motif. As early as 1874, he was recognized as a specialist in depicting the ballet. He was especially interested in the strained postures of the younger dancers at the barre. Although he stated that "the dancer is only a pretext in drawing," his admiration for the dancers' submission to their strenuous discipline in order to achieve seemingly effortless grace on stage is a direct parallel to his own art. In addition, the dance subject allowed him to contrast subtly the stage art and backstage vice of prostitution in the Opéra of the time. His initial interest in painting popular ballet subjects may also be due to their saleability — he had to pay off large family debts after the collapse of the family bank in the 1870s.

The present drawing is a study for the painting *Two Dancers at the Barre* (circa 1876-77), now in the Metropolitan Museum, New York.

Naked Figure with Folded Arms

circa 1895 pastel 290 x 170 mm

inscription: signed *Degas*

The figure is strongly reminiscent of Rodin's *Naked Balzac with Folded Arms* of 1892-93, although it cannot be said for certain that Rodin is the source for this drawing. Rodin's highly controversial, powerful depiction of the inspired Balzac may well have appealed to Degas. In *Autre Étude de Femme*, Balzac describes Napoleon: "A man is depicted with his arms folded, but who did everything! . . . A man who could do everything because he willed everything." The paradoxical juxtaposition of the passive gesture with a fiery personality would strike a chord in Degas. Besides, throughout his life, Degas was a great mimic; he posed with his family in a photograph in 1885 parodying Ingres' *Apotheosis of Homer*. Degas and Rodin were good friends and had mutual respect for each other's works. Degas was a frequent visitor to Rodin's studio at Meudon, and there is a close parallel between many of the female figure sculptures, especially dancers, of Degas and Rodin from the 1880s onwards.

Naked Figure with Folded Arms

circa 1895 pastel

290 x 170 mm

inscription: signed *Degas*

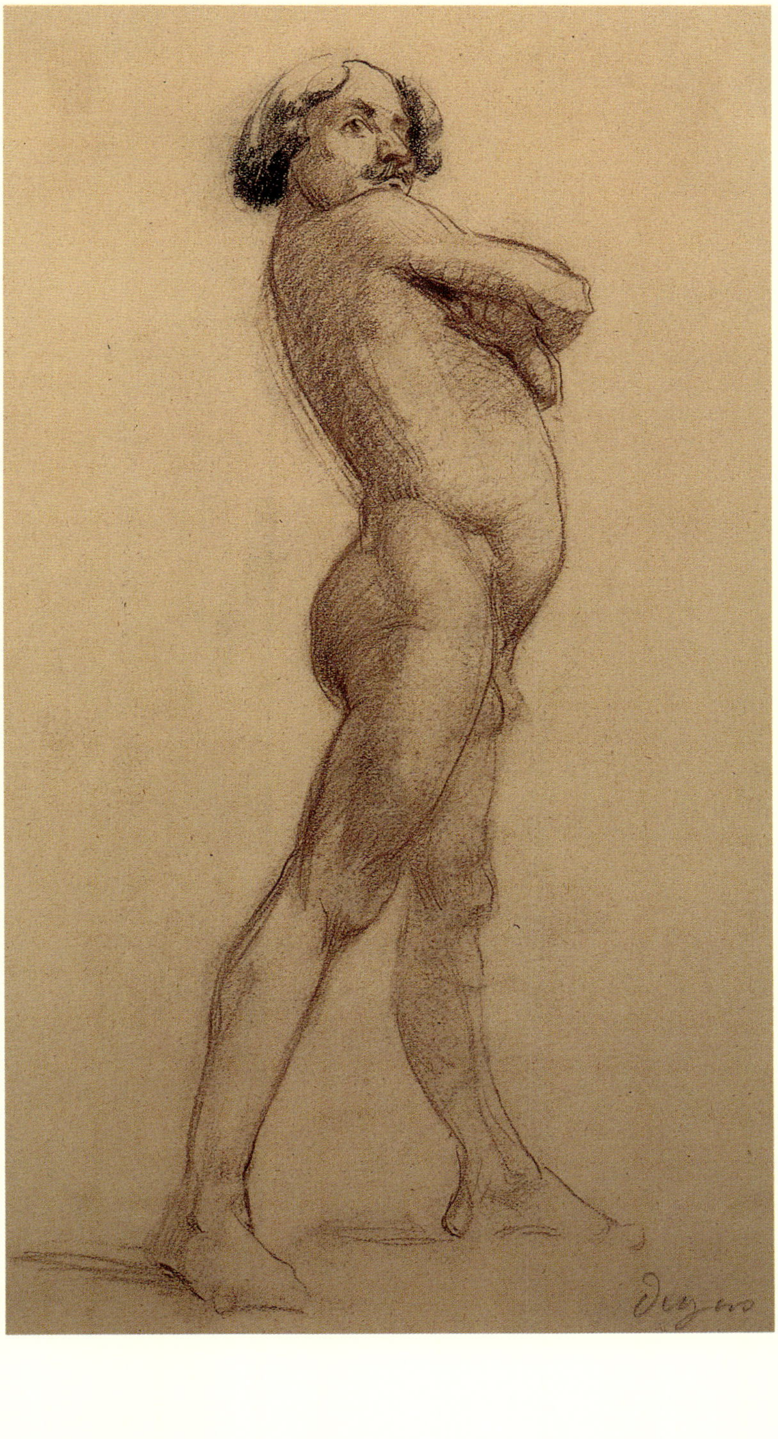

Eugène Delacroix

1798 – 1863 | French

Galloping Horse

circa 1820-25

graphite

145 x 230 mm

Delacroix was the son of Charles Delacroix, minister of foreign affairs under the Directoire and later ambassador of the French Republic to Holland. (It has been rumoured that his true father was Talleyrand, Charles Delacroix's successor in the foreign ministry.) Delacroix showed an early gift in classics and drawing. In 1815, he entered the studio of Neoclassicist Pierre-Narcisse Guérin. There he met Theodore Géricault and Richard Bonington, and soon became an ardent admirer of Géricault's modern heroic subjects. Bonington, in the meantime, introduced him to the British tradition of watercolour and the works of Shakespeare, Byron, and Scott, the chief literary sources of his Romanticism. He also studied in the Louvre, especially the works of Titian, Veronese, Rubens, and Gros. With the exception of *Dante and Virgil* of 1822, his Salon paintings in the 1820s — *Massacre at Chios* (1824) and *Sardanapalus* (1827) — were bitterly criticized. Following the Revolution of 1830, his painting *Liberty Leading the People on the Barricades* received great acclaim in the Salon of 1831, and he was awarded the Legion of Honour. In 1832, he visited North Africa in the suite of the comte de Mornay. There he recorded scenes of Arab and Jewish life. From the 1830s on, he was in official favour; besides Salon exhibits, he received large-scale decorative commissions: the Salon du Roi in the Palais Bourbon (1833-37), the library of the Chambre des Députés in the Palais Bourbon (1838-47), the library of the Senate in the Palais du Luxembourg (1840-46), the chapel at St. Sulpice (1849-61), the ceiling of the Galerie d'Apollo in the Louvre (1850-51), and the ceiling and frieze of the Salon de la Paix in the Hôtel de Ville (1851-54). In 1849, he was appointed to the fine arts commission and the Salon hanging committee. In 1851 he even became a city councillor of Paris. The government of Louis Napoleon honoured him in the Paris World's Fair of 1855 with a large retrospective; the other artist so honoured was his great rival, Ingres. He was elected to the Institute française in 1857. Throughout most of his life, he kept a journal — from 1822 to 1824 and from 1847 to 1863 — an indispensable source regarding his life and work as well as a rich social, intellectual, and artistic documentation of the Parisian art world.

Delacroix's violent, sulphuric but completely self-controlled character, well described by his early biographers — Baudelaire compared him to a "volcano artistically concealed beneath bouquets of flowers" — is best reflected in his many dramatic historical and contemporary subjects, as well as his depictions of lion and tiger hunts and galloping horses. During the 1820s, he painted and drew horses more than any other animal. He wrote in 1823: "Il faut absolument se mettre à faire des chevaux. Aller dans une écurie tous les matins; se coucher de très bonne heure et se lever de même." Undoubtedly this interest was derived from the works of Rubens, Gros, Géricault, and Vernet, in addition to the English sporting tradition. The highly strung type of horse, as in this drawing, appeared in a number of notable works in the 1820s — in *Massacre at Chios* of 1822 and the lithograph of *Giaour and the Pasha* of 1827. About 1824, Delacroix executed a series of sketches and drawings illustrating the popular theme of *Mazeppa*, inspired by Lord Byron's poem of 1819, which tells of a Polish nobleman bound naked to a wild horse and let loose on the plains of Ukraine as punishment for his affair with a count's wife.

Figure Study for "The Death of Sardanapalus"

1827 red chalk 254 x 151 mm

inscription: signed *Eug. Delacroix*

This female nude is a study for Delacroix's largest (395 x 495 cm), most important, and most controversial painting in the Salon exhibitions. The subject was inspired by Lord Byron's poetic stage drama, *Sardanapalus* (1821). Facing defeat and rejecting surrender to the governors of Media and Babylon, Sardanapalus, the last Assyrian king, committed suicide. Delacroix embellished Byron's hero by portraying him as a self-indulgent and licentious monarch who ordered, and observed indifferently, the voluptuous slaughter of the harem and the burning of the royal treasures on the funeral pyre. As a public Salon picture, *Sardanapalus* embodied Delacroix's sudden explosion of suppressed fury and his disdain for public values and bourgeois taste and morality. The *danse macabre* of this intimate boudoir scene is succinctly captured in this female nude, placed in the foreground of the composition. Conceived as an object of erotic desire and possession similar to others found in many of Delacroix's works, this female nude, about to be stabbed by an African slave, also reveals the unsettling Romantic fantasy of imaginary violence against women.

A nearly identical sketch of this figure, larger in size and done in pastel, is now in the Louvre, as are the majority of the sketches and drawings for *Sardanapalus*.

Medea

1836-38 graphite 210 x 123 mm

inscription: *Eug. D.*

Delacroix first noted his interest in *Medea* in 1824, just months after his purchase of Marantonio's engraving after Raphael's *Massacre of the Innocents*. Although the painting was not begun until 1836, the figure of Medea was indeed derived from Raphael'swoman holding an infant in the foreground of *Massacre*.

Of all of the literary sources Delacroix might have consulted — Euripides, Seneca, Corneille, Longepierre, Glover, or Legouvé, Corneille's tragedy is the only drama that includes a scene of Medea in her magic grotto. Delacroix chose the moment when the enchantress Medea, blinded by jealous rage, turns back towards the unfaithful Jason and grabs her two sons before killing them. The fascination with the abnormality of maternal infanticide belongs to the Romantic theme of the *mauvaise mère*, popular since the early nineteenth century, and mirrors a general mistrust of and contempt for women. However, Delacroix's depiction is psychologically ambivalent: looking back in fear, anger, and guilt, Medea also inherently displays her maternal tenderness by exposing her breasts. Medea's emotional conflict thus allows Delacroix to synthesize the voluptuous and the pathetic.

Delacroix painted four versions of *Medea* — the original, dated 1838, is in the Musée des Beaux-Arts, Lille; three later, reduced variants are known: one, dated 1859, is in the National Gallery, Berlin; two, dated 1862, are in the Louvre and the collection of Vicomtesse de Noailles, Paris.

Figure Study for "The Death of Sardanapalus"

1827 red chalk

254 x 151 mm

inscription:

signed *Eug. Delacroix*

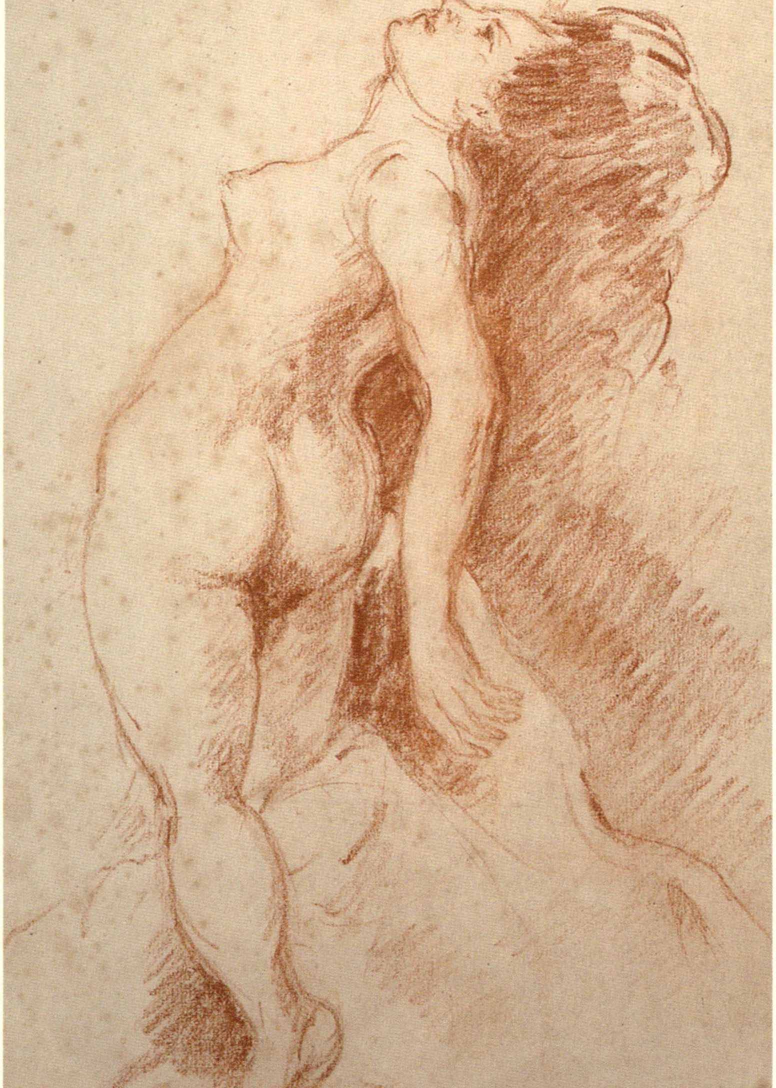
Eug Delacroix

James Ensor

1860 – 1949 | Belgian

Town Hall, Brussels

1885
conté crayon
and graphite
254 x 110 mm
inscription:
signed *J. Ensor*

Born in Ostend, Ensor began his art studies with two local painters. In 1877, he entered the Académie Royale des Beaux-Arts in Brussels, where he learned to despise formal art training, later referring to the Académie as an "establishment for the near blind." While in the Académie, he met Professor Ernest Rousseau and his wife. Rousseau was a physicist and rector of the Université Libre de Bruxelles; his wife, also a scientist, often provided Ensor with canvases and sustained him in his times of depression. Ensor returned to Ostend in 1880 and set up his studio in the attic of his family house; it was here, with a view of the whole city and the North Sea, that his future art would be formulated. In 1883, together with Guillaume Vogels, Théo van Rysselberghe, Willy Finch, and Fernand Khnopff, he founded the stormy avant-garde group, Les XX. Often rejected by the Brussels Salon, he now exhibited with Les XX in Brussels. But his most ambitious and important work, *The Entry of Christ into Brussels 1889,* was rejected by Les XX in 1889. Four years later, Les XX was disbanded. In the mid-1890s, Ensor's reputation began to grow. In 1898, the Parisian journal *La Plume* organized an exhibition of his work and devoted a special issue to him. In 1903, he was honoured with a knighthood of the Order of Leopold. King Albert named him a baron in 1929, the year in which the Palais des Beaux-Arts in Brussels devoted its inaugural exhibition to his works. Two years later, Edmond de Valeriola's monument to Ensor was unveiled. Finally in 1933, he was proclaimed "Prince of Painters" in Brussels and awarded the Legion of Honour by the French minister, Anatole de Monzie.

From the very beginning, Ensor showed a strong contempt for the moribund art establishment, and his works mark a notable departure from the contemporary aesthetics of Paris and Brussels. He represents more than the later nineteenth-century revolution liberating form and colour; his work is an intensified enquiry into urgent psychological, religious, social, and political issues. Tellingly, Ensor liked to call himself *le peintre des masques.*

The drawing *Town Hall, Brussels* is related to the painting of the same subject now in the Liege-Musée des Beaux-Arts. They belong to a group of Ostend and Brussels cityscapes executed around 1885. Shown from Ensor's usual elevated viewpoint, undoubtedly inspired by the familiar perspective from his attic studio, these cityscapes and street scenes resemble the French Impressionist boulevard representations of the 1870s. Ensor had come into contact with French Impressionism through Les XX and Brussels' growing cosmopolitanism — the noted French art dealer Durand-Ruel exhibited Degas, Monet, and Renoir in a Brussels hotel in 1885; and Monet, Renoir, and Rodin were invited to participate in Les XX in 1886. Yet unlike the works of Monet, Renoir, or Pissarro, Ensor's cityscapes frequently convey symbolic meanings — they were often settings for carnival celebrations, labour strikes, and military repressions. Brussels, in particular, had special significance for Ensor. It was here that his father was born (his father had recognized his unusual gifts early and encouraged him to come to terms with his own needs and aspirations; as a result, both suffered much torment under family domination). Brussels was also the place where he studied art and faced early public and academic hostility. Thus, the dominating structure of Brussels' city hall may be Ensor's symbol of authority and paternalism. His criticism of politicians, doctors, judges, magistrates, bankers, and other dignitaries is well known. As he said, "Who bears the torch of truth among the crowd singes here a beard and there a wig."

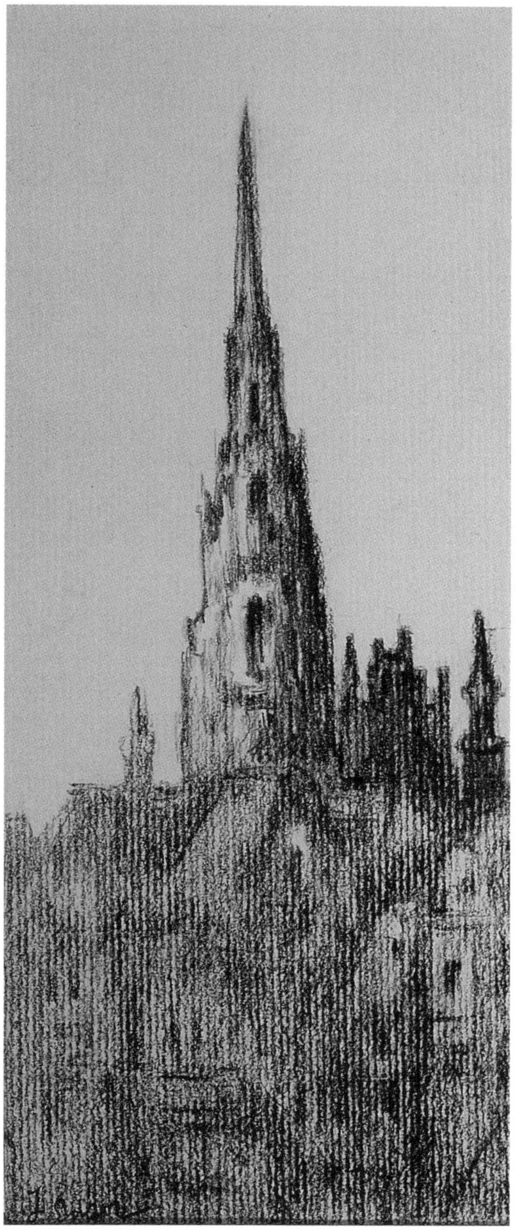

Town Hall, Brussels

1885
conté crayon
and graphite
254 x 110 mm
inscription:
signed *J. Ensor*

John Flaxman

1755 – 1826 | British

Figure Study for "Elektra Leading the Procession to the Tomb of Agamemnon"

circa 1794-95

pen and brown ink

160 x 120 mm

Born in York, Flaxman was the son of a plaster-cast maker and sculptor. In 1756, his family moved to London, and in his father's shop Flaxman learned to read, draw, and model. In 1767-68, he exhibited in the Free Society of Artists; two years later he showed in the Royal Academy and entered the Royal Academy School to study sculpture. Between 1775 and 1778 he was employed as a Wedgwood pottery designer. In 1787, he went to Italy to continue his studies of classical art. Returning to England in 1794, he was elected associate of the Royal Academy in 1797. Following the Treaty of Amiens in 1802, he visited Paris; David received him and praised his work. In 1810, he was appointed professor of sculpture at the Royal Academy. The remainder of his life was largely spent designing sculptural grave monuments.

In the late eighteenth- and early nineteenth-centuries, Flaxman's fame was founded primarily on his outline illustrations of classical authors: Homer, Aeschylus, Dante, Hesiod, and Milton. These simple outline designs, engraved by Thomas Piroli and published in the 1790s, became the undisputed international artistic currency for the dissemination of Neoclassical aesthetics. The spartan austerity of Flaxman's outline compositions, inspired by eclectic sources ranging from Greek vases and Etruscan incised mirrors to medieval and Renaissance art, was admired for its primitive purity, heroic manliness, and visual sincerity. The phenomenon of "Flaxmania" made a tremendous impact on the Neoclassical and Romantic generations and those beyond.

This drawing is a study for one of the Trojan women in the composition *Elektra Leading the Procession to the Tomb of Agamemnon* for an edition of the tragedies of Aeschylus. (The finished drawing is in the Royal Academy, London.) The Aeschylus drawings were commissioned by the Countess Dowager Spencer in 1792 when Flaxman was still in Rome working on Homeric illustrations for the countess's cousin, Mrs. Hare-Naylor. The entire series of Aeschylus illustrations was published in London in 1795 following Flaxman's return from Italy.

The Aeschylus drawings are especially noted for their visual "echoes" of the hieratic composition, deliberate repetition, ritualistic, and incantatory qualities of the original plays. Typical of his outline drawings, the composition is completely devoid of any suggestion of colour, light, space, and modelling. The figure is defined by strong continuous contours. Clearly Flaxman conceived these works with subsequent engraved illustrations in mind. At the dawn of the Industrial Revolution, these simple outlines replaced the traditional line engravings and thus streamlined the entire reproductive publishing culture.

The Giant "Fiery Passions"

circa 1796 pen and brown ink 200 x 321 mm

This drawing is an enlarged study of the group of "Giant Passions" from Plate 7 of *The Knight of the Blazing Cross*, a poem that was written and illustrated by Flaxman for his wife's birthday in 1796. (The sketchbook is in the Fitzwilliam Museum, Cambridge.) Inspired by John Bunyan and influenced by Swedenborg, the allegory of the knight who struggles against vice and triumphs in virtue is about human-kind's search for the ideal life. In his confrontation with the fiery passions, the knight is coming to face his "inward self." Flaxman wrote in the poem: "What — does thou fear this sight?/Thou only seest thine inward self/These are the fiery passions, gigantic, furious, fell/Who dance and play on thine imagination/Till they have whirl'd thy brains into an eddy/Within the which thy ship-wrecked reason sinks."

A Cloaked Figure

circa 1810 pen and brown-gray ink 165 x 105 mm

This sheet belongs to a group of studies related to principles concerning the fall of draperies extensively discussed in Flaxman's Academy Lecture VIII of 1810. Other sheets are in the University College, London.

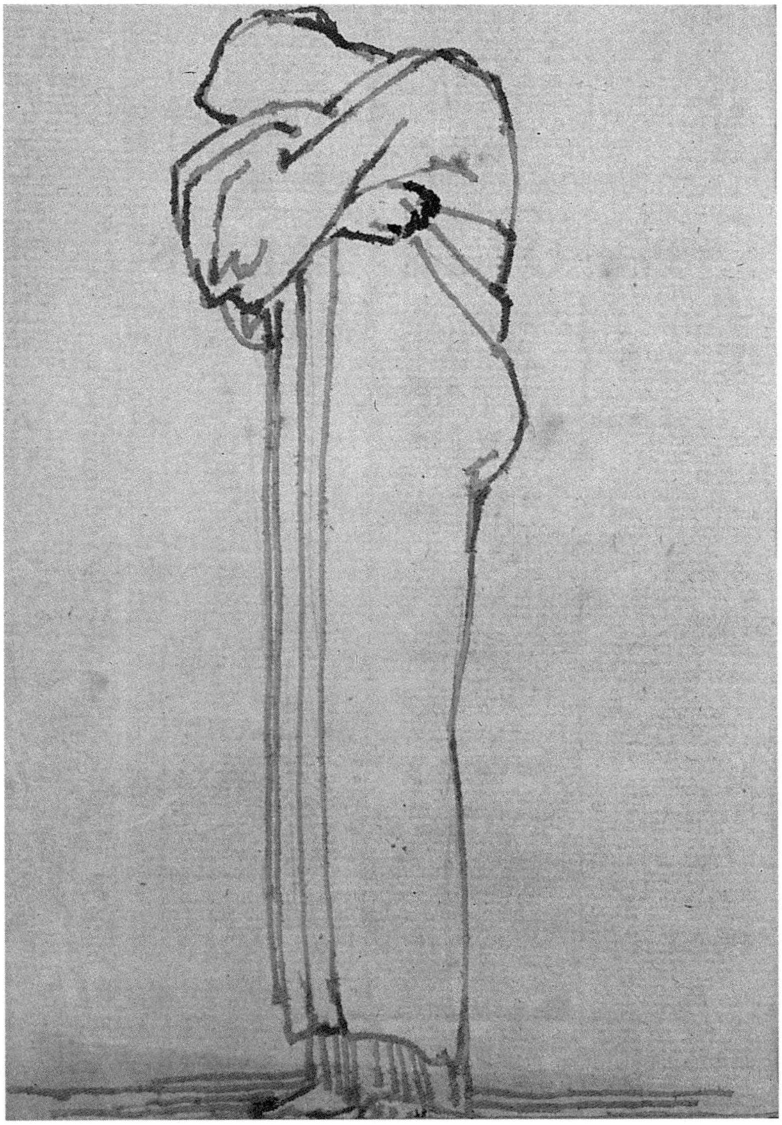

A Cloaked Figure

circa 1810

pen and brown-gray ink

165 x 105 mm

Jean Honoré Fragonard

1732 – 1806 | French

Copy After Watteau's "Columbine"

circa 1755

red chalk

170 x 100 mm

Born in Grasse, Fragonard moved with his family to Paris in 1738. After a brief but difficult apprenticeship to Chardin, he became a student of François Boucher in 1751. In 1752, he won the Prix de Rome. Between 1753-56, he studied with Carle van Loo at the École Royale des élèves protégés to prepare for his Italian sojourn. In Italy (1756-1761), he made prolonged visits to the Villa d'Este in Tivoli, Venice, Naples, and Sicily, and was in close association with the painter Hubert Robert and the dilettante Abbé de Saint-Non. He returned to Paris in 1761. Four years later, the Académie française admitted him as an *agréé,* and in the Salon of 1765, he exhibited the theatrical *Corésus Sacrificing Himself for Calirhoé.* Fragonard seems to have disliked official commissions, and exhibited publicly only once more, at the Salon of 1767. In the 1760s and 1770s he painted many moderate-size erotic and domestic scenes. His erotic pictures, while continuing the tradition of Watteau and Boucher, reveal a wilder, more extravagant, wittier temperament. His paintings, marked by a distinctive calligraphic line of the brush, reflect a special poetry of passion, of sweeping motion, storm, and decay, and almost Romantic enthusiasm. Increasingly his work showed northern, especially Dutch, influences. He was very much in demand for decorative work. Between 1771 and 1773, he executed a series of four large panels, *The Progress of Love* (Frick Collection, New York) for Madame du Barry's palace at Louveciennes, but it was rejected in favour of Vien's. He was hard hit by the French Revolution. He did obtain a few art-administrative posts after the Revolution, including the curatorship of the newly established Central Museum, which David had procured for him. He retired to Grasse during the Terror.

From the beginning of Fragonard's career, Watteau exerted a considerable influence. More than Boucher, Watteau's stylistic virtuosity and inherently Romantic temperament suited Fragonard's personality. This drawing, a copy of the figure of Columbine from Watteau's painting (circa 1716) *Harlequin and Columbine* (Wallace Collection, London), probably dates from the period just before Fragonard's 1756 Italian journey. As a student of the École Royale his curriculum consisted of drawing from life and from statues, as well as making copies after great masters from Parisian private collections and neighbouring châteaus.

A Young Woman

circa 1770 red chalk 155 x 100 mm

inscription: *Fragonard f.*

Although Fragonard is known for his many erotic representations, he also produced numerous scenes of domestic virtues, especially the education of children. In the late 1760s, these domestic scenes may be related to his marriage (1769). The figure in this drawing may be his pupil and wife, Marie-Anne Gérard. In any event, by the 1770s, the moral climate in France was already demanding the replacement of licentious subjects with bourgeois dramas. In the wake of the popularity of the novels of Rousseau and Richardson, and Diderot's proclamation of Greuze as the ideal painter of virtue, Fragonard's more serious subjects show his exploitation of an increasingly popular view.

An Old Man

circa 1780-88 graphite 230 x 190 mm

This drawing is a separate study of the figure symbolizing old age for a larger chalk and wash drawing entitled *Les Sept Ages de la Vie.* (Sold at Christie's, London, 1973, its present location is unknown.) Thematically this work belongs to a group of allegorical and mythological pictures Fragonard produced in the 1780s; the best known in this group is *The Fountain of Love* (Wallace Collection, London), which shows an aging couple rushing towards a fountain to renew their youth and love. The concept of time, of human transience, is an inherent aspect of the Rococo love theme, especially in the works of Watteau and Fragonard.

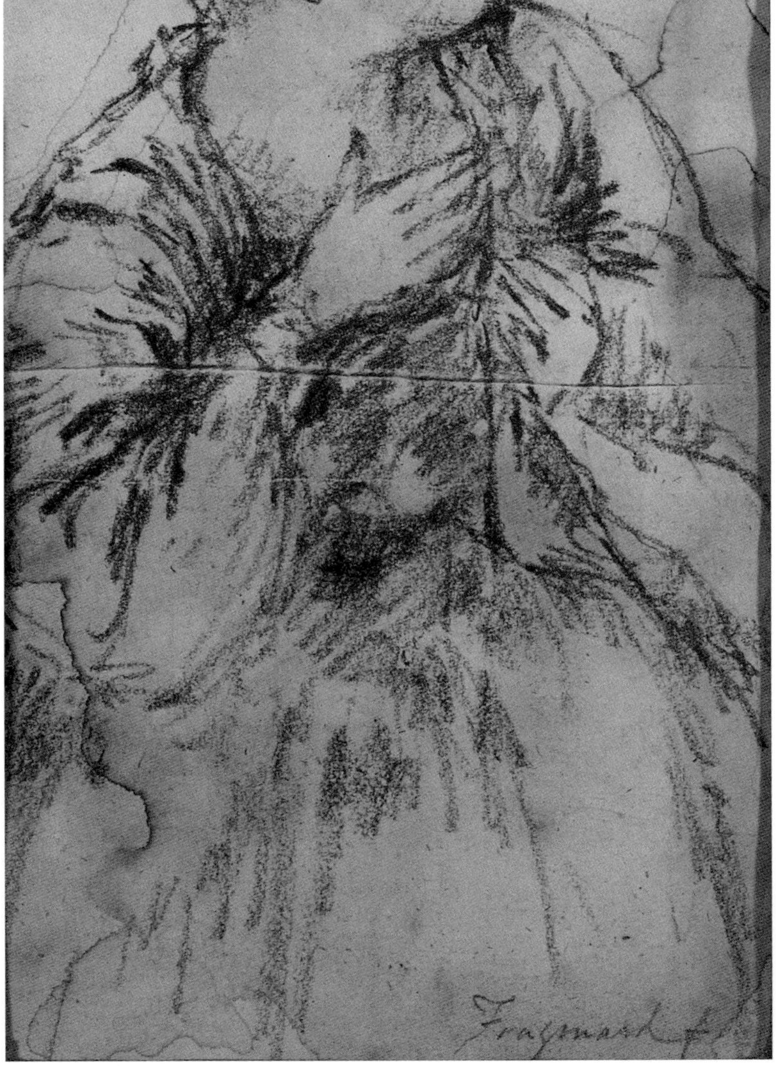

Copy After Watteau's "Columbine"

circa 1755

red chalk

170 x 100 mm

Caspar David Friedrich

1774 – 1840 | German

Dolmen Near Gützkow

1802 graphite
180 x 235 mm
inscription:
dated *19 Marz 1802*

Friedrich was born in Greifswald, Pomerania, on the Baltic coast. He studied drawing (1790-94) under Johann Gottfried Quistorp at the University of Greifswald. In the Copenhagen Academy (1794-98), he was taught by landscape painter Christian August Loventzen, Neoclassicist Jens Juel, and history painter Nicolai Abildgaard. After a brief stay in Berlin, he settled permanently in 1798 in Dresden, then the centre of German Romanticism. Here he became involved in the literary circle of the German Transcendentalists, including Kleist, Tieck, Arnim, Schlegel, and Schelling, whose writing and theories on art and nature-philosophy made a strong impression on him. Friedrich's early works are detailed topographical landscape drawings. In the solitary hills of Saxony and along the Baltic coast, he discovered the lifelong motifs of his art: the rocky beaches, barren mountains, gnarled trees, ruins of Gothic churches, and ancient dolmen tombs. He began to paint in oils around 1806. Very quickly, works such as *Cross in the Mountain* (1808) and *Monk by the Sea* (1810) drew great attention and even controversy. In these works, Friedrich was attempting to replace traditional religious subject matter with landscape symbolism. Like his fellow Dresden artist, Philipp Otto Runge, he was trying to invent a new pictorial language for the expression of religious and philosophical ideas. In his symbolic landscapes, the natural world is transformed into magical apparitions; his visionary approach represents an introspective, and often existentially pessimistic, meditation on nature's silent sublimity. Throughout his works, discipline and Romantic sensibility, stylistic artifice and observation of nature, national sentiment and concern for modernity are precariously balanced. Elected a member of the Dresden academy in 1816, he became a professor in 1824.

Friedrich's art possesses enormous emotional power. It developed in deliberate isolation, confined to its North German milieu: Friedrich refused even to make the art student's traditional pilgrimage to Rome. He believed strongly in the spiritual over the material; as a result, his landscapes are less physical depictions than expressions of his inner life. Even many of his early topographical studies, such as this drawing of a dolmen tomb near Gützkow, are symbolic and meant to be understood as allegories of transience and the promise of eternal life, and a reflection of a Nordic, semi-mythical, and heroic prehistoric past. Friedrich's eschatological interpretation of nature, in this instance, was undoubtedly influenced by the Pomeranian poet and Protestant pastor, Ludwig Theobul Kosegarten, who was especially interested in these dolmen tombs, generally known as *Hünengräber* (giants' graves), on the island of Rügen. Friedrich drew and painted these dolmens many times. A similar drawing, done and dated on the same day, is now in the Wallraf-Richartz Museum in Cologne.

Ship on the High Seas

circa 1815 graphite 205 x 127 mm

This sheet is a study for two painted versions of the same subject, one in a Hamburg private collection and the other in the Städtische Kunstsammlungen in Karl-Marx-Stadt. Although the ship is a traditional symbol of the individual soul, in this case it represents the Christian religion. The three masts are an allusion to the Trinity, while the anchor on the ship's prow suggests the shape of the cross. The voyage thus symbolizes a pilgrimage, the journey through life.

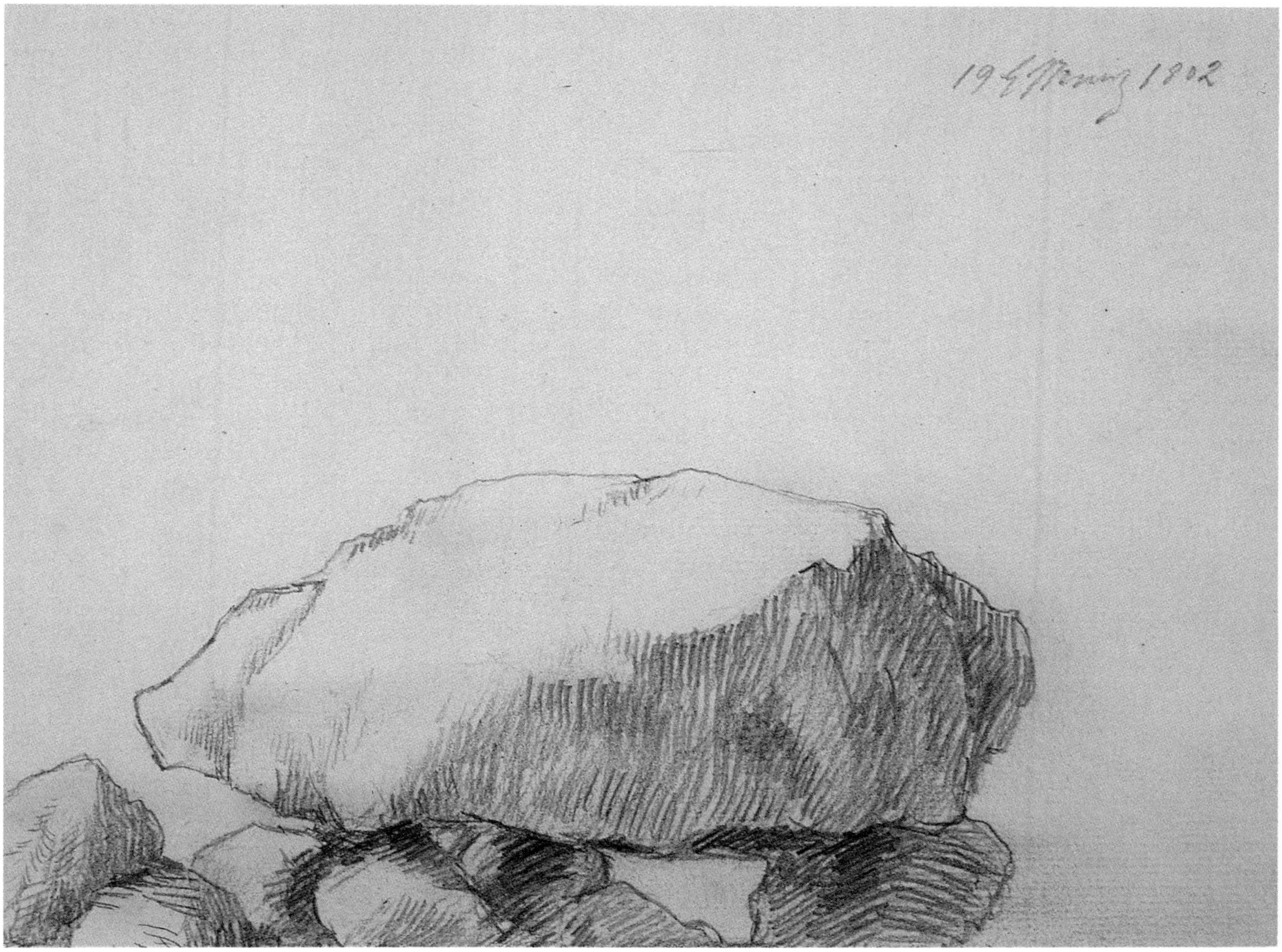

Dolmen
Near Gützkow

1802 graphite

180 x 235 mm

inscription:

dated *19 Marz 1802*

Johann Heinrich Füssli (Fuseli)

1741 – 1825 | Anglo-Swiss

Studies of the Furies

circa 1820 graphite

204 x 275 mm

inscription: (in Greek)

They guard the body of the slain mother — Fusely

Füssli was born in Zurich, the son of a painter and publicist. He studied theology and was ordained in 1761. The most important formative influence on him was that of the antiquarian and philologist, J.J. Bodmer, who introduced him to medieval literature, the Niebelungen epic, Dante, and Shakespeare. In Bodmer's circle, he met the physiognomist, Lavater. He left Zurich in 1763 and arrived in London the following year. He was at first active as a publicist and translated Winckelmann's *Reflections on the Imitation of Greek Art*. In 1766 he visited Paris and met Rousseau; the following year he published *Remarks on Rousseau*. Encouraged by Sir Joshua Reynolds, he decided to become a painter in 1768. He was by this time already one of the leading figures in the German literary movement Sturm und Drang ("Storm and Stress"). Between 1770-78, he travelled and worked in Italy, mainly in Rome, and was strongly influenced by ancient art and Michelangelo. Back in London in 1779, he exhibited regularly at the Royal Academy. In 1782, his painting *The Nightmare* was a great success (later Sigmund Freud owned an engraving of it). He was elected to the Royal Academy in 1788 and became a full member in 1790. In 1789, he was one of the contributors to John Boydell's ambitious *Shakespeare Gallery*. In 1799, he exhibited his *Milton Gallery*, a series of paintings in a grand Michelangelesque style illustrating *Paradise Lost*. That year he also became professor of painting at the Royal Academy and, finally, its keeper in 1804.

Füssli's art is a fusion of Mannerist, Baroque, and Neoclassical traits. His ability to digest eclectic impressions, gathered with incredibly diligent scholarship, prompted him to consider himself an untrammelled natural genius. The daemonic stance Füssli maintained throughout his life, which was viewed as notorious in England, was only for show. Although his works often consist of bombast and spoofing, he did possess rare insight into the realm of the subconscious, a gift shared by two of his contemporaries, Blake and Goya.

In 1821, Füssli exhibited the painting *The Erinyes Drive Alemaeon from the Corpse of His Mother, Eriphyle, Whom He Has Killed* in the Royal Academy. The subject was probably derived from Hyginus's *Fables* and Statius's *Thebais*. Füssli described the picture in a catalogue: "Amphiaros, a chief of the Argolic league against Thebes, endowed with prescience, to avoid his fate, withdrew to a secret place known only to Eriphyle his wife, which she, seduced by the presents of Polynices, disclosed: thus betrayed, he on departing, commanded Alemaeon his son, on being informed of his death, to destroy his mother; Eriphyle fell by the hand of her son, who fled, pursued by the avenging Furies."

This drawing appears to be a preliminary sketch for a more finished drawing for the painting. The finished ink and wash drawing, made in the house of Lavinia de Irueje, is in the collection of Kurt Meissner in Zurich. The exhibited painting is now in the Kunsthaus, Zurich.

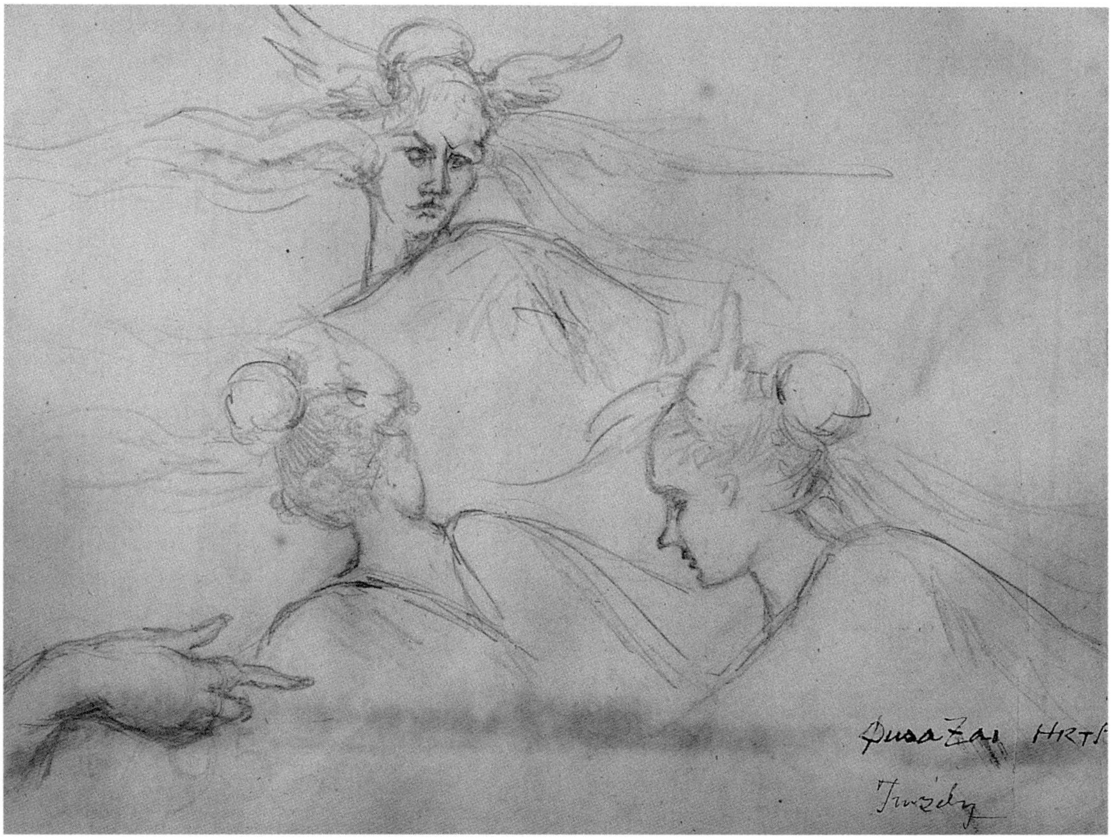

Studies
of the Furies

circa 1820 graphite

204 x 275 mm

inscription: (in Greek)

They guard the body of
the slain mother — Fusely

Paul Gauguin

1848 – 1903 | French

Self-portrait

1889 graphite

147 x 116 mm

inscription:

signed and dated

P. Gauguin 89

Born in Paris, Gauguin spent his early childhood in Peru, whence his mother's family came. There he developed an affinity for the tropics. From 1865-71, he was at sea working on cargo ships, travelling to Rio de Janiero and India. He became a stockbroker's agent in 1871. About this time he also became the unofficial pupil of Camille Pissarro, collected Impressionist works, and participated in their exhibitions between 1881 and 1886. Affected by the collapse of the Union Général des Banques, he left his firm in 1883, moved to Copenhagen, and devoted himself to art. Returning to France, he lived and worked in Brittany, at Pont-Aven and Le Pouldu from 1886 to 1890. In 1888, he met Emile Bernard, who encouraged him to abandon Impressionism in favour of Synthetism, a style drawing on a variety of western and non-western sources. Ultimately his search for the primitive and exotic and for an escape from western materialism led him to Tahiti in 1891. But his utopian hopes were dashed by numerous difficulties, and he returned to Paris in 1893. Yet two years later, he went back to the South Sea islands to stay. His remaining years in Tahiti and the Marquesas were a continuous struggle with finances, health, and the French colonial authorities. He died at Atuana in the Marquesas.

This *Self-Portrait* was executed in Brittany in the months following Gauguin's return from his stay with van Gogh at Arles in early 1889. It was an unsettling time for him. The Café Volpini exhibition at the Paris World's Fair, which he organized to show his own works and others' in 1889, proved to be disappointing, as did his participation in the spring salon of Les XX in Brussels. Thus during 1888 and 1889, he repeatedly portrayed himself as Victor Hugo's fictional hero, Jean Valjean, and as the crucified Christ. At the Paris World's Fair of 1889, he turned his attention to non-western art and renewed his interest in the Mayan, Javanese, and Cambodian sculptures there. It was about this time that he produced a ceramic cup in the form of a head (Konstindustrimuseet, Copenhagen), on which this drawing and the self-portrait pot in the painting of *Still-life with Head-Shaped Vase* (1889, in the Ittelson collection, New York) were based. The idea of making the pot in the shape of a head probably derived from the Peruvian head pots of the Chicama Valley, with which Gauguin had been familiar since childhood. In all these representations — ceramics, painting, and drawing — he portrayed himself as the Man of Sorrows.

A Polynesian Woman

circa 1896 graphite 235 x 160 mm

inscription: signed *P. Gauguin*

The figure is related to a wooden mask that Gauguin produced about 1896 (destroyed during the Second World War and known only through a photograph). Both the mask and this drawing suggest the sitter was probably Pahura, Gauguin's companion during his second stay in Tahiti after 1895. In 1896, Pahura gave birth to a girl who survived only a few days. Moved by this event, Gauguin painted *The Nativity* (Bayerische Staatsgemäldesammlungen, Munich), which is inscribed "Te Tamari no atua" and shows the mother watching from the bed her infant, cradled by a hooded death-spirit. During his last years in Tahiti, when he was forced to move to the suburbs of Papeete, Gauguin sued Pahura for housebreaking when she would not accompany him; the case was dismissed. In 1899, they had a son.

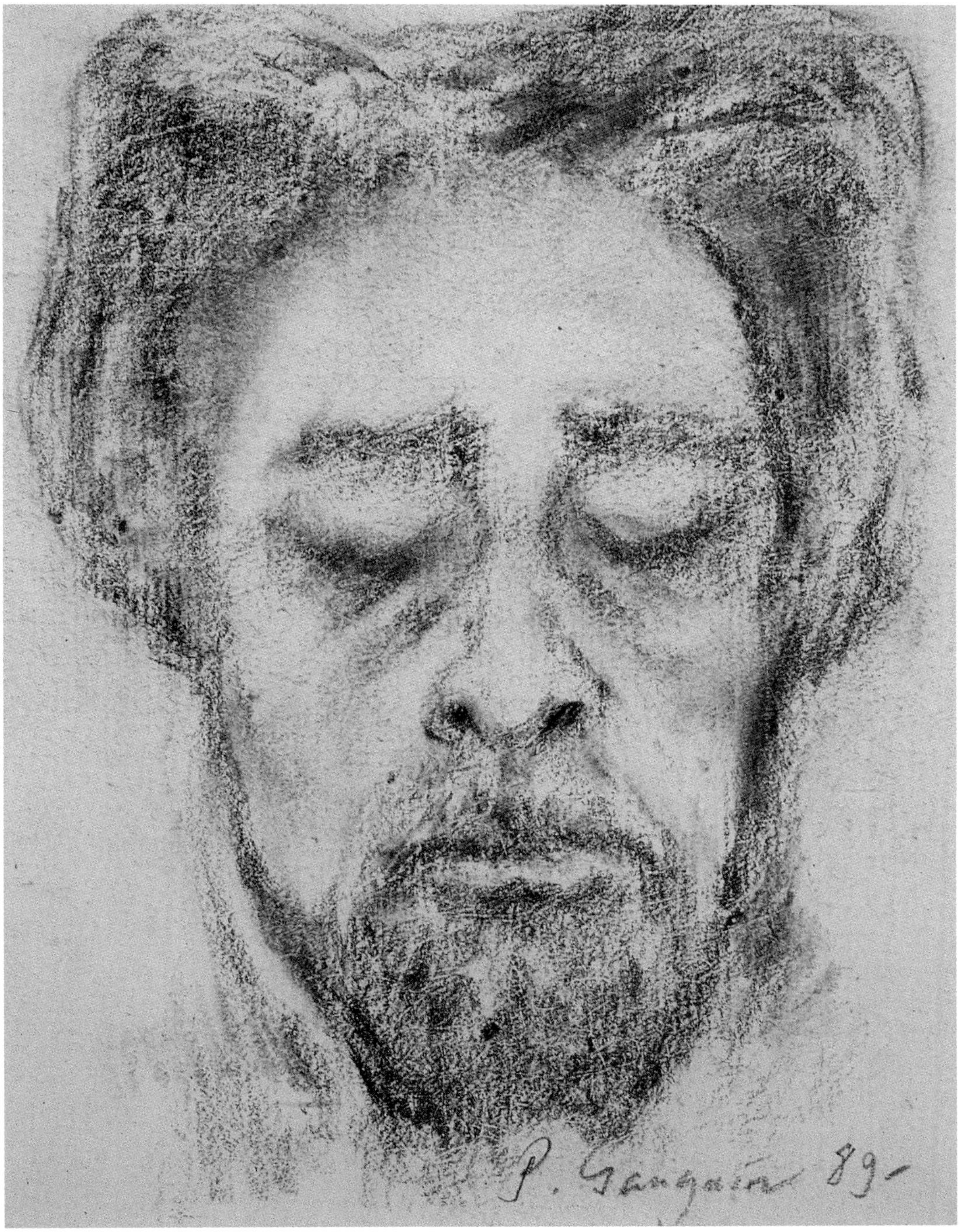

Self-portrait

1889 graphite

147 x 116 mm

inscription:

signed and dated

P. Gauguin 89

Theodore Géricault

1791 – 1824 | French

Study of a Man's Arm

1818-19

graphite

187 x 150 mm

Born in Rouen, Géricault moved with his parents to Paris in 1796. In 1808 he started to study with Carle Vernet, a popular painter specializing in elegant, modern equestrian and military genres. By 1810, he had entered the studio of Pierre Guérin, an orthodox classicist of melodramatic subjects. Even in Guérin's studio, Géricault began a program of self-training by copying the masters in the Louvre.The Baroque works of Rubens, van Dyck, and Caravaggio, and modern artists such as Gros were of particular interest to him. About the time of Napoleon's final abdication in 1815, Géricault developed his "antique" manner, inspired by studies of Michelangelo. He failed to win the Prix de Rome in 1816. The same year, attempting to escape from his troubled love affair with his aunt, he went to Italy. Returning to Paris in 1817, he chose the subject of *The Raft of the Medusa* for his next Salon painting. For two years he laboured on the project. The picture, however, received mixed reviews in the Salon of 1819. Exhausted physically and mentally, he took the *Raft* to England in 1820, exhibited it in London, and spent the next two years absorbing the English sporting genre and landscape painting.

He returned to Paris in 1822 and was commissioned to do a group of ten *Portraits of the Insane*, for Dr. Georget, a well-known psychiatrist specializing in the treatment of monomanias, who might have treated Géricault in 1819-20.Towards 1823, Géricault was working on two contemporary subjects, *Liberation of the Prisoners of the Spanish Inquisition* and *The African Slave Trade*; they remained unfinished at his death in 1824.

This sketch of an arm is a study for a dead African figure in the painting *Raft of the Medusa*, shown in the Salon of 1819. In terms of build, the person who posed for this life study is probably the same as the one for the signalling African figure on a barrel at the apex of the compositional pyramid in the *Raft*. He has been identified as a professional model named Joseph, who worked for Géricault at this time. For the painting of the *Raft*, Géricault produced a large series of studies and sketches; nearly a hundred have survived.

The subject of the *Raft* was the shipwreck of the *Medusa* in 1816 off the Senegal coast, and the abandonment of 150 of its crew and passengers on a make-shift raft by an incompetent, aristocratic captain. The disaster resulted in the loss of 135 lives. Géricault traced the politically explosive event by following the account by the surviving surgeon and engineer on the raft (*Naufrage de la Frégate la Medusa*, Paris, 1817). He also interviewed other survivors and even had a model of the raft constructed for studio use. His response to the scandalous *Medusa* episode — his dramatic depiction of the sea-tossed raft — is political, humanitarian, and even philosophical; the raft is a contemporary metaphor for the tragic condition of humanity. In his prominent placement of the two African figures — one alive and the other dead — in the composition of the *Raft*, Géricault has underlined his Romantic concern for all oppression. His sympathy for the African slaves is paralleled by his feelings for the monomaniac patients and Inquisitional victims later on.

Severed Legs and Arm

1818-19 graphite 270 x 335 mm

inscription: signed *Géricault*

A study for a painting now in the Musée Fabre in Montpellier, this drawing represents a special group of studies of severed heads and dissected limbs that Géricault produced while working on the *Raft of the Medusa*. He obtained the body parts from medical friends on the staff of the nearby Beaujon hospital. Although these studies did not serve any direct purpose for the *Raft* painting, Géricault needed to stay close to the horrible reality of his subject in order to convey the experience of the passengers on the raft whose suffering, including cannibalism, he was trying to express. Delacroix, who posed for the *Raft of the Medusa*, saw some of these studies and considered them to be "truly sublime . . . the best argument for Beauty as it ought to be understood."

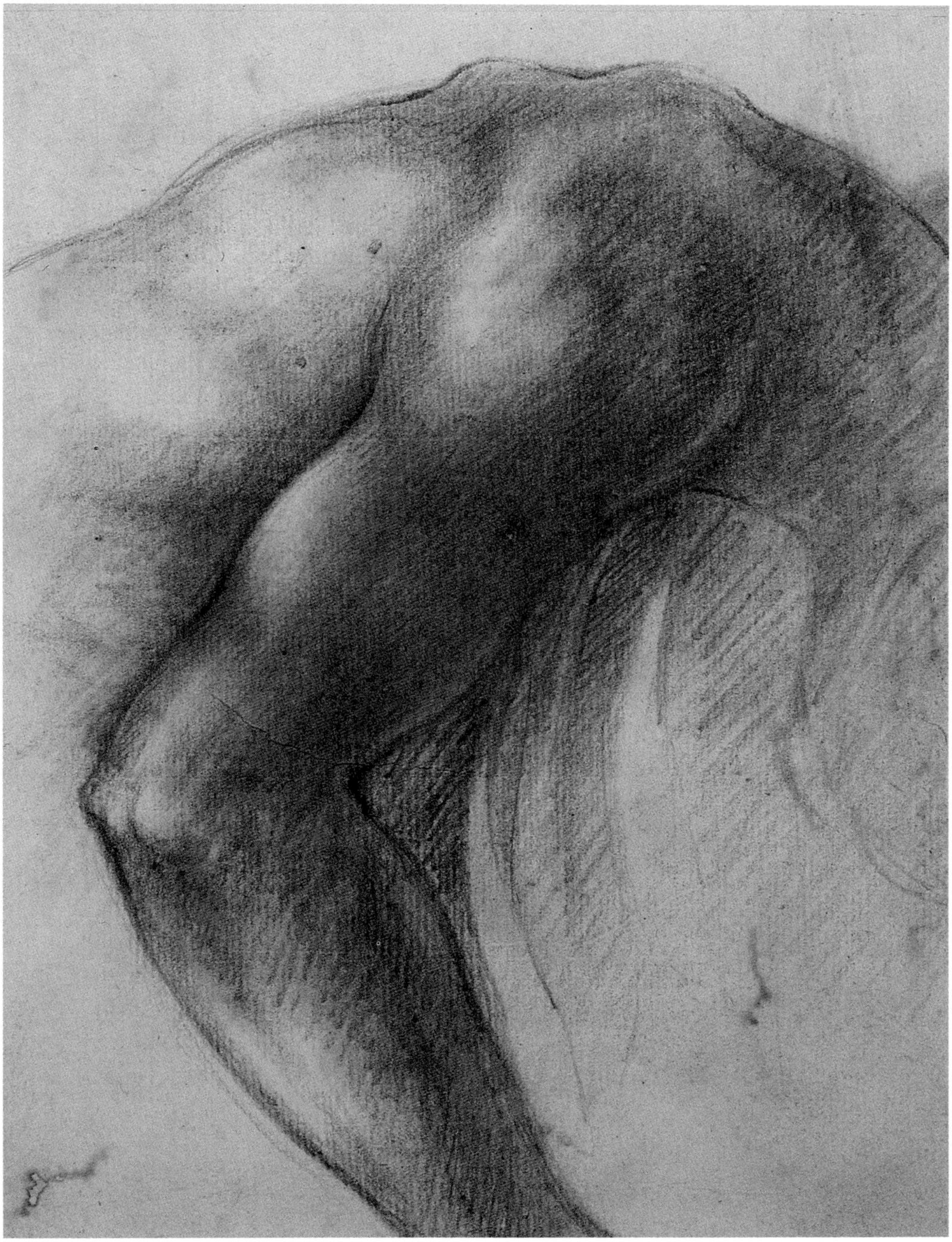

Study of
a Man's Arm

1818-19

graphite

187 x 150 mm

Anne-Louis Girodet de Roucey-Trioson

1767 – 1824 | French

Study for the Arm of Hippocrates

1791 graphite

128 x 175 mm

Girodet began his art lessons with a local artist, Luquin. After his father's death in 1784, he joined the studio of David in 1785. He competed unsuccessfully for the Prix de Rome in 1787 and 1788, but won first prize in 1789. He spent the following five years, the years of the Revolution, in Italy. In 1790, while staying in the Villa Medici, he painted *Endymion's Sleep*, a Romantic interpretation of a classical myth, which was a great success in Rome and in the Paris Salon of 1793. Returning to Paris in 1795, he worked for the Parisian publisher Didot, providing illustrations for the works of Homer, Virgil, Anacreon, and Racine. During the Directoire and Consulate when a taste for luxury was re-established — as a reaction against the Revolution's austerities — Girodet's affectatious and extravagant art came into fashion. In the Salon of 1799, he created a great sensation and scandal with the clever *Portrait of Mlle. Lange as Danaë*, his revenge on the fashionable actress for rejecting his earlier portrait of her. In 1801 in the service of Napoleon, he painted, for the Malmaison, *Ossian Receiving the Shades of Napoleonic Officers*, inspired by James Macpherson's Erse pseudo-epic. This was followed by *Napoleon Receiving the Keys of Vienna* in 1808 and *Revolt of Cairo* in 1810. During 1809, he also decorated the Compiègne apartments of the emperor and the empress. The Salon of 1814 showed fifteen of his paintings, a mounting to a retrospective. He became a member of the École des Beaux-Arts in 1815. His later works, however, were uneven; after the death of his adopted father, the military surgeon Dr. Trioson (who adopted him in 1806), he came into a considerable inheritance and his productivity noticeably declined.

Girodet's art is manneristic, and his compositions often anti-Davidian; they are filled with tortuous complexities and refinements. More than a painter, he was also an ambitious intellectual, a writer, and a theorist. Well-read and deeply cultivated, he chose a great variety of complicated subjects, ranging from ancient history to contemporary literature. The present drawing is a study for the figure of Hippocrates in his painting *Hippocrates Refusing the Presents of Artaxeres*, produced while he was in Rome in 1792 (École de Médecine, Paris). The painting, intended for the decoration of Dr. Trioson's house at Bourgoin, was also a homage to Dr. Trioson. According to the 1814 Salon description, Girodet derived his inspiration from Abbé Barthélemy's *Voyage du jeune Anacharsis en Grèce* of 1788. It is the story of the famous Greek physician Hippocrates who, remaining loyal to his own people, rejected the gifts with which the ambassadors of the Persian king, Artaxeres, hoped to persuade him to come and assist in their plague-stricken country. The classical tale of the rejection of wealth on moral and patriotic grounds was clearly meant to convey the importance of public virtue in the years of the French Revolution. Girodet himself described the subject as "un des plus beaux de l'antiquité, tant par la vénération attachée à Hippocrate, que par le bel exemple de patriotisme et de désintéressement dont il offre le tableau." And nowhere is the sense of patriotism and psychological characterization of virtue and steadfastness more apparent than in the gesture of the left hand of Hippocrates, as depicted in this drawing. The stern gesture emphasizes the moral contrast between the hero's virtue and the Persian's hypocrisy. Theatrical and symbolic, the gesture was undoubtedly intended to bring to mind for comparison's sake those firm, outstretched hands in David's famous *Oath of the Horatii* (1784) and the oath-taking motif in the context of the French Revolution (such as the Oath of the Tennis Court in 1789). Later, illustrating Racine's *Phèdre* (Didot, 1801) Girodet reused the gesture for the figure of Thésée, shown reproachfully ordering Hippolyte to leave him (IV, ii).

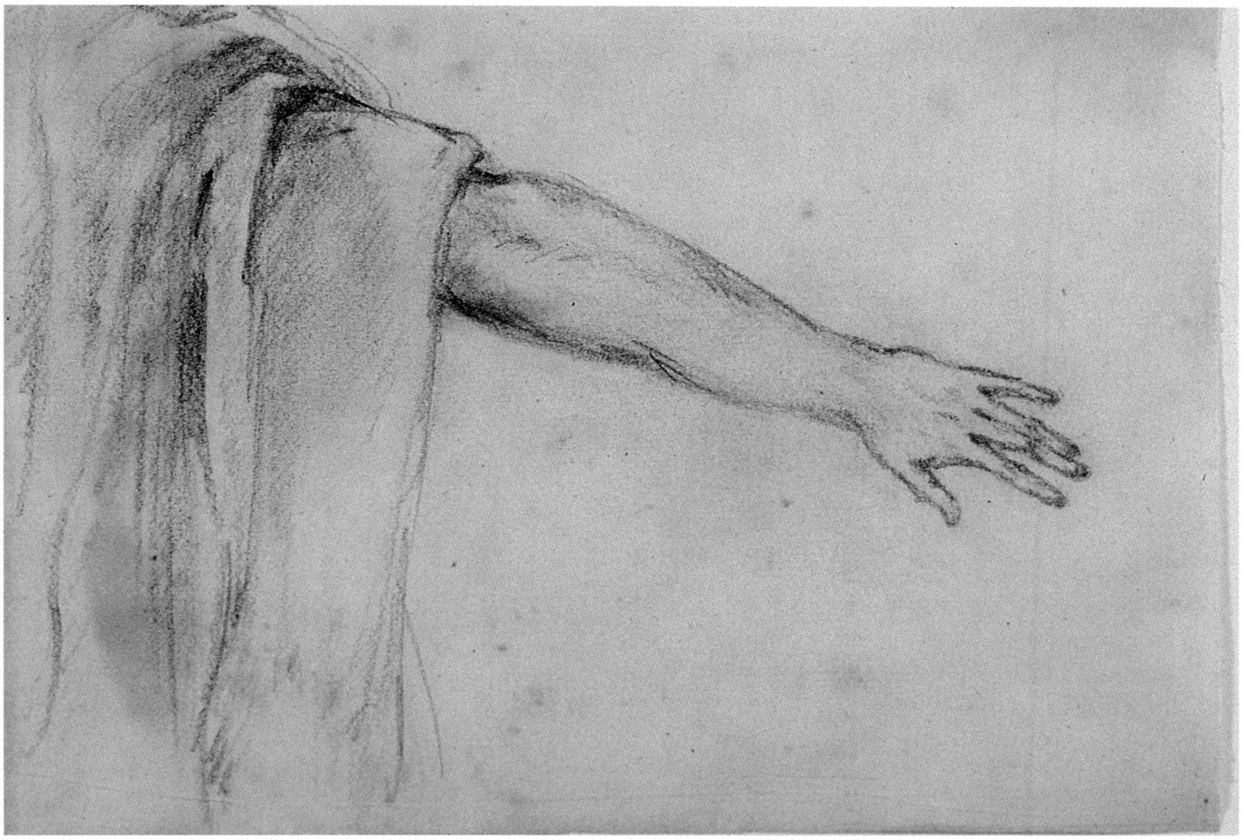

Study for the Arm of Hippocrates

1791 graphite

128 x 175 mm

Francisco Goya y Lucientes

1746 – 1828 | Spanish

Maja

circa 1825
brush and brown ink
158 x 90 mm
inscription:
La Maja de la Mantilla.
Goya

Goya was born at Fuendetodos, near Saragossa. He began his apprenticeship in 1760 with José Luzan. In 1763, he went to Madrid and continued his studies at the Academy of San Fernando with Francisco Bayeu, a court painter and Goya's future brother-in-law. He travelled to Italy some time after 1766, and returned to Spain in 1771. Supported by Bayeu, he acquired a position in 1774 as cartoon designer for the royal tapestry factory of Santa Barbara, a position he held until 1792. During that period, he produced seven series of tapestry cartoons for various royal palaces, studied and inventoried the royal collection, and copied Velázquez. His worldly success came in the early 1780s with commissions from the Spanish high aristocracy. In 1785, he became deputy director of painting in the Madrid academy and its director ten years later. Throughout the 1780s, he was also a court painter, first to Carlos III and then Carlos IV, the latter appointing him first court painter in 1799. Besides his painting commissions, he also produced etchings. His first major series of prints, *Los Caprichos*, was issued in 1799 but the Inquisition forced its withdrawal from sale. When Spain was occupied by the French forces between 1808 and 1814, he continued to work for Joseph Bonaparte, who awarded him the Royal Order of Spain in 1811. At the same time he also painted portraits of Fernando VII (1808) and the duke of Wellington (1812), and began another series of etchings, the *Disasters of War* (1809-1820). Following the restoration of Fernando VII in 1814, he commemorated the War of Independence with two paintings, *The Charge of the Mamelukes: 2nd May 1808* and *The Execution of the Hostages: 3rd May 1808*. Two years later he published the print series of bullfighting, the *Tauromaquia*. By this time his liberal associations under the absolutist government of Fernando VII forced him to withdraw more and more from public life. Before his final departure from Spain in 1824, he painted, between 1819-23, a series of fourteen murals (known as *The Black Paintings*) for his country villa, the Quinta del Sordo. Productive to the end, he spent the last ten years of his life in Bordeaux.

This drawing was produced in the Bordeaux years. A similar drawing showing the figure in reverse, done in black chalk and now in the A. Santa Marina collection, Buenos Aires, was originally part of the "Bordeaux Album," which Goya sketched between 1824 and 1828. Both these *Maja* drawings were probably preparatory studies for the two etchings Goya made about 1825-27. The "Bordeaux Album" drawing corresponds to the etching on a dark ground whereas this drawing corresponds to the reversed figure on white ground in the second etching. The pose of the figure in these drawings and prints is reminiscent of the figure of the *maja*-costumed Duchess of Alba in the *Portrait of the Duchess of Alba* that Goya painted in Sanlúcar in 1797 (Hispanic Society of America, New York).

The *maja* is the female counterpart of the *majo*. Together they formed a special group of strutting, picaresque characters from the lower working class of Spanish society, distinguished by their colourful costumes and behaviour. The *majos* and *majas* considered themselves representatives of Spanish popular (*pueblo*) culture, the true Castilian spirit. Maintaining a sense of superiority, they were hostile towards any foreign innovations. They also observed a strict anti-establishment moral code. Socially rebellious, they showed an ambivalent loyalty to the king and the church. Rather than opposing their way of life, the Spanish aristocracy deliberately imitated their dress, speech, and behaviour as a direct reaction against the French styles of the *illustrados*, those enlightened new Spaniards. Throughout his life, Goya held a precarious, and often ambiguous, balance between these two cultures — he considered himself a man of the *pueblo* and supported *majismo*, yet many of the views expressed in his works and behaviour were derived from his circle of friends belonging to the *illustrados* of the Madrid intelligensia.

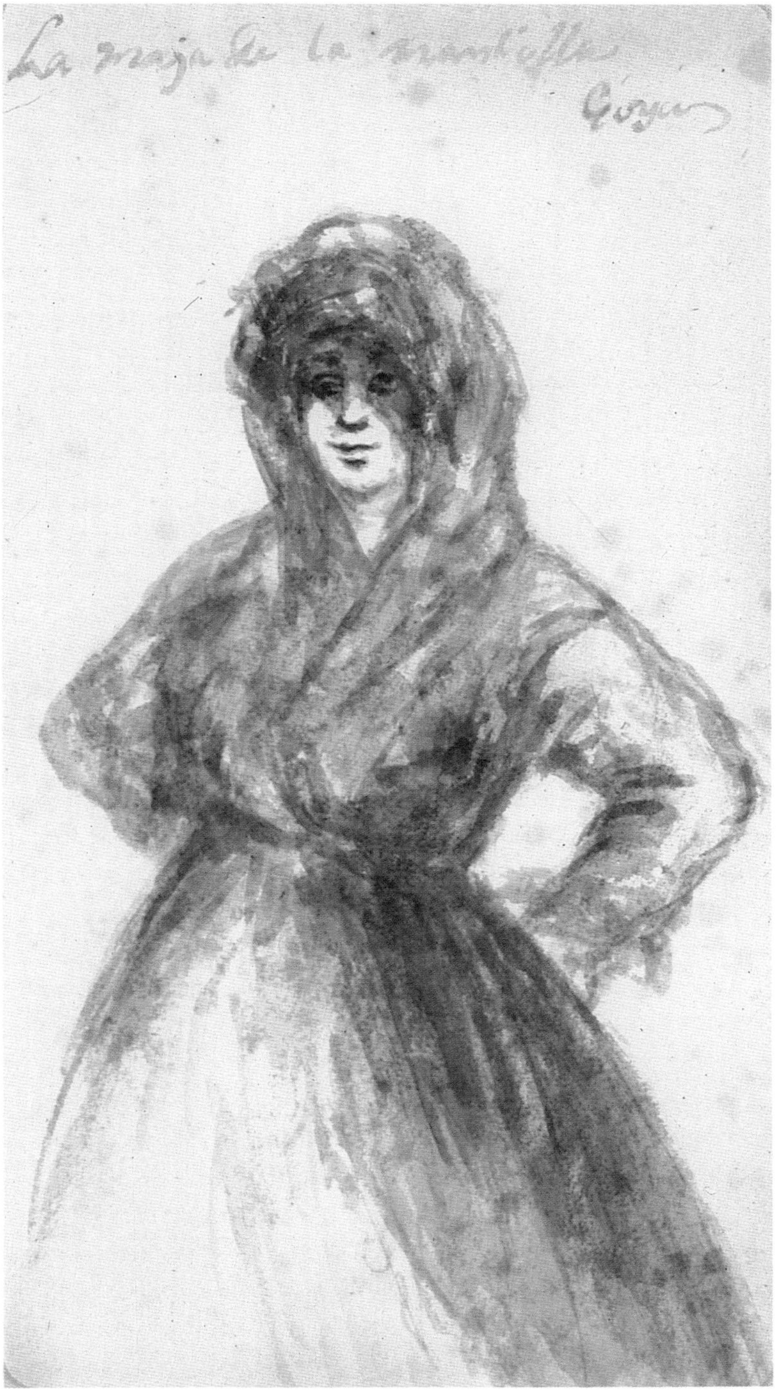

Maja

circa 1825

brush and brown ink

158 x 90 mm

inscription:

La Maja de la Mantilla.

Goya

Jean Baptiste Greuze

1725 – 1805 | French

Figure Study for "La Paressense Italienne"

1757 red chalk

180 x 125 mm

Greuze was born in Tournus and pursued his early studies in Lyon under Charles Grandon. Some time in the early 1750s, he went to Paris. He was admitted to the Académie Française as an *agréé* in 1755. Shortly after, he spent two years, 1755-57, in Italy. Following his return to Paris in 1757, his patrons included La Live de Jully, Julienne, Damery, the comte de Vence, and the duc de Choiseul. His novel representations, influenced by Dutch and Flemish masters, increasingly attracted the middle class. In 1759, he met the art critic and encyclopedist, Denis Diderot, who would be a great influence on his work and in furthering his career by publicly proclaiming him to be the "pictorial preacher of good behaviour." In the Salon of 1761, his *L'Accordée de Village* (Louvre) was a spectacular success. Taking subjects from the life of the "humble poor," he developed his specialty: dramatizing moral conflicts. He was particularly concerned with the corruption of innocence, a theme he gave an erotic and sentimental flavour. His pictorial narratives have a direct parallel in the middle-class, realistic, and sentimental novels and stage-plays of the time — Voltaire, Rousseau, Diderot, Moissy, Beaumarchais, and Richardson provide the obvious comparisons. In 1763, his *Death of the Paralytic* won great acclaim; two years later, compositional sketches for *The Father's Curse* and *The Bad Son Punished* caused a sensation in the Salon and won Diderot's fervent praise. Until the arrival of David, Greuze had no competitors. In the years of the Revolution, he painted portraits of revolutionary leaders and scenes of contemporary life. He was a favourite of the Bonaparte family.

This sheet is a study for the painting *La Paressense Italienne* (Wadsworth Atheneum, Hartford), one of a group of pseudo-Italian pictures Greuze exhibited in the Salon of 1757, the year he returned from Rome. The image of the pensive seated woman with only one shoe on — the other is lying on the floor — is a typical moral allegory of the corruption of innocence and virtue. The unshod foot is a symbol of lost virginity. (The shoe is a symbol of female sexual favour, best exemplified in Fragonard's *The Swing* of 1767.)

Figure Study for "The Return"

circa 1778-79 red chalk 180 x 125 mm

The crouching female in this drawing is a separate study of a centrally placed figure in a large ink, wash, and chalk drawing now in the Wadsworth Atheneum, Hartford. The entire scene, representing the joyful welcome of the returning son by his family, is typical of the moralizing, sentimental narratives Greuze had popularized since the early 1760s.

Portrait of a Man

circa 1778-80 red chalk 180 x 125 mm

inscription: *Greuze fecit*

Greuze's powerful pictorial talent is best reflected, and is least flawed by overt sentimentality, in his many portraits. Compared to contemporary Rococo productions, his portraits are extremely naturalistic. Not surprisingly, the Bonaparte family patronized him with many portrait commissions in his last years. He also painted Benjamin Franklin in 1778.

Study of a Boy

circa 1770-80 red chalk 180 x 125 mm

Study of a Boy in Profile

circa 1770-80 red chalk 180 x 125 mm

Inscription: *Greuze*

Since Greuze's moralizing genres centred around the concept of the family and its unity — and the inherent conflict between parents and their offspring provided a theme for most of his large-scale figure compositions — he made many tender studies of children throughout his career, some of them, including these two perhaps, used in such compositions as *Le Gâteau des Rois* (1774), *La Dame de Charité* (1775), *La Malédiction Paternalle* (1777), *Le Fils Puni* (1778), *Le Donneur de Chapelets* (1780), and *La Belle-Mère* (1781).

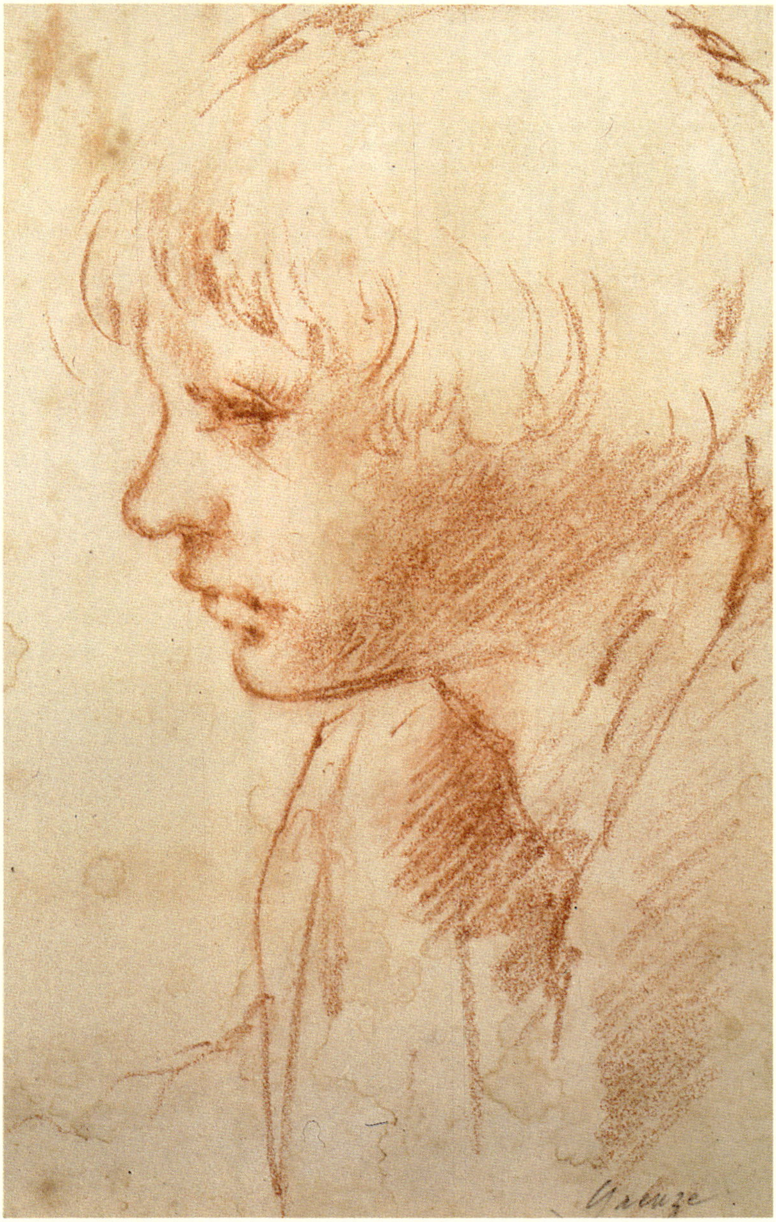

Study of
a Boy in Profile

circa 1770-80

red chalk

180 x 125 mm

Inscription: *Greuze*

Constantin Guys

1802 – 1892 | French

Promenading Along the Seine: Pont Royal

circa 1870

pen and wash
in red-brown ink
over graphite

155 x 115 mm

Guys, often known as the "chronicler of the Second Empire," was born in Flushing, Holland; his father was chief purser in the French navy. Growing up in a naval family, he was very much drawn to the excitement of travel and adventure. He travelled extensively throughout his life, to Spain, England, and Turkey. In 1824, he joined Lord Byron in the Greek War of Independence and three years later, he enlisted in a French regiment of dragoons. During the Crimean War in 1854, he was the artist correspondent for the *Illustrated London News*. An acknowledged modern dandy, he was as comfortable in society as in the demi-monde. He was an incessant draughtsman; his rapid, witty drawings and watercolours documented not just wars, but also the fashions, manners, and attitudes of Europe — from soldiers and horse-drawn carriages to quayside prostitutes. While he never received any formal training in drawing, and he never painted in oils, his talent for the improvised sketch shows the influences of Callot, Rembrandt, and Goya. Daumier, a fellow artist-journalist and amoralist, held him in great esteem. As one of the best examples of the Realist principle of "il faut être de son temp," Guys fully embodied the mid-nineteenth-century avant-garde mission of contemporaneity. Among his noted portrayals of fashionable modern urban life are vignettes of the Parisian bourgeoisie promenading along the newly created boulevards and parks of Louis Napoleon's Second Empire capital, as in this drawing. Guys' works are far removed from the stifling world of official academic art and thus exercised a decisive influence on a whole generation of artists from Manet to the Impressionists and Toulouse-Lautrec. In the rapidity of their execution, Guys' drawings underline his modern vision of an ever-changing world and quick-moving life.

The poet and art critic Charles Baudelaire chose Guys as a pretext and the basis for his theory of modernity. In his now familiar "Painters of Modern Life," first published in 1863 in *Figaro*, Baudelaire writes of Guys' technique: "M.G. [Monsieur Guys] begins with slight pencil marks which scarcely indicate the place the objects are to occupy in space. The principal planes are then indicated with wash tints, in masses that are at first vaguely and lightly coloured, but then taken up again later to have stronger colours laid on successively. At the very last, the outline of the object is traced with ink." He then goes on to describe Guys' art: "M.G. loves mixing with the crowds, loves being incognito, and carries his originality to the point of modesty. . . . We are betting on a certainty when we say that in a few years the drawings of M.G. will become precious archives of civilized life. His works will be sought after by discerning collectors, as much as those of all those exquisite artists who, although they have confined themselves to recording what is familiar and pretty, are nonetheless, in their own ways, important historians. Several of them have been sacrificed too much to the 'pretty-pretty,' and have sometimes introduced into their compositions a classic style foreign to their subject. . . . Less skillful than they, M.G. retains a profound merit, which is all his own; he has deliberately filled a function which other artists disdain, and which a man of the world above all others could carry out. He has gone everywhere in quest of the ephemeral, the fleeting forms of beauty in the life of our day, the characteristic traits of what, with the reader's permission, we have called 'modernity.' Often bizarre, violent, excessive, but always full of poetry, he has succeeded, in his drawing, in distilling the bitter or heady flavour of the wine of life."

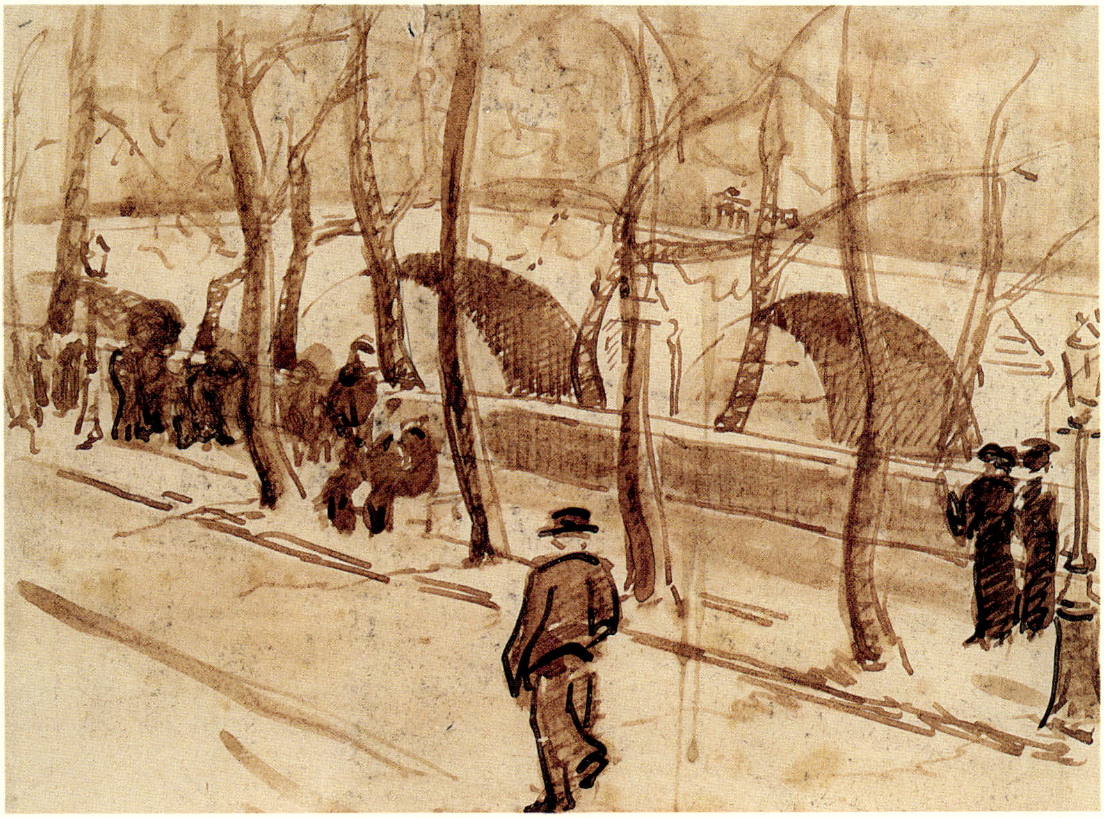

Promenading Along the Seine: Pont Royal

circa 1870

pen and wash in red-brown ink over graphite

155 x 115 mm

Victor Hugo

1802 – 1885 | French

Character Studies: Two Heads

circa 1873

pen and wash in brown ink

154 x 201 mm

inscription: signed *V. Hugo*

Son of an army officer, Hugo was born in Besançon. After spending some years in Corsica, Elba, and Italy, his family returned to Paris in 1808. Even in his teens, Hugo was recognized for his poetry: he received an award from the *Jeux floraux de Toulouse* in 1819, he published *Odes et Poésies diverses* in 1822 and in 1822-23, Louise XVIII granted him two pensions. By 1830, his prolific career began with the publication and performance of a series of novels and dramas: *Hernani* in 1830; *Notre Dame de Paris* and *Marion de Lorme* and *Les Feuilles d'automne* in 1831; *Le Roi s'amuse* in 1832; *Lucrèce Borgia* and *Marie Tudor* in 1833; *Claude Gueux* in 1834; *Angelo* and *Les Chants du crépuscule* in 1835; *Les Voix intérieures* in 1837; *Ruy Blas* in 1838; and *Les Rayons et les Ombres* in 1840. He continued to write and publish for the next four decades until 1878; his newspaper, *L'Evénement* first appeared in 1848. He was made an officer of the Legion of Honour in 1837, elected to the Académie française in 1841 and named peer of France in 1845. First elected to the legislative assembly in 1849, he campaigned on universal suffrage and freedom of the press, and opposed the death penalty and church-controlled education. His continuous opposition to the government of Louis Napoleon forced him into exile after the coup d'état of 1851. Inspired by his official expulsion from France in 1852, he wrote *Histoire d'un crime* and *Napoléon le petit.* Throughout his exile in the next nineteen years, he lived in Belgium, Jersey, and finally Guernsey. When the Third Republic was proclaimed in 1870, he returned to France and served briefly in the national assembly. In 1876, he was elected to the senate. On his death in 1885, he was given a state funeral and buried in the Panthéon.

Hugo was one of those literary figures with a strong visual artistic bent; drawing was almost a natural extension of his writing. He drew nearly all his life. Calling himself "homme de caprice et de fantaisie" in the preface *Les Orientales* (1829), he began producing caricatures in the 1830s, satirizing corrupt politicians such as the comte de Cessec and even his pretentious brother-in-law, the writer Paul Foucher. About 1870, he started to organize many of his caricatures from the previous decades into a collection entitled *Théâtre de la Gaité*, followed by another, *Poëme de la sorcière*, in 1873. It is to the last series that the present drawing is related.

Hugo's taste for the grotesque appeared early in his novels. Half-comic and half-terrifying figures first emerged in *Han d'Islande* (1823) and *Bug-Jargal* (1826). Then came the famous hunchback Quasimodo in *Notre Dame de Paris* (1831) and the tragic clown Triboulet in *Le Roi s'amuse* (1832). Bestialized beings continued to populate his writings and drawings in subsequent decades. Hugo drew his inspiration from a variety of sources: from the prints of Callot and Goya and contemporary caricatures as well as the travelling musicians and actors he encountered on his picaresque journeys. While some of the drawings have been compared to coastlines in maps, his caricatures — similar to contemporary social and political cartoons — were intended to satirize the established authorities: monarchy, church, army, and above all, bourgeois values and stupidity.

The majority of Hugo's drawings are located in the Maison de Victor Hugo in Guernsey and the Bibliothéque Nationale in Paris.

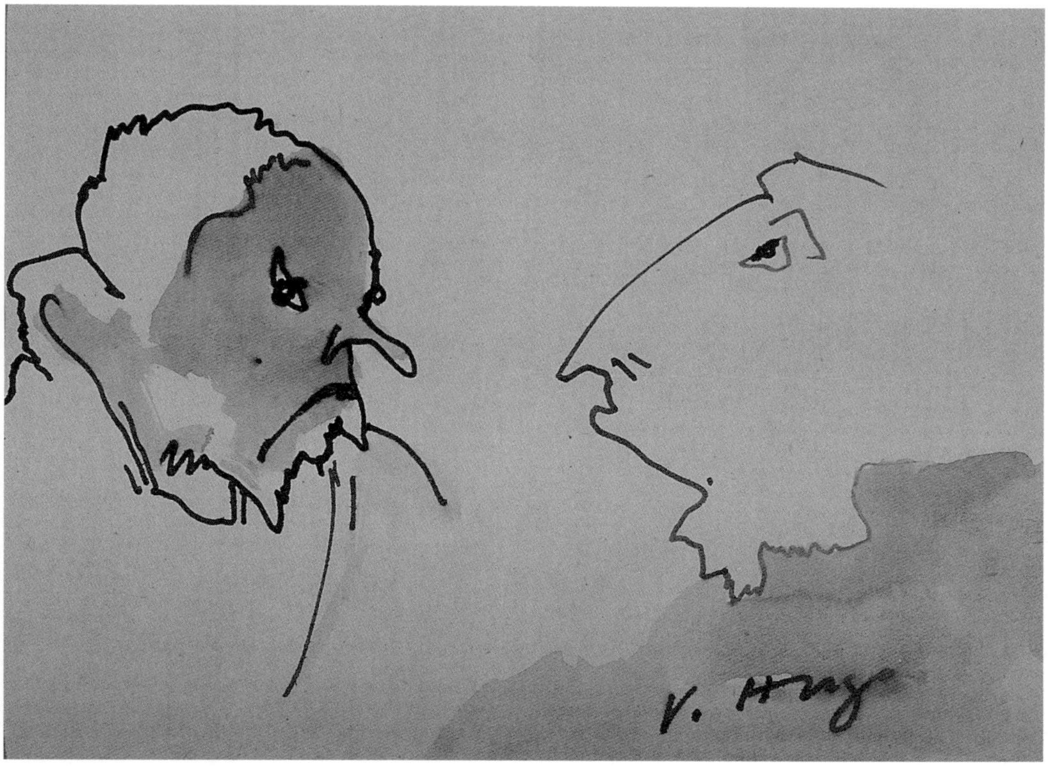

Character Studies: Two Heads

circa 1873

pen and wash

in brown ink

154 x 201 mm

inscription:

signed *V. Hugo*

Jean-Dominique Ingres

1780 – 1867 | French

Ares Borghese

1793 black chalk
275 x 204 mm
inscription:
signed and dated
J D Ingres 1793
and *Ve Ingres*

Son of a Montauban decorative painter and sculptor, Ingres showed an early interest in music and drawing. In 1791, he enrolled in the Toulouse academy and won a series of prizes for figure drawings. He also became an accomplished violinist, playing in the orchestra of the Toulouse theatre. He went to Paris in 1797 and entered the studio of J.L. David at a time when a group of David's radical students — calling themselves Primitifs or Barbus — were demanding a purer, more archaic style, perhaps influenced by John Flaxman's Homeric designs. Although officially he was not a member of this radical group, Ingres was sympathetic to their cause and shared many of their aesthetic principles. In 1801, he won the Prix de Rome with *The Ambassador of Agamemnon in the Tent of Achilles* and became a *pensionnaire* of the Académie française in Rome in 1806. He stayed in Italy until 1824, long after his stipend had expired, and produced in those Italian years many pencil portraits and works for the Bonaparte family. By 1824, he was recruited by the government to be the new leader of the French art establishment, which was then in a state of crisis due to the absence of David (exiled in Brussels) and their dissatisfaction with David's faltering students. Awarded the Legion of Honour and elected to the Académie in 1825 shortly after his return to Paris, he became David's heir. Later he was named president of the École des Beaux-Arts in 1834 and director of the Académie française in Rome between 1835-41. He was honoured by the government of Louis-Philippe with several important commissions. In the Paris World's Fair of 1855, he, like Delacroix, was given a large retrospective exhibition.

Ingres' works occupy an important but paradoxical position in nineteenth-century art. On the one hand, he was an intimidating proponent of the classical doctrine in his official capacity at the École des Beaux-Arts and the Académie française in Rome; his works in this area are unyieldingly austere and represent the immutable authority of tradition. Yet on the other, his private works are characterized by great sensitivity and sensuality, best reflected in his numerous female nudes, and thus reveal an unmistakable Romantic temperament. But throughout both public and private works, he remained an unrivalled, fluent technician. His drawings are at once intellectual and sensuous, powerfully constructive and at the same time taut with feeling.

This drawing of the *Ares Borghese*, copied after the Roman copy of the Greek fifth-century B.C. original (Louvre), belongs to a group of drawings Ingres carefully saved most of his life and gave to his second wife, Delphine, probably some time after their marriage in 1852. They were all signed by Madame Ingres (Ve Ingres — Widow Ingres), who gave them to Léon Bonnal, then *conservateur* of the Musée Ingres in Montauban. (Eleven drawings in this group now belong to a private American collection.) This group of academic copies after antique sculptures dates to Ingres' early career in Toulouse, some from when Ingres was only thirteen years old. The present sheet is most likely a subject assigned while Ingres was studying in his father's workshop on drawing in Montauban, prior to his admission to the Toulouse academy. Nearly 500 of his youthful studies and sketches still exist in the collection of the Musée Ingres in Montauban; one-third of them date from the Montauban and Toulouse years.

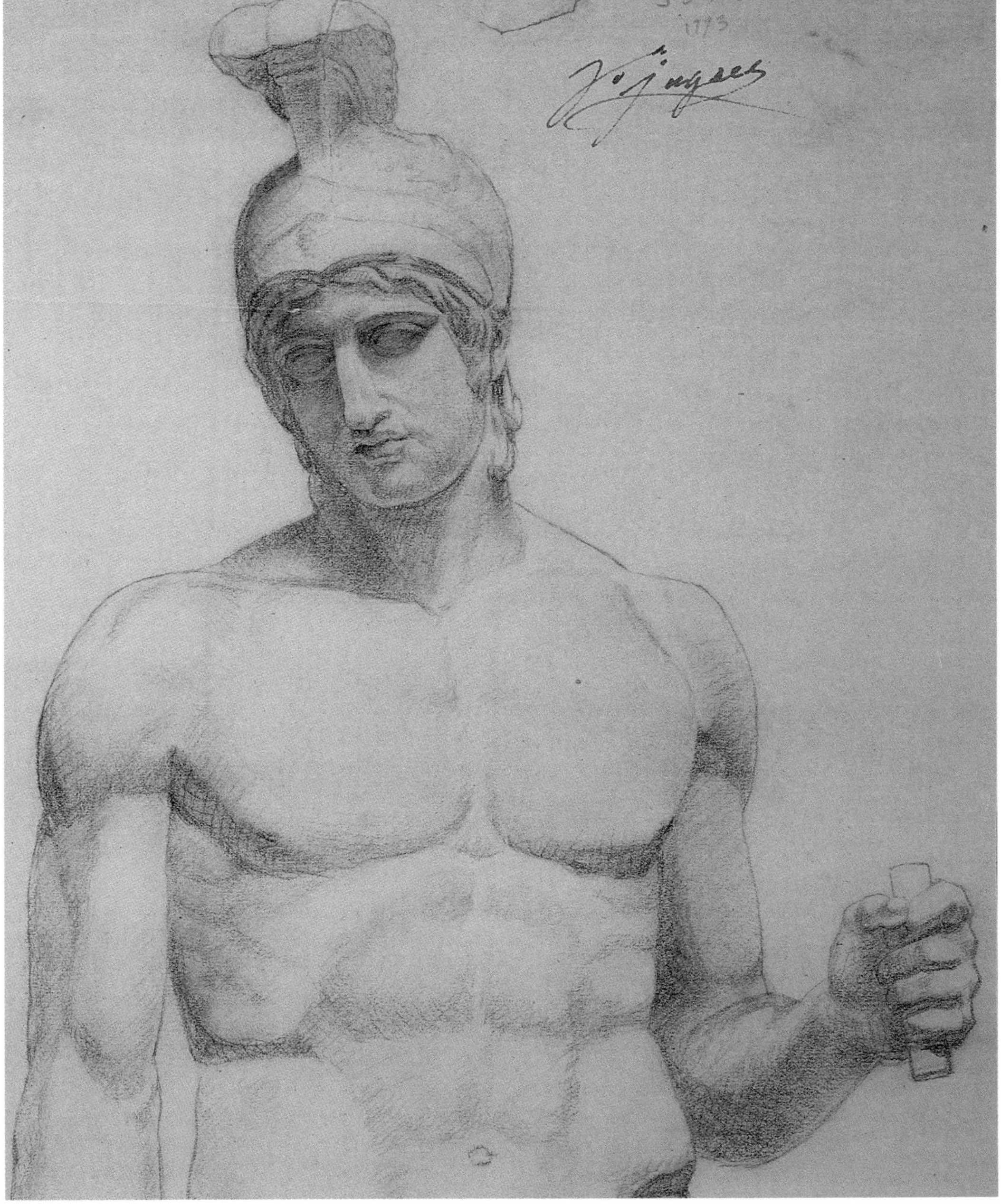

Ares Borghese

1793 black chalk

275 x 204 mm

inscription:

signed and dated

J D Ingres 1793

and *Ve Ingres*

Fernand Khnopff

1858 – 1921 | Belgian

Under the Bridge

circa 1888-90

pastel

167 X 214 mm

inscription: signed *Fernand Khnopff*

Born in the château of Grembergen near Termonde, Khnopff moved with his family to Bruges in about 1860. After Bruges, the family moved to Brussels. Following a brief period of studying law at the university in 1875-76, Khnopff enrolled in the Académie des Beaux-Arts. In 1877, he visited Paris and its museums, where he studied the Renaissance and Baroque masters, especially admiring the Romantic works of Delacroix. Between 1876 and 1879, he was at the Académie Royale des Beaux-Arts, where James Ensor was also a student at the time. Visiting the Paris World's Fair in 1878, he first discovered the works of Gustave Moreau and Edward Burne-Jones. During 1879-80, he was studying in the studios of Jules Lefebre and G. Boulanger. Returning to Brussels in 1880, he started an independent art career and produced, in the 1880s, mostly realistic portraits and landscapes. He came to engage in an intensive study of Symbolist literature and the art of Gustave Moreau. In 1883, he became a founding member of the progressive Belgian art group Les XX. By the late 1880s, his works had become dominated by allegorical and emblematic representations. These were also the years of his international success. In the Paris World's Fairs of 1889 and 1900, he won second-class medals. He also exhibited in London, Munich, and Vienna. In 1892, he became a member of the Society of Portrait Painters in London and from 1894, he was a regular correspondent for the British art journal, *The Studio*. Clearly his Anglomania had been influenced by his admiration for the Pre-Raphaelites with whom he formed friendly relations and shared many aesthetic and social affinities. From 1892 to 1897, he was a leading contributor to the annual Salon de la Rose + Croix in Paris and was invited to participate in the first exhibition of the Vienna Secession in 1898. In 1892 he was made a chevalier of the Order of Léopold in Belgium and in 1898, a member of the Order of St. Michael of Bavaria. Beginning around 1900, he formed a fruitful collaborative relationship with Maurice Kufferath, director of the Théâtre de la Monnaie, and produced many designs for sets and costumes. In 1900, he erected and opened his Symbolist villa in Brussels. Seven years later, he became a member of the Belgian academy. Besides his academic duties, he taught regularly at the independent Atelier Labor.

Throughout his life, Khnopff had a particular attachment to the Flemish city of Bruges, where he spent five years of his childhood. Although he later frequently declared that he had never returned to this Gothic city of canals and churches because he preferred to preserve the city in magical memory, the image of Bruges haunted many of his compositions. His first depictions of the bridges, canals, and buildings of Bruges, often done with the assistance of photographs, began in 1888-89 with the frontispiece to Gregoire Le Roy's book of verse, *Mon coeur pleure d'autrefois*. This was followed by his illustrating *Une ville morte* of 1889, to which this drawing may be related. Khnopff's love of Bruges and his evocation of the city's melancholy silence clearly are inseparable from his childhood and his dream of a simpler age of religious piety and mystery. But his medievalism is also connected to late nineteenth-century nationalism, especially in relation to art: Bruges was the city of Hans Memling and associated with the works of Jan van Eyck, Dirk Bouts, and Quentin Massys. Finally, his attachment to the past charm of Bruges suggests a form of passive social protest and criticism of the inferior quality of life in the modern city, also revealed in much of his art criticism published in *The Studio*.

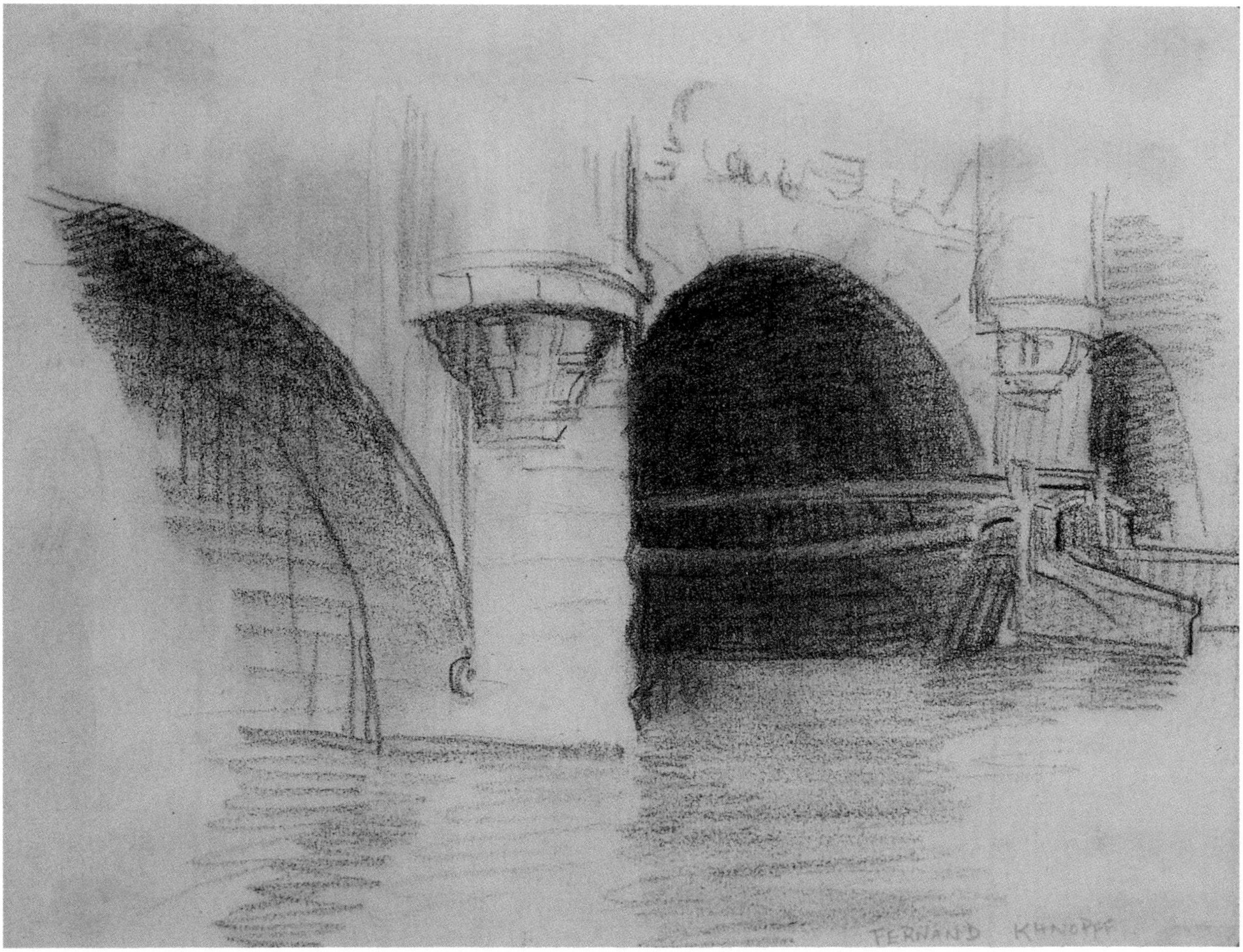

Under
the Bridge

circa 1888-90

pastel

167 X 214 mm

inscription: signed

Fernand Khnopff

Paul Klee

1879 – 1940 | Swiss

Dragon-flies

1926 graphite

248 x 242 mm

inscription:

signed and dated

Klee 1926

Klee was born in Münchenbuchsee near Berne. He showed an early aptitude for the violin and was an associate member of an orchestra between 1886 and 1897. In 1898, he enrolled in Heinrich Knirr's private school of drawing in Munich. Two years later, he joined the painting class of Franz von Stuck at the Munich academy. Between 1902 and 1905, he travelled to Italy and to Paris. His contact with modern art began in 1911 when he met Alfred Kubin, August Macke, and Wassily Kandinsky, the founding members of *Der Blaue Reiter* ("The Blue Rider"). In the following year, he met Robert Delaunay in Paris, where he also saw the works of Picasso and Matisse. During the First World War, Klee was drafted into the German army, but was discharged in 1918 and returned to Munich. In 1920, he was invited to join the Staatliches Bauhaus in Weimar. In 1926, he participated in the first group exhibition of the Surrealists in Paris. In 1930, he taught in the Düsseldorf academy, and three years later, he emigrated to Switzerland after being dismissed from the Bauhaus. During the 1920s and 1930s, he had a number of large exhibitions in Munich, Berlin, and Berne. In 1937 seventeen of his works were shown in the exhibition of Degenerate Art in Munich, and 102 of his pictures from public collections in Germany were seized by the Nazis.

For Klee the Surrealist, with Art Nouveau roots, the use of the popular, sinuous Art Nouveau dragon-fly represented a return to biomorphic imagery and a renewed concern with the process of life itself. Almost one-third of Klee's works was based on subjects drawn from the entire range of organic life. He published *Ways of Studying Nature* in 1923 and frequently mentioned art's relationship to nature and the secret of creation in his lectures and writings. He was particularly fascinated with the theme of avian evolution. Even from the beginning of his career, he drew birds and figures with wings.

The miraculous power of flight, unhindered by the law of gravity, embodied his continual quest to free himself and his creations from earthly bonds. In his diary and images, he also associated flight with planes (he was stationed at the flying school in Gerstenhofen from 1917 to 1919). In 1918, he produced drawings of *Bird Airplanes* (Collection Felix Klee, Berne). Although such representation is connected with war, destruction, and the evolutionary extinction of species, flight is often his metaphor for fleeing from destruction and death to a new life. He wrote: "To work my way out of my ruins I had to fly. And I flew." Thus it is tempting to relate this drawing to Klee's life in 1926. The right-wing Thuringian government had revoked its contract with the Bauhaus and its teachers in 1924, the culmination of the attacks on the Bauhaus by Nazi circles since its establishment in 1919. The Bauhaus was forced to move students and teachers, including Klee and Kandinsky, to Dessau in 1925. In 1926 Klee participated in the first group exhibition of the Surrealists in Paris.

Angel

1939 graphite 255 x 201 mm

inscription: signed and dated *Klee 1939*

In 1939, a very productive year for Klee, he completed over 1,200 works, mostly drawings. Of these, at least thirty represent angels. These winged creatures, although related to the theme of aviation, are uncharacteristically grounded and given human imperfections and foibles. Klee labelled them "forgetful," "ugly," "incomplete," and "poor." Childlike in appearance, these angels are probably connected to Klee's repeated reference to his own artistic offspring as "*Kinder.*" At the same time, these spiritual beings, appearing just months before his death, must have had a special meaning for Klee, who was diagnosed in 1936 as suffering from a rare and incurable disease that slowly led to the drying up of his bodily fluids, scleroderma. Klee wrote that his final resting place would be "beside an angel of some kind." This *Angel* drawing is similar to the one in the Paul Klee Foundation, Kunstmuseum, Berne, entitled *Schellen-Engel*, also dated 1939.

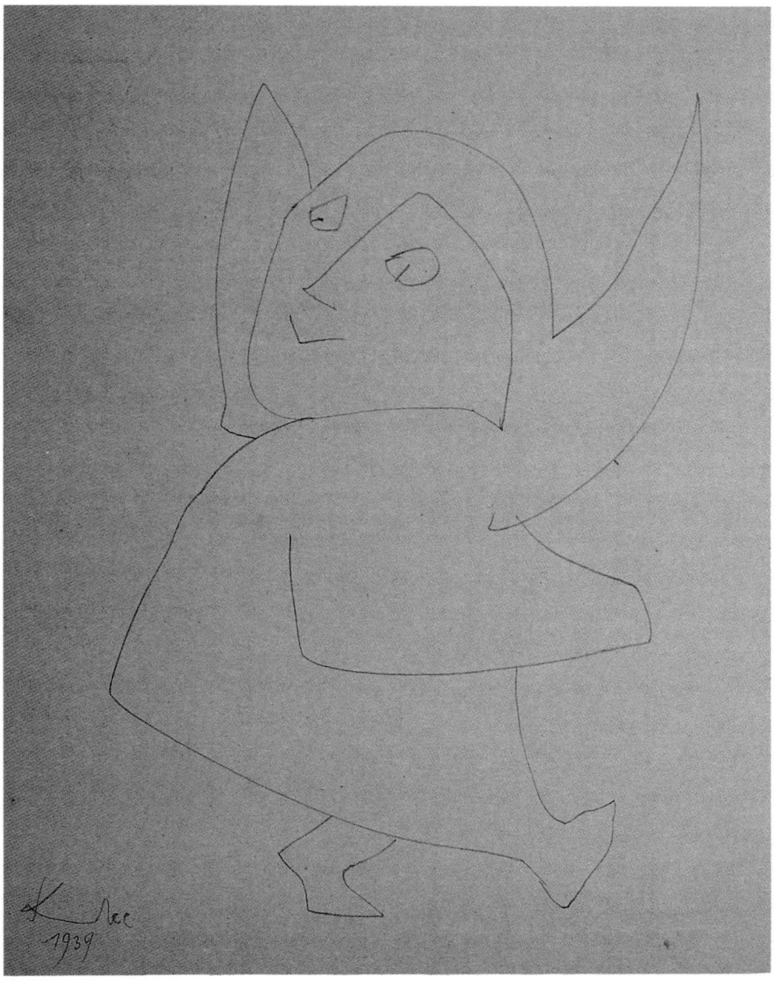

Angel

1939 graphite

255 x 201 mm

inscription:

signed and dated

Klee 1939

Gustav Klimt

1862 – 1918 | Austrian

Hygieia

1899-1900

graphite

259 x 264 mm

inscription:

signed *Gustav Klimt*

The principal Austrian Jugendstil (Art Nouveau) painter, Klimt was born in Baumgarten, near Vienna, the son of a Bohemian engraver. From 1876 to 1883 he took art lessons from Ferdinand Laufberger and Julius Viktor Berger in the Kunstgewerbeschule of the Österreichische Museum für Kunst und Industrie in Vienna. Sharing a studio with his brother, Ernst, and fellow student, Franz Matsch, Klimt began his career by decorating many important Vienna buildings: paintings for the courts of the Kunsthistorische Museum in 1879, the ceiling of the Sturany Palace in 1880, the Hermes Villa at Laniz in 1885, and the stairwell of the Kunsthistorische Museum in 1890. During this period, the three men also decorated a number of theatres: the Stadt Theater in Fiume in 1885, the Stadt Theater at Karlsbad in 1886, and the Burgtheater in Vienna in 1886-88. In 1897, Klimt became a founding member and the first president of the Vienna Secession, contributing regularly to Secession's exhibitions and the periodical, *Ver Sacrum*. Between 1894 and 1903, he was occupied with painting commissions from the ministry of education for the Vienna university hall. The principal paintings for this project — *Philosophy*, *Medicine*, and *Jurisprudence* — generated great controversy when they were exhibited in the Vienna Secession; *Philosophy*, however, received the gold medal in the Paris World's Fair in 1900. The university commission was temporarily abandoned in 1905; returning the honorarium to the ministry, Klimt said: "I want to escape from all the unedifying absurdities and feel free again." The university paintings were finally completed in 1907 and exhibited in Vienna and Berlin. In this period he also completed two series of paintings related to music: *Schubert at the Piano* and *Music* for the Palais Dumba in 1899; in 1902, he showed in the Secession exhibition the *Beethoven Frieze*, a free interpretation of the Ninth Symphony on the theme of humankind's evolution. In his remaining years, after refusing a professorship at the Vienna Academy, he travelled to London, Brussels, Paris, Madrid, Rome, and Florence. He also exhibited frequently in the international art exhibitions in Vienna and Munich (1909), the Berlin Secession (1909), the Venice Biennale (1910), Rome (1911), and the Great Exhibition in Dresden (1912).

The drawing of *Hygieia* represents the ancient Greek goddess of health. It is a study for *Medicine* (1900-07), one of the paintings commissioned for the university hall by the ministry of education in 1894. When *Medicine* was exhibited in 1901, it drew a divided response from Vienna's academics and received violently hostile reviews in the daily press, to the delight of the public. In Klimt's theatrical conception, Hygieia is an uncaring, immobile, sphinx-like priestess. A hollow civilized emblem concealing the unpleasant reality of the cult of medicine, she stands for the institution that enchains humankind. In the painting *Medicine* (destroyed at Schloss Immendorf in 1945; an oil sketch is in a Vienna private collection and other related working drawings are in the Albertina, Vienna), Death waits for the mass of suffering humanity, entangled in their decrepit bodies on the Wheel of Life and forever trapped in cyclic motion. And Hygieia, symbolizing the powerlessness of progress, proclaims a new matriarchy. At the centre of Klimt's interpretation, it is art, rather than medical progress, that would relieve human agony and bring life and reality into a complete, meaningful aesthetic harmony. Thus Klimt's sense of superiority, revealed in the Schopenhauer-Nietzsche-inspired philosophical interpretation of human fate, offended the Viennese university professors. They considered *Medicine* a blasphemous distortion of the role of science.

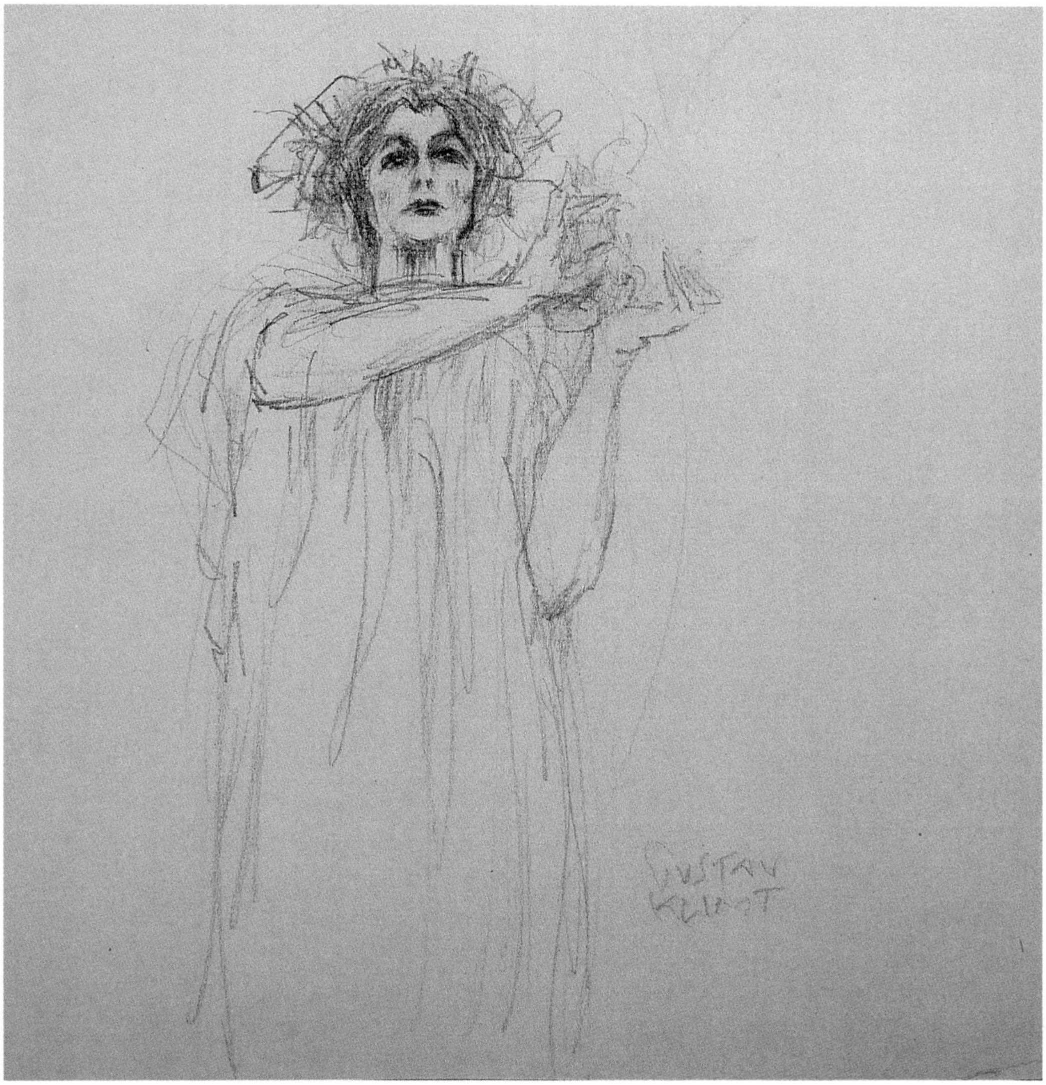

Hygieia

1899-1900

graphite

259 x 264 mm

inscription:

signed *Gustav Klimt*

Käthe Kollwitz

1867 – 1945 | German

Mother and Child

circa 1899

black chalk

220 x 135 mm

inscription:

signed *Kollwitz*

Kollwitz was born in Königsberg in East Prussia. In 1885-86, she studied painting and drawing in Berlin under the Swiss painter, Karl Staoffer-Bern. Two years later, she attended the Women's Art College in Munich, studying with Ludwig Herterich. She married Karl Kollwitz, a medical doctor, in 1891, and settled in Berlin. Through her husband's clinic, she came into contact with Berlin's industrial workers. In 1893, she saw a private performance of Gerhart Hauptmann's *The Weavers*, a play about the Silesian weavers' revolt of 1844. Deeply moved by the censored political play, she began a print series (half lithographs and half etchings) on *The Weavers' Revolt*, completed in 1898. Although censored by Kaiser Wilhelm II, *The Weavers' Revolt* attracted much attention when exhibited, and as a consequence, she obtained a teaching appointment at the Berlin Women's Art College. Her concern with the oppressed lower classes led her to another cycle of etchings, *The Peasants' War* (1902-07), which dramatizes the early sixteenth-century peasants' revolt in Germany. In 1909, she began a diary, and the following year, she produced her first sculpture (her most ambitious sculpture is the war memorial at the Roggevelde cemetery in Belgium, done in 1932). The First World War brought suffering and great sadness: her son Peter was killed in 1914. After the War, she was appointed a member of the Prussian art academy. In 1920, she joined the leftist group, International Workers Aid, producing several posters to raise funds for administering relief to starving Germans. In the same year, she began making woodcuts, inspired by the powerful works of Ernst Barlach. Her most impressive woodcuts are from the series *War*, produced in 1922-23. She visited Moscow in 1927 at the invitation of the Soviet government. She was appointed head of graphic arts at the Prussian Academy in 1928, but relieved from teaching five years later by the Nazis who also considered her work "degenerate" and officially forbade her from exhibiting. Under these circumstances, she began her final series of lithographs, *Death*, in 1934. The Second World War was as tragic for her as the First. Her husband died in 1940; two years later her grandson Peter was killed in battle. Her home and studio in Berlin, containing most of her work, were both destroyed by bombs in 1943.

The drawing *Mother and Child* is probably related to the 1899 etching *Gretchen*. In theme, both print and drawing are closely linked to *The Downtrodden* of 1900 and *The Carmagnole* of 1901. They show Kollwitz's growing preoccupation with the exploited peasants and their rebellion, misery, and helplessness. The subject of mother and child conveys the tenderness and the hardship of the proletarian family. Chronologically it stands between her two great series representing working-class struggles, *The Weavers' Revolt* (1895-98) and *The Peasants' War* (1902-08).

Self-portrait

1927 graphite 260 x 210 mm

inscription: signed *Kollwitz*

Throughout her career, Kollwitz produced many self-portraits, both in drawings and prints. The present self-portrait in profile is identical to a lithograph she produced in 1927. Kollwitz is sixty years old in this *Self-portrait*. That year she and her husband were invited by the Soviet government to celebrate the country's tenth anniversary. Kollwitz wrote in her diary on New Year's Eve in 1927: ". . . the sadness of the previous year, the sadness of old age, has decreased. This is due to the wonderful experience we were granted; Ascona in the spring. Then my sixtieth birthday, with all the joy it brought. Then Hiddensee with my loved ones, and after that, Russia. . . ." Her longtime friend and biographer, Otto Nagel, wrote in the *Sozialistische Monatshefte*: "Käthe Kollwitz is sixty years old, and yet she stands nearer to the youth of today than any other artist. . . . She identified passionately with working class life . . . [was] involved in the working class struggle, and [worked] for all suffering humanity . . . Käthe Kollwitz's art is active and alive . . . an exhortation and a faith in a . . . better future."

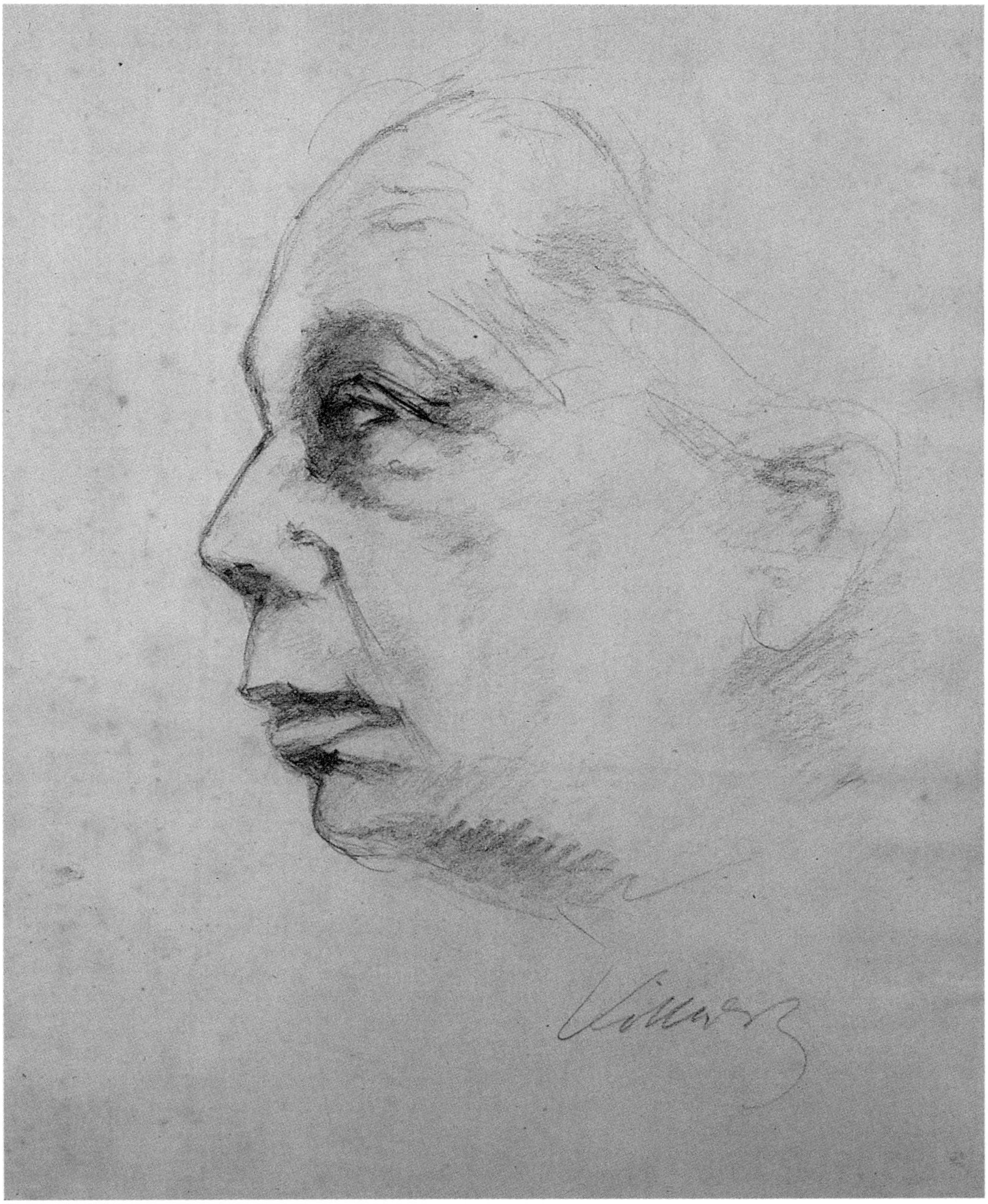

Self-portrait

1927 graphite

260 x 210 mm

inscription:

signed *Kollwitz*

Nicolas Lancret

1690 – 1743 | French

Drapery and Hand Studies

circa 1720-25
pen and brown ink
with red chalk
110 x 142 mm
inscription:
Nicolas Lancret

Lancret was born in Paris, the son of artisan parents. Most likely he began his early training in engraving, since his older brother, François-Joseph, was an engraver. About 1707, he was apprenticed to an obscure history painter, Pierre Dulin. Shortly after, he was enrolled in the Royal Academy school. In 1711, he competed unsuccessfully for the Prix de Rome. The following year he joined the studio of Claude Gillot, who, though an Academician, was able to pursue a successful outside career. Gillot had a special fondness for the theatre, especially the improvisatory Italian theatre, *commedia dell' arte*. Wry wit and rhetorical posturing characterized much of Gillot's works; he even designed costumes and stage sets for comedies, ballets, and operas. The elements of fantasy, together with the performers' physical grace and expressive gestures in *commedia dell' arte,* were transmitted from Gillot to both Watteau and Lancret. Watteau's influence on Lancret was immense. Lancret probably met Watteau around 1712, when Watteau presented several *fêtes galantes* at the Académie. By 1719, Lancret was admitted to the Académie as a painter of *fêtes galantes*, a category that had been created for Watteau only two years earlier. Following the untimely death of Watteau in the early 1720s, Lancret, benefiting from the popular taste for Watteau among connoisseurs, acquired important court patrons, including the duc d'Antin, Pierre Crozat, Tessin, Jean de Boullongne, Jean-François Leriget de la Faye, the prince of Carignan, and Frederic II. In the 1730s and 1740s, his works became more distinguishable from Watteau's: the figures are more robust and their execution smoother. With his noticeable pedestrian realism and a lively eye for topical manners, he was more detailed, narrative, and factual in his work than Watteau.

Yet in spite of his individual style, Lancret retained a great many elements from Watteau throughout his career. Frequently he transcribed favourite Watteau figures, poses, and other motifs in his own compositions, with only minor changes. But what is missing in these borrowings and variations is Watteau's subtlety, which neither Lancret, nor his contemporary Jean-Baptiste Pater, was able to imitate. As the contemporary art dealer Edme-François Gersaint had recognized: "Lancret and Pater were the only two painters who stumbled into the taste for fashions and for gallant subjects of which Watteau was the inventor and the model." The present sheet, showing the study of drapery and the hand of Il Matto holding the stick jester, might have been derived from Watteau's *Les Comédiens Italiens* of 1720 (National Gallery, Washington D.C.).

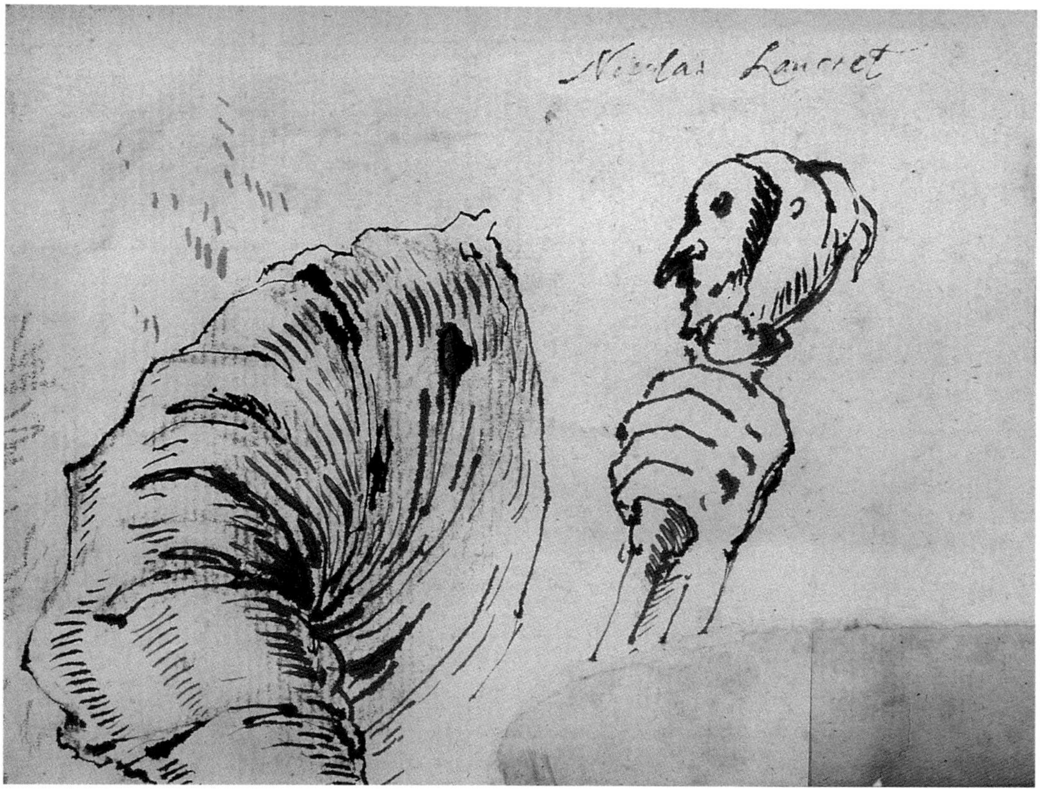

Drapery and Hand Studies

circa 1720-25

pen and brown ink with red chalk

110 x 142 mm

inscription:

Nicolas Lancret

Edouard Manet

1832 – 1883 | French

Sketching in the Studio

circa 1860-65
graphite
271 x 165 mm
inscription: *Manet*

An urbane, fastidious aristocrat, Manet was born into a Parisian family of the *haute bourgoisie.* During the early 1840s, he showed a gift for drawing at the College Rollin, where he met his future protector and biographer, Antonin Proust. From 1850 to 1856, he was a student of Thomas Couture, a highly acclaimed academician who had recently exhibited the sensational *Romans of the Decadence* in the Salon of 1847. Manet soon turned increasingly to independent study, copying the works of Dutch, Spanish, and Venetian masters, and visiting museums while travelling with his brother, Eugène, to Italy in 1853. In 1856, the year he set up his own studio with the animal painter Albert de Belleroy, he also travelled to Holland, Germany, Austria, and Italy. About this time he met Fantin-Latour, Delacroix, and the poet Charles Baudelaire, who encouraged him to take up modern subjects. *Concert in the Tuileries* (1860-62) is his earliest modern work, depicting modish society in public gardens; other works of the period represent his own social and artistic environments. In the 1860s, he replaced Courbet as the spokesman for Realism. This was a period of enormous productivity and experimentation. He gathered a group of progressive artists and literary figures at the Café Guerbois, including Whistler, Fantin-Latour, Degas, Monet, Renoir, Bazille, the photographer Nadar, the poet Astruc, and the critics Duranty and Silvestre. Two of his most controversial paintings also made their debut. *Le Déjeuner sur l'Herbe,* originally entitled *Le Bain,* was rejected by the Salon of 1863, but exhibited in the notorious *Salon des Refusés;* its stylistic eccentricities and its subject, amounting to an impudent modernization of Giorgione's famous *Pastoral Concert* in the Louvre, angered the conservative public and critics. His *Olympia,* shown in the Salon of 1865, was even more scandalous; the blatant display of a modern Parisian courtesan, exposing society's moral and social hypocrisy, deeply offended Salon viewers. During the 1860s, Manet's Hispanism also grew; he painted many Spanish subjects, and travelled to Spain in 1865. Inspired by Goya's etchings after Velázquez, he began etching many of his own painted compositions. By the late 1860s, through his sister-in-law, the painter Berthe Morisot, he became more artistically involved in the Impressionist circle. Without renouncing the Salon, and while refusing to show in the Impressionist exhibitions, he did adopt Impressionist techniques and subjects. Beginning in the 1870s, his outdoor scenes become lighter, brighter, and freer in handling. At the same time, the urban, nocturnal subjects — cafés, bars, and brothels — inspired perhaps by Degas and the novels of Huysmans, Halévy, and Zola, fascinated him: he produced *Nana* (1877), a painting on the theme of prostitution; and later *The Bar at the Folies-Bergère* (1881), a work dealing with the complex psychology and murky activities of nocturnal entertainment.

Always concerned with modernity, but equally mindful of tradition, Manet's works and career contain curious contradictions. Many of his modern subjects, including *Le Déjeuner sur l'Herbe* and *Olympia,* were based on quotations from past art; likewise the theme of artists in their studio, as in this drawing. Manet could trace the theme from ancient to modern times: from Apelles to St. Luke, from Velázquez's *Las Meninas* (1656) to Courbet's *Artist's Studio: A Realist Allegory* (1855), and from Manet's own *Luncheon in the Studio* (1868) to his *Monet in his Painting Boat-studio at Argenteuil* (1874). Indeed, for Manet, the subject of the artist's studio underlines both the traditional and modern process of creativity and the artist's social status. About 1860, it might even have a more personal meaning: his young studio assistant, Alexandre, who modelled for his painting *Boy with Cherries* in 1859, hanged himself in Manet's studio in a fit of despair.

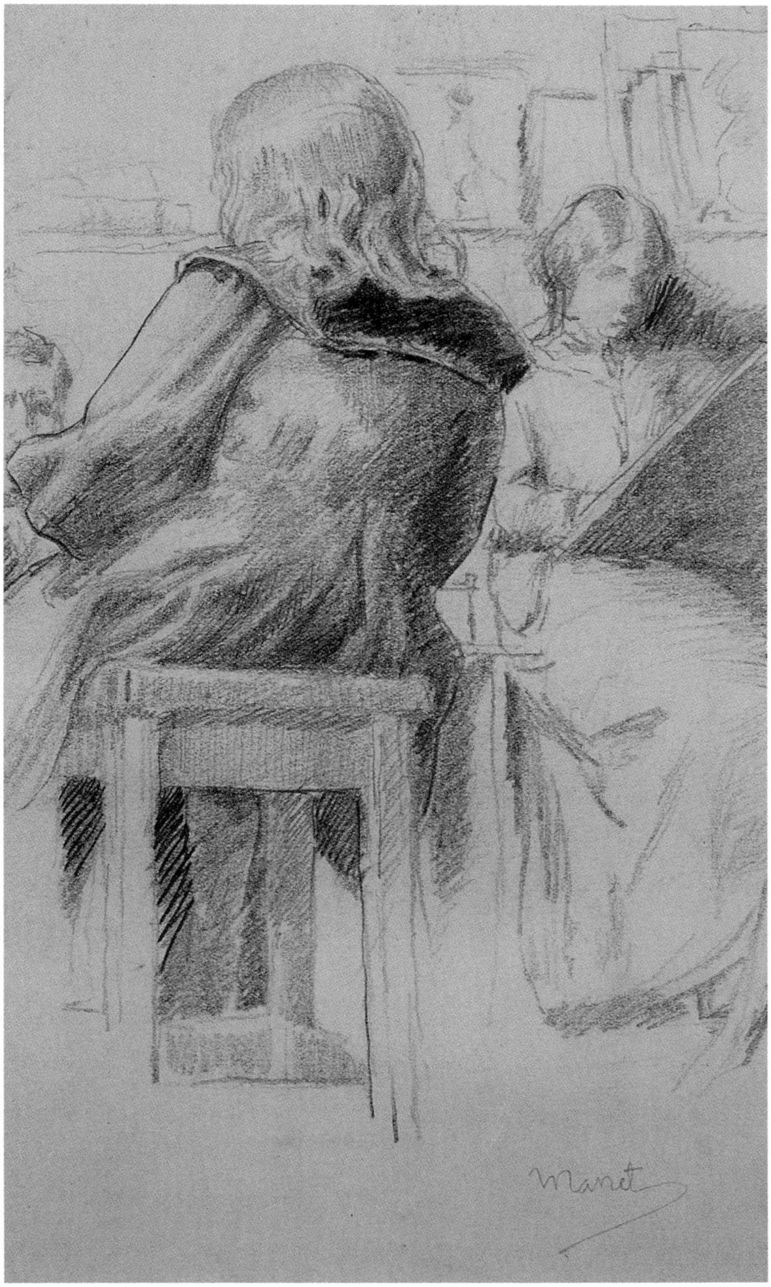

Sketching
in the Studio

circa 1860-65

graphite

271 x 165 mm

inscription: *Manet*

Carlo Maratta

1625 – 1713 | Italian

Study of a Foot

circa 1675

red chalk highlighted with white

132 x 145 mm

Maratta — or Maratti — hailed by his contemporaries as the greatest painter of his age, was a precocious talent from Camerino. At the age of twelve, he began his long apprenticeship in the studio of Andrea Sacchi, the master of High Baroque classicism. His early works show the influence of the Carraccis and Correggio. Like his master Sacchi, Maratta had the greatest respect for Raphael. He was also interested in the dynamic Baroque frescoes of Pietro da Cortuna and Giovanni Lanfranco. By the 1650s, his reputation was firmly established; and until his death near the beginning of the eighteenth century, his career was a continual success. His friendship with the influential theorist, Giovanni Pietro Bellori, no doubt furthered his career. Bellori was an antiquarian and a close friend of the French classicist, Nicolas Poussin, and he wrote about those he considered the most important artists of his age. Although his writing on the life of Maratta was left unfinished at his death in 1695, Bellori championed Maratta as the new Raphael, the redeemer of the art of painting, which he thought had been contaminated by the Baroque. In late seventeenth-century Rome, Bellori's view was shared by the artistic elite. But Maratta, whose reputation has been much devalued in our own century, was not merely a classicist of the grand style; he was a highly talented painter whose work, in a number of styles, is at times as dynamic and theatrical as Gianlorenzo Bernini and Giovanni Battista Gaulli. In many ways, Maratta's works represent a pragmatic reconciliation of the Baroque and the classical.

During the 1670s, Maratta, then the leading painter in Rome, was clearly in competition with Gaulli. Between 1672 and 1685, Gaulli was transforming the ceiling of the Church of Gesù, culminating in the great, illusionistic nave ceiling decoration of *The Adoration of the Name of Jesus.* Maratta, on the other hand, began his fresco on the ceiling of the grand salon (used as an audience chamber) in the Palazzo Altieri in 1676; the subject is *The Clemency of Pope Clement X.* Clement X came to the papacy in 1669 at the age of eighty, and his family, the Altieri, was eager to complete the new family palace they built next to the Church of the Gesù (to the great indignation of the Jesuits). Maratta consulted Bellori concerning the iconography of the Altieri ceiling. Deliberately in contrast to the infinite, complex celestial vision of Gaulli's Gesù decoration next door, Maratta's ceiling was simple and clearly framed with few figures, emphasizing classical principles. The present drawing may be a study for a foot of one of the supporting angels in the lower portion of the Altieri fresco.

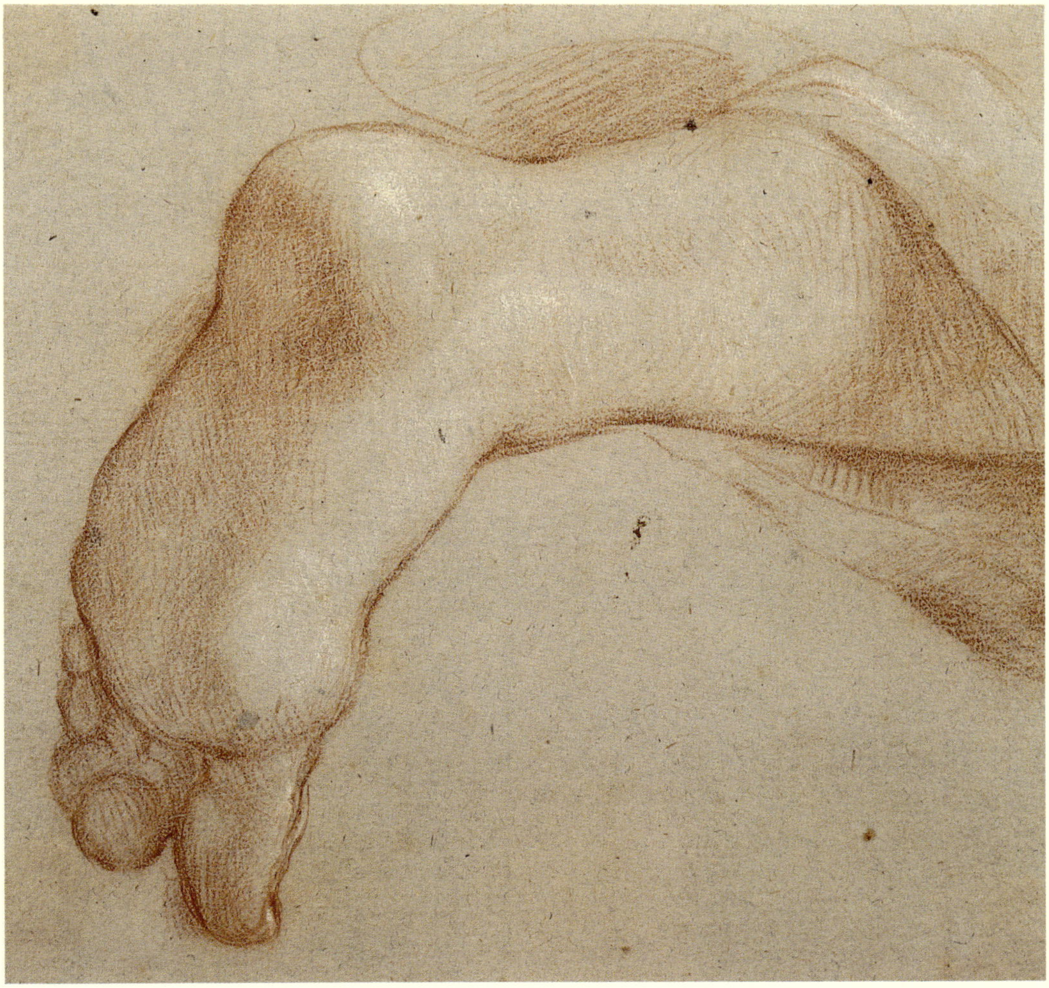

Study of a Foot

circa 1675

red chalk highlighted

with white

132 x 145 mm

Henri Matisse

1869 – 1954 | French

Portrait of Charles Baudelaire

circa 1932

graphite

255 x 202 mm

inscription:

signed *Matisse*

Born in Le Cateau-Cambrésis, Matisse first studied law in Paris in 1887-88. Abandoning law, he became a student of William-Adolphe Bouguereau at the Académie Julian. He entered the studio of Gustave Moreau in 1892 and enrolled in the École des Beaux-Arts in 1895. During the late 1890s, he became interested in the works of the Impressionists and Turner, and took sculpture lessons in the Paris Ecole Communale. In 1904, he had his first one-man show at Ambroise Vollard's Paris gallery and began exhibiting in the Salon d'Automne. The famous Fauve Salon d'Automne came in 1905. His first U.S. exhibition took place in 1908 at Alfred Stieglitz's Little Galleries of Photo-Secession ("291") in New York. The Russian collector S.J. Shchukin started to acquire his works in 1908 and commissioned *Dance and Music* the following year. For the installation of Shchukin's decorations, he visited Moscow in 1911; there he studied Russian icons. During those years he travelled widely — to Switzerland, Germany, Italy, Spain, Algeria, and throughout France. He developed an interest in Islamic and African art. In 1918, he moved to Nice; by now his works were shown internationally. He was made chevalier of the Legion of Honour in 1925 and awarded first prize at the Carnegie international exhibition in Pittsburg in 1927. Following his visit to the Barnes Foundation at Merion, Pennsylvania, in 1930, he accepted Dr. Barnes' commission to paint murals for the walls of the Foundation, which he installed in 1933. Besides paintings, drawings, and prints, his works in the 1930s include book illustrations, tapestry designs, and scenery and costumes for the Ballets Russes of Monte Carlo. In 1940, he moved to Bordeaux, then to Ciboure; in 1943, he lived in Vence and began the paper cut-outs for *Jazz* (published in 1947). In 1950, he received the highest prize at the twenty-fifth Venice Biennale. Retrospectives were held in the Philadelphia Museum of Art in 1948, in the Musée des Beaux-Arts at Lucerne in 1949 and at the Museum of Modern Art in New York in 1951. In 1952, two years before his death, he inaugurated the Musée Matisse at Le Cateau-Cambrésis.

In 1930, Matisse accepted a commission from the publisher Albert Skira of Lausanne to illustrate a new edition of Mallarmé's poems. After a great deal of painstaking struggle, *Poésies de Stéphane Mallarmé* was published in 1932. It was his first illustrated book, and he was clearly in competition with Picasso, who was then engaged in the illustration of Ovid's *Métamorphoses* for Skira and Balzac's *Le Chef-d'oeuvre inconnu* for Vollard. The variety of subjects in Mallarmé's poems provided Matisse with an opportunity to expand his iconography greatly. While he admired Mallarmé's verse, he also desired to complement, not merely to illustrate, the poetry. As he said, the artist "must be careful not to adhere too closely to the text. On the contrary he must work freely, his own sensibility enriched through contact with the poet he is to illustrate." In preparation for the *Mallarmé* etchings, he produced numerous graphite drawings. These designs, he said use "an even, very thin line, without hatching, so that the printed page is left almost as white as it was before printing." The highly condensed, precise, and pure lines are intended to produce light, space, and symbol. For the etching illustrating, "Le tombeau de Charles Baudelaire" (*Poésies* page 136), to which this drawing is related, Matisse worked from a composite image of daguerreotypes and other portraits of Baudelaire, delineating and characterizing the Symbolist poet. The result is a luminous image transforming object into sign, as Baudelaire did in his poetry.

Jackie

1947 conté crayon 305 x 255 mm

inscription: *Jackie*; signed and dated *H. Matisse 47*

This cursory line drawing depicts Matisse's granddaughter, Jacqueline Matisse. Matisse did a suite of eleven portrait drawings of Jacqueline, including this one, in Vence in 1947. They represent a cinematic sequence of front, three-quarter, and profile views of the sitter. They are now in various private collections and in the Musée National d'Art Moderne, Paris (Centre Georges Pompidou).

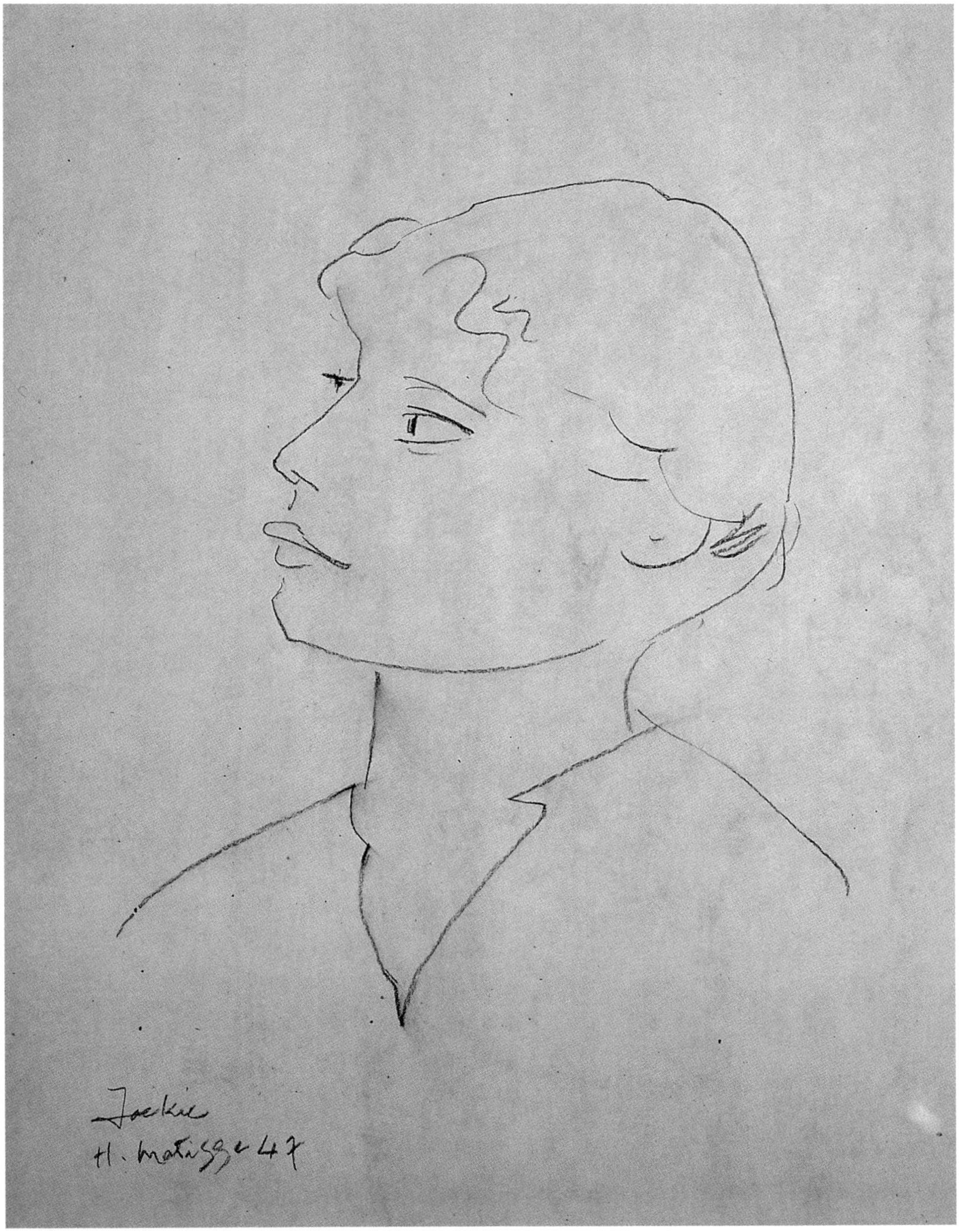

Jackie

1947 conté crayon

305 x 255 mm

inscription: *Jackie*

signed and dated

H. Matisse 47

Jean François Millet

1814 – 1875 | French

Washerwomen

1853-55

conté crayon

205 x 200 mm

inscription:

signed *J.F. Millet*

Millet was born in Gruchy, in Normandy. He took art lessons during the period 1833-37 in Cherbourg, first with Mouchel and later with L. Langlois. With a scholarship from Cherbourg, he went to Paris in 1837 and began studies with the renowned history painter, Paul Delaroche, at the École des Beaux-Arts. Two years later he left the École and lost his stipend. Towards the mid-1840s, he met the Barbizon painters, Constant Troyon, Narcisse Diaz, Theodore Rousseau, Charles Jacques and the dealer Durand-Ruel. He also befriended Daumier and Barye, and found a patron and agent in the government functionary, Alfred Sensier. In 1849, he settled permanently in Barbizon. In the Salon of 1850, his *Sower* was hailed as a success by republican and leftist critics. During the 1850s and 1860s he produced some of his most controversial works depicting peasants: *The Gleaners* in the Salon of 1857 and *Man with a Hoe* in 1863. On the other hand, his *Angelus* of 1857 became his most celebrated work. By the mid-1860s, Millet enjoyed his growing recognition, and his works were exhibited and sold by dealers in England, Belgium, and America. The Paris World's Fair of 1867 gave him a retrospective, and the following year he became a chevalier of the Legion of Honour.

This drawing is a study for the painting *Washerwomen* in the Museum of Fine Arts, Boston. It shows a pair of silhouetted washerwomen loading their wash on a river bank against the fading light of the sunset. In Millet's conception, these peasant women, in their natural and symbolic roles, are performing their tasks as isolated beings in a non-gregarious society. Nearly two dozen related drawings are known in various public and private collections.

Maternal Care

circa 1855-57 conté crayon 175 x 135 mm

inscription: *J.F. Millet*

Until about 1860, Millet achieved more sales in drawings than paintings. This drawing belongs to a large group of works that he produced in the 1850s and 1860s on the popular nineteenth-century subject of mother and child, without resorting to sentimentality or undue sweetness. A very closely related but more elaborate drawing of *Maternal Care* is in the Musée des Beaux-Arts, Budapest, and the painting is in the Louvre.

Death and the Woodcutter

1857-59 graphite 230 x 293 mm

inscription: *J.F. Millet*

This is a study for the painting *La Mort et le bucheron* (Ny Carlsberg Glyptotek, Copenhagen), which Millet submitted to the Salon of 1859, where it was rejected; the painting was subsequently exhibited in the Paris studio of C. Tillot and defended by Alexandre Dumas in *L'Independance belge.* Most likely the subject of the woodcutter was taken directly from La Fontaine's fable: the weary and dejected woodcutter, alone in the depths of the forest, summons Death to help him bear his load. In 1857 Millet was very much involved in the abortive project of illustrating La Fontaine. As early as 1851, Millet, in a letter to Sensier, wrote about La Fontaine's woodcutter: "What has he had since the day of his birth?/Who so poor as he in the whole wide earth?" Millet's allegory of suffering, which offended the Parisian public, may reflect an undertone of social protest concerning the contemporary issue of rural poverty and serve as a reminder of the recent violence and social unrest that resulted from forest clearances.

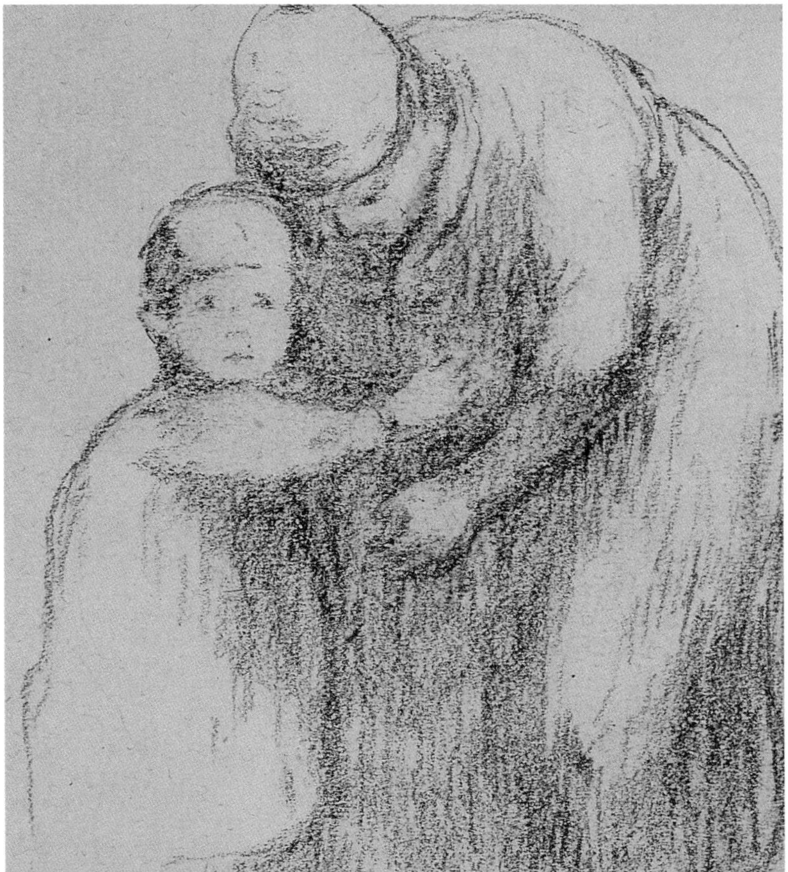

Maternal Care

circa 1855-57

conté crayon

175 x 135 mm

inscription:

J.F. Millet

Amedeo Modigliani

1884 – 1920 | Italian

Caryatid Head

circa 1912-13

graphite

355 x 260 mm

inscription:

signed *Modigliani*

Caryatid

circa 1912-13

graphite

410 x 280 mm

inscription:

signed *Modigliani*

Modigliani was born in Livorno. He showed an early interest in literature, and began his art studies in 1898 with Guglielmo Micheli in the Livorno academy. In 1900, his tuberculosis forced him to leave Micheli's studio. During his convalescence, he visited Rome and studied the old and modern Italian artists. In 1902, he enrolled in the art academy in Florence and a year later, in the art institute in Venice. He came to Paris in 1906 and lived in Montmartre, then the artistic centre of the capital. He concentrated on two subjects — portraits and nudes, evolving an expressive vocabulary of line and form. At this time, he developed close friendships with other Jewish artists: Chaim Soutine, Moïse Kisling, Jacques Lipchitz, and Max Jacob. He also acquired a taste for absinthe, hashish, and cocaine. Initially, he focused more on sculpture than painting. His sculptures reflected the influence of African and Polynesian masks, then the craze of Paris, and the works of Elie Nadelman and Constantin Brancusi. By 1914, he had shifted towards painting, and met the dealers Paul Guillaume and Leopold Zborowski. He had his first one-man exhibition in 1917, at the Galerie Berthe Weill. The show was a scandal — no sales, and the police ordered the removal of five of the nudes. The following year his health rapidly deteriorated, in spite of his growing recognition. Tragically, his wife, Jeanne Hébuterne, committed suicide the day following his own death in 1920.

Modigliani had been introduced to Brancusi by Dr. Paul Alexandre in 1909. The meeting was crucial. From Brancusi he learned to extract the essentials from non-European sculptures. That year he also saw the exhibited works of Elie Nadelman, whose human geometrics deeply impressed him. Fusing these influences together with his admiration for archaic Greek and Ivory Coast sculpture, he began making designs in 1910 for great monuments on the subject of caryatids, those female figures that held up ancient temples and African thrones. He conceived a large temple of beauty, dedicated to humanity, with hundreds of huge, sinuous, graceful figures, which he described as "colonnes de tendresse." Devoid of individuality, these figures represent Modigliani's ideal love object. The ambitious project was never completed — with his alcohol and drug addiction, he could afford neither the cost nor the energy for the physically demanding work. The group of drawings and watercolours of caryatids, including these two, are now scattered in various public and private collections.

Portrait of Chaim Soutine

circa 1916-17 graphite 410 x 280 mm

inscription: signed *Modigliani*

In Paris, as a result of the recently concluded Dreyfus affair, Modigliani developed a keen sense of his Jewish identity. The First World War intensified France's xenophobia and further isolated the small colony of foreign artists. Around 1915, Modigliani was welcomed into the ghetto of Jewish painters from eastern Europe, among them was Chaim Soutine. Soutine, originally from Lithuania, worshipped Modigliani, while Modigliani recognized Soutine's nascent talent. In spite of their tremendous personal differences — Modigliani was highly literate, urbane, and sophisticated; Soutine hardly articulate, unhygienic, and obsessed with violence — Modigliani patiently introduced Soutine to his friends and his own dealer, Zborowski, guided him through the Louvre, and taught him French and proper manners. Soutine later acknowledged that it was Modigliani who gave him self-confidence. Modigliani drew and painted Soutine many times around 1915 to 1917 (other portraits of Soutine are in the National Gallery, Washington D.C.; Staatsgalerie, Stuttgart; and various private collections).

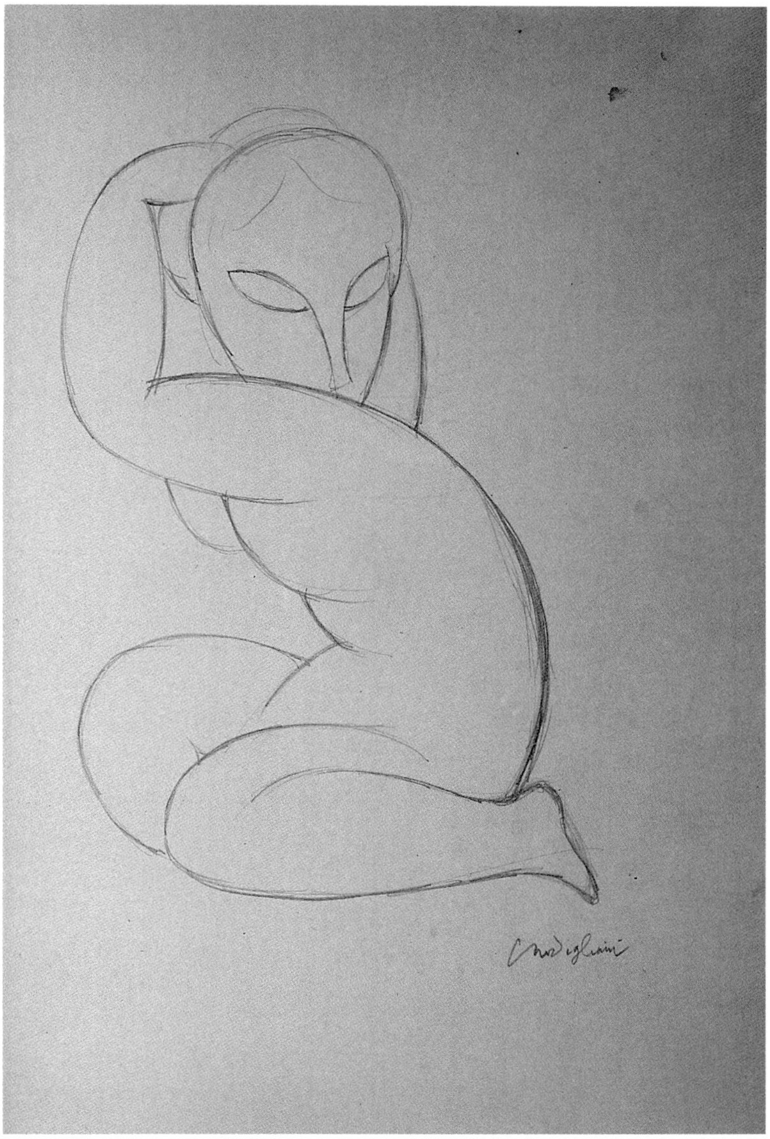

Caryatid

circa 1912-13

graphite

410 x 280 mm

inscription:

signed *Modigliani*

Piet Mondrian

1872 – 1944 | Dutch

Washerwomen

circa 1896-99
graphite and pastel
161 x 250 mm
inscription:
signed *P. Mondriaan*

Boat Work

circa 1896-99
graphite
160 x 250 mm
inscription:
signed *P. Mondriaan*

Mondrian was born in Amersfoort, Holland. His uncle, Friytz Mondriaan, an artist, gave him his first lessons in painting. In 1892, he enrolled in the Amsterdam academy of fine arts. There he painted many landscapes and still-lifes in the Dutch naturalist tradition, influenced by August Allebé and George Breitner. The 1890s was a period of financial and personal struggles with art and religion. In 1904, he lived in Uden, Brabant, and came under the influence of the works of van Gogh. Returning to Amsterdam in 1905, he continued his realistic themes of rustic cottages, windmills, polders, barges, and trees on river banks. During his first visit to Doomburg in 1908, he met Jan Toorop, whose mysticism appealed to his theosophical leanings. His painting style underwent a radical change. This was the beginning of his Zeeland period: the abandonment of naturalist illusionism in favour of abstraction. In 1911, he went to Paris and was attracted to Braque and Picasso, whose Cubist ideas and techniques he adopted; he also changed his name from Mondriaan to Mondrian. Returning to Holland in 1914, he was forced to remain in Amsterdam, and then Zeeland, for the war. In this period, he developed the inviolable axiom of Neo-Plasticism: the vertical-horizontal scheme on a flat, geometric surface. In 1917, with the painter Theo van Doesburg, he founded the magazine *De Stijl* to promote Neo-Plasticism. The first De Stijl group exhibition took place in Paris at Léonce Rosenberg's in 1923, the second in the Brooklyn Museum in the U.S. in 1926. In 1929, Mondrian became a member of the group Cercle et Carré. He exhibited with the Abstraction-Création group between 1932 and 1938. In 1938 he went to London; two years later he arrived in New York, where he met many European war refugee artists, including Marcel Duchamp, Max Ernst, and Fernand Léger. Two years before his death, in 1942, he had his first one-man exhibition, at Valentin Dudensing's gallery in New York.

The realism of Mondrian's early figurative and landscape works was derived from the open-air tradition of the Barbizon school and The Hague and Amsterdam schools of Impressionism. Throughout the 1890s, his first rural scenes — farm houses, canals and boats, washerwomen and workers, as found in these two drawings — revealed the influence of Amsterdam artists Isaac Israels and George Breitner. But unlike their works, Mondrian's restrained realism lacked the human and social interest in either industrial progress or the working class. Rather, they showed the concern for pictorial structure that would characterize his later compositions. Working in the picturesque settings at Uden, in Twente, and along the Gein, Mondrian began to evolve the structural elements of design and expression.

Windmill

circa 1905 graphite and watercolour 270 x 195 mm

This drawing is related to a series of windmills and summer houses from the post-Brabant period, around 1905 and early 1906. At this time Mondrian often went painting in the area of the Gein river in the company of two artists, A. Hulshoff Pol and A.M. Gorter; many of his entries in exhibition catalogues between 1905 and 1906 make reference to this area. The artists, staying at the Hotel-Cafe "de Vink," would work in the open air from morning until late evening, along the meandering tributory of the Vecht River. Here Mondrian searched for solitary prospects and found in the grid pattern of windmills a model of equilibrium crucial to his theory of Neo-Plasticism, a reflection of an inherently stable and tranquil world with the possibility of rhythm that would unite, as he put it, "the individual with the universal."

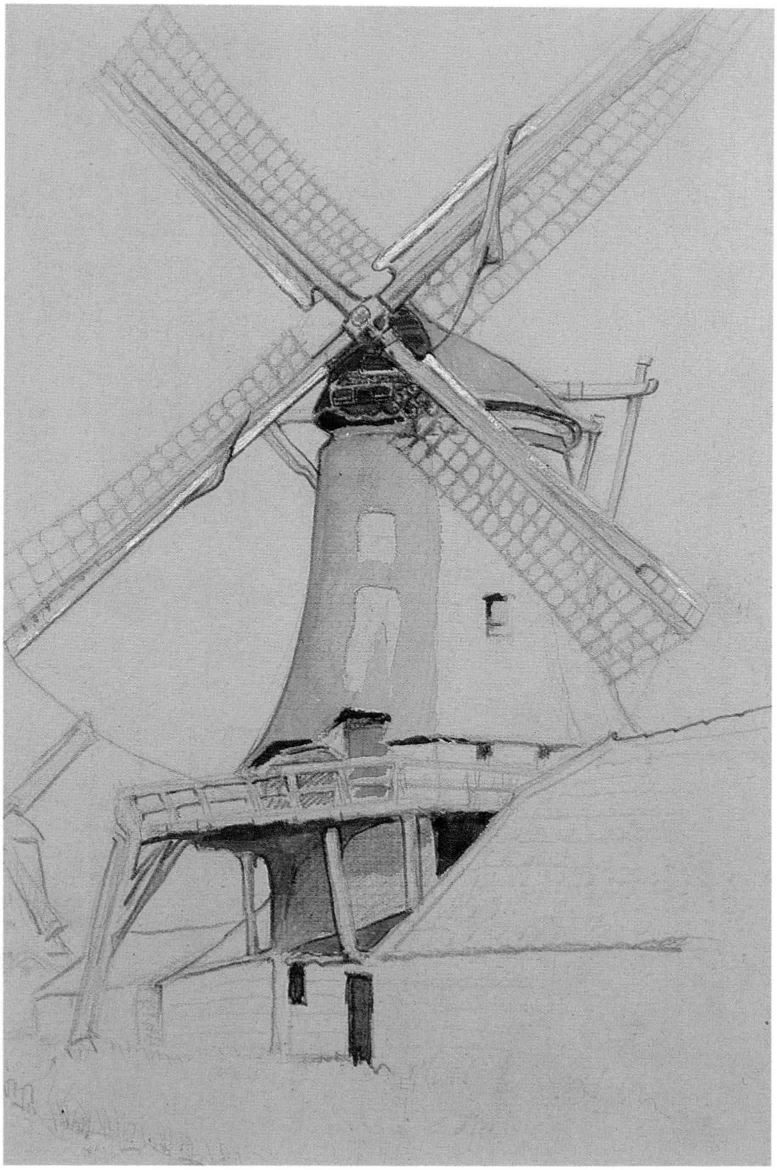

Windmill

circa 1905

graphite and watercolour

270 x 195 mm

Claude Monet

1840 – 1926 | French

A Shipyard

circa 1865
graphite
155 x 250 mm
inscription:
signed *Claude Monet*

Born in Paris, Monet moved with his family to Le Havre in 1845. He had a precocious talent for drawing and, as a youth, developed a local reputation as a caricaturist. In 1857, he met Eugène Boudin, a specialist in seascapes and beach scenes, who introduced him to outdoor painting. He went to Paris in 1859 and was impressed by the Barbizon painters in the Salon; he also began to frequent the Académie Suisse and was in touch with Courbet's circle. Drafted into the army in 1861, but released the following year, he met J.B. Jongkind, whose atmospheric and luminous landscapes made a deep impression on him. In 1862, he entered the studio of Charles Gleyre, where he met Bazille, Renoir, and Sisley, the core of the future Impressionist group. During those years, in the company of other artists, he often painted along the coasts of Normandy, on the beaches around Trouville, near Honfleur and St. Simeon. While he had some success in the official Salons of 1865 and 1866, his works were rejected by the jury throughout the late 1860s. At the outbreak of the Franco-Prussion War in 1870, he left for London, where he met his future dealer, Durand-Ruel, and the painter Pissarro. After travelling in Holland, he returned to Paris in 1871 and rented a house at Argenteuil on the Seine just outside the city, where he lived until 1878. In 1873, he painted two important Impressionist works: *Impression: Sunrise* and *The Boulevard de Capuccine.* He was one of the chief organizers of and contributors to the first Impressionist exhibition in 1874. A satirical review by Louis Leroy in *Charivari* dubbed Monet and his colleagues "Impressionist," from Monet's painting's title. In the summer of 1874, joined by Renoir and Manet at Argenteuil, Monet reached the high point of Impressionism. He continued to participate in the Impressionist exhibitions until 1886, abstaining only from the fifth and sixth in 1880 and 1881. During the 1870s, he met two patrons, Victor Chocquet and Ernest Hoschedé, and began painting views of the Gare St. Lazare in Paris. In 1883, he had a large retrospective at Durand-Ruel's gallery, painted at Etretat on the Normandy coast, and rented a house at Giverny. Throughout the 1880s, he worked at different sites in Holland, Belle-Ile off southern Brittany, the Mediterranean, and the Creuse Valley. By the 1890s, having purchased the house at Giverny, he worked on the various series of *Poplars, Haystacks, Rouen Cathedral, Morning on the Seine,* and *The Thames in London.* In 1908 and 1909, he made two trips to Venice and produced several views of that city. In 1903, after enlarging the water-lily pond in his Giverny garden, he began the new series of water-lily paintings. Forty-eight water-lily paintings were shown at Durand-Ruel in 1909. Encouraged by his friend Clemenceau, the prime minister, he undertook a large decorative cycle of water-lilies, constructing a new studio to carry out the project. The cycle was dedicated in the Orangerie des Tuileries in 1927, just months following his death.

This drawing dates from the beginning of Monet's career, around 1865, when he was working at several sites along the familiar Normandy coast where he grew up. Here, the site is probably Honfleur. Under the influence of Boudin, Jongkind, and Manet, and supported by a new group of young artists from Gleyre's studio where he studied — Renoir, Sisley, and Bazille — Monet produced many seascapes and related subjects. In this instance, the depiction of ships and boats around the Normandy beaches does not merely represent a familiar sight in his neighbourhood, it is also connected with his family background. His family had moved to Le Havre when he was five, and achieved a measure of affluence in the wholesale grocery and ships' provisioning business. For him, ships were vehicles both of pleasure and of business. Such an implication is clearly seen in many of his representations of *Boats in the Pool of London,* in 1871, and more significantly, in the painting *Impression: Sunrise* (1873), from which the Impressionist movement received its name, showing small barges sailing towards merchant ships in the misty harbour of Le Havre.

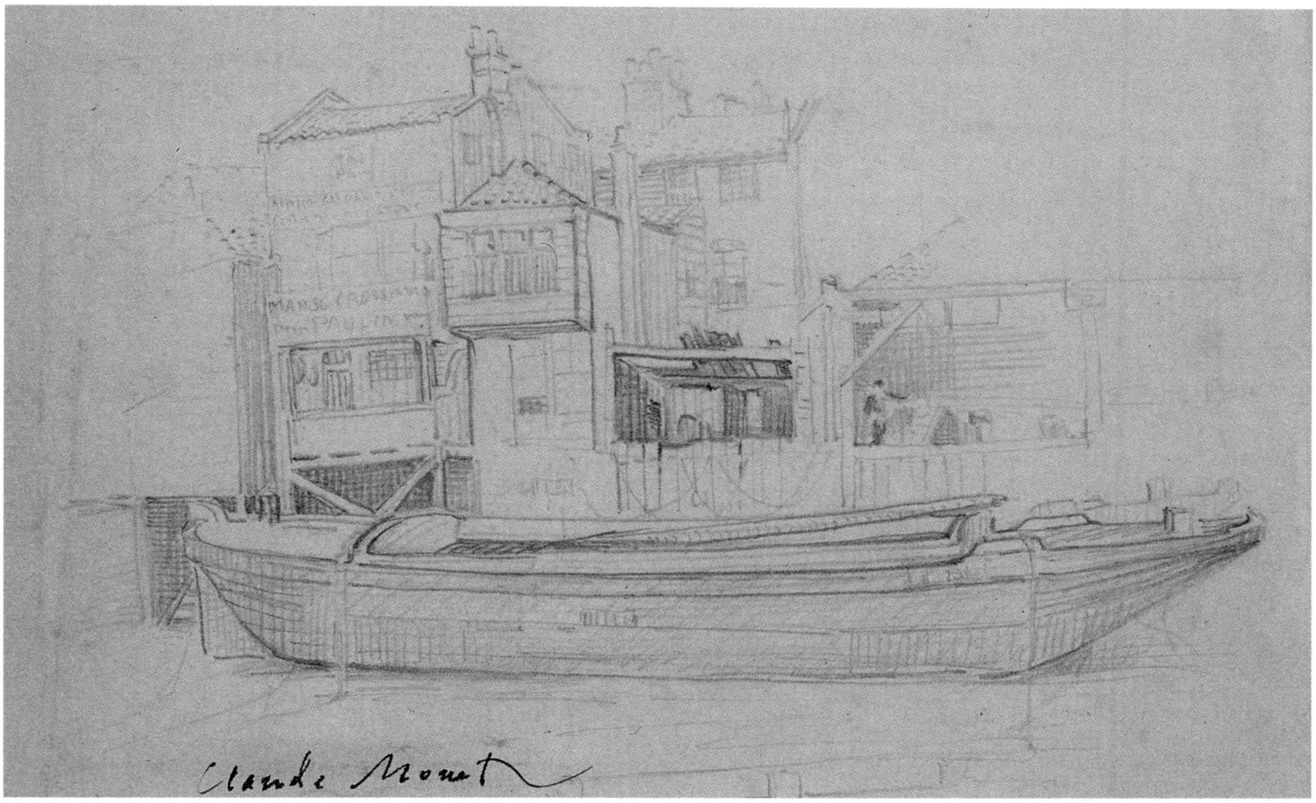

A Shipyard

circa 1865

graphite

155 x 250 mm

inscription:

signed *Claude Monet*

Gustave Moreau

1826 – 1898 | French

Study of the Nurse Eurycleia

1849 graphite

270 x 220 mm

inscription:
signed *G.M.*

Son of a Paris architect, Moreau entered the École des Beaux-Arts in Paris as a student of François Picot in 1846. In 1851, he began a close friendship with the painter Théodore Chasseriau. Like Chasseriau, he attempted a synthesis of Ingres' Classicism and Delacroix's Romanticism. In 1864 his *Oedipus and the Sphinx* won a medal and critical acclaim in the Salon. Throughout the 1860s, he exhibited regularly at the Salon, until 1869 when his *Prometheus* and *Europe* were strongly criticized by the press. He returned to the Salon in 1876 with two of his best-known works, *Salome* and *The Apparition*. In the Paris World's Fair of 1876, he exhibited nearly a dozen paintings and won the second-class medal. After his last Salon appearance in 1880, he cloistered himself in his studio to work on large allegorical compositions and watercolours, many of which were inspired by the fables of La Fontaine. He was named chevalier of the Legion of Honour in 1875, and officer in 1883. In 1884, Huysman's shocking novel *À Rebours,* in which Moreau's works were highly praised, gained him notoriety. In 1892, he succeeded his friend Elie Delaunay as professor at the École des Beaux-Arts. His teaching career was distinguished by two students, Matisse and Rouault. Between 1895 and 1896, he remodelled his house to create a museum for his works, which the state accepted as the Musée Gustave Moreau in 1902.

Eurycleia is a study of the nurse in the painting *Ulysses Recognized by His Nurse Eurycleia,* which Moreau submitted to the Prix de Rome competition in 1849. Moreau's painting has not survived, but the preparatory drawings and sketches are in the Musée Moreau. The prescribed competition subject was from Homer's *Odyssey.* Ulysses, arriving home in Ithaca incognito and planning to trap and kill the suitors of his faithful wife Penelope, is immediately recognized by his old servant Eurycleia, who notices the scar on his leg.

Minotaur

1854 graphite 325 x 220 mm

inscription: signed and dated *Gustave Moreau 1854*

This drawing is a sketch of the minotaur for *The Athenians Delivered to the Minotaur in the Labyrinth on Crete,* a painting exhibited in the combined Salon and Paris World's Fair of 1855. (The painting is in the Musée de l'Ain, Bourg-en-Bresse.) Inspired perhaps by a contemporary account *(Magasin Pittoresque,* 1854) of the discovery of remains of a Cretan labyrinth, Moreau drew on the myth of the fourteen Athenian youths King Minos ordered sacrificed to the minotaur, a monster half human and half bull.

Salome

1872-75 graphite 112 x 85 mm

inscription: signed *G.M.*

This drawing belongs to a group of studies for the large painting *Salome,* which Moreau exhibited in the Salon of 1876 and the Paris World's Fair of 1878 (the painting is in the Armand Hammer collection, Los Angeles; other drawings and clay models are in the Musée Moreau). The subject is based on the biblical story of the young princess Salome, who danced for her stepfather in order to win the head of St. John the Baptist for her mother, Herodias. Moreau's *femme fatale* conception of Salome was influenced by Flaubert's descriptions of the Carthaginian priestess in his novel, *Salammbô* (1862), one of Moreau's favourite books. Moreau might also have had in mind Baudelaire's "Spleen et Idéal xxvii" in *Les Fleurs du Mal* (1857), Mallarmé's *Hérodiade* (1864-69), and Theodore de Bauville's *Les Princesses* (1874). Huysmans, who saw Moreau's painting *Salome* in the 1876 Salon, provided perhaps the most celebrated description in his novel *À Rebours* of 1884: "She had become in some way the symbolic deity of indestructible lust, the goddess of immortal Hystera, the accursed Beauty exalted above all other beauties . . . the monstrous Beast. . . . "

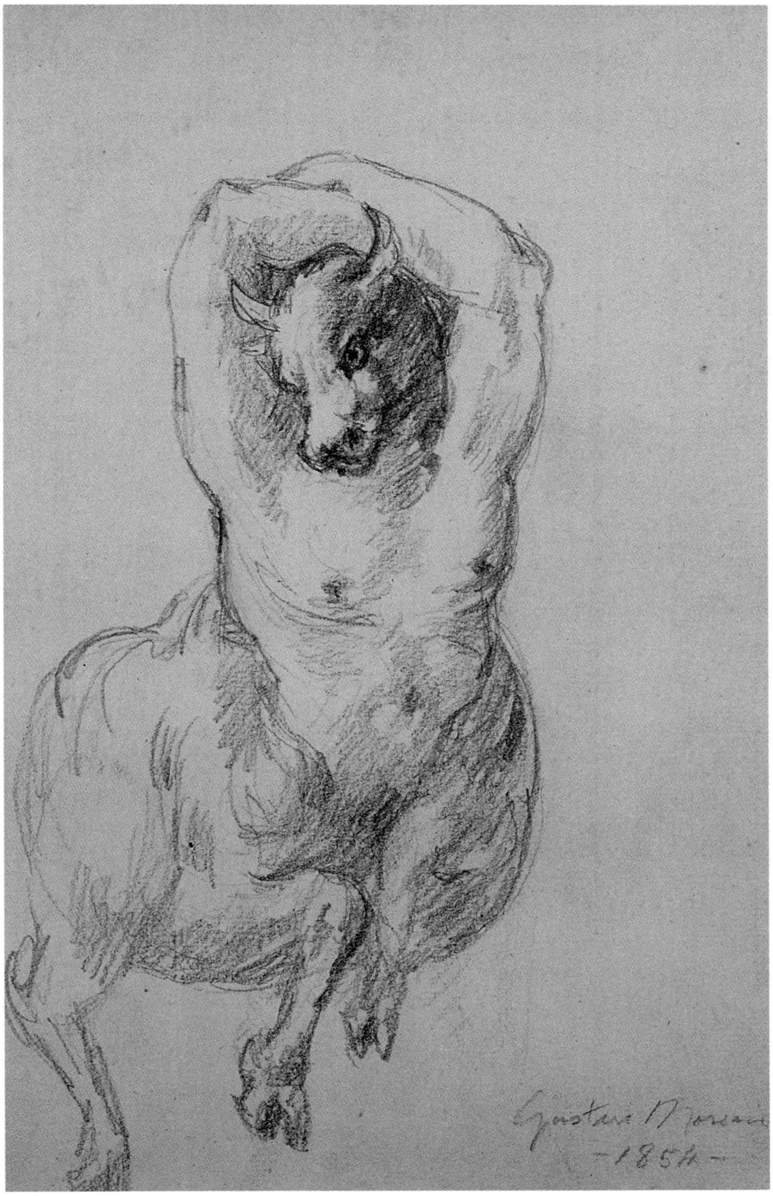

Minotaur

1854 graphite

325 x 220 mm

inscription:

signed and dated

Gustave Moreau 1854

Edvard Munch

1863 – 1944 | Norwegian

Man with Umbrella

1891 graphite
345 x 260 mm
inscription:
signed *E. Munch*

Munch came from a bourgeois family of doctors, pastors, officers, and professors. His childhood and adolescence were overshadowed by family illness and death: his mother died of tuberculosis when he was five; his sister Sophie, when he was fourteen; his father suffered from chronic depression. Munch later wrote, "Illness, madness and death are the black angels who watched over my cradle and who have accompanied me through my life." His father had planned an engineering career for him, but Munch, after a year of technical college, enrolled in the Oslo school of arts and crafts. His early works showed the influence of Norwegian artists such as Christian Krohg, Hans Heyerdahl, and Fritz Thaulow; Impressionism also had an impact on him. In 1885, he visited the Antwerp World's Fair and went on to Paris, where he came into contact with the avant-garde. Four years later he won a three-year scholarship to study in Paris, where he stayed briefly in the studio of Léon Bonnat and discovered the works of Manet, Gauguin, van Gogh, Seurat, Whistler, Böcklin, and the Nabis. In 1892, his Berlin exhibition led him to become a member of the Berlin Secession. At this time he began his *Frieze of Life,* a series of twenty-two paintings representing humankind's spiritual journey through life, love, anxiety, and death. *The Scream,* with its distorted figure of existential fear, is the best known. (The entire *Frieze of Life* was first exhibited in the Berlin Secession in 1902.) In the 1890s, he also developed his techniques in etching, woodcut, and lithography. His impact on the development of Expressionism in France and Germany during this period was decisive. But in 1908, after years of restlessness, nervous disorders, and alcoholism, Munch broke down and was treated in Dr. Jacobson's clinic in Copenhagen. Returning to Norway, he decorated the banquet hall at Oslo university with the monumental paintings *History, The Sun,* and *Alma Mater* (1910-16). In 1912, he was honoured in the Sonderbund exhibition in Cologne, and the following year, in the Berlin exhibition, along with Picasso. During the 1920s and 1930s, he led a withdrawn life on his property, Ekely, outside Oslo, often reworking motifs from the earlier *Frieze of Life.* At his death, he left the city of Oslo 1,200 paintings, 7,500 drawings, 18,000 prints as well as his personal collection of documents.

As early as the 1880s, when he was under the spell of Impressionism, Munch's approach was inclined towards Symbolism in his emphasis on subject matter, on moods and recollections. He said: "I don't paint what I see, but what I have seen." The drawing *Man with Umbrella* is a haunting rendition of a mysterious solitary figure enveloped by empty space. It belongs to a series of studies and paintings representing Oslo street scenes, as well as lonely figures on endless barren roads. The series culminates in the psychologically oppressive *Evening on Karl Johan Street* of 1892 (Casino Communal, Knokke-le Zoute, Belgium). Together, the works form part of the *Frieze of Life.* Here, the Impressionist subject of city boulevards has been transformed into an image of alienation and growing anxiety. The "man with the umbrella" is but the beginning of a series of gradual metamorphoses of isolated figures marking the evolution of the figure of terror and despair in *The Scream* (1893).

Woman by the Seashore

circa 1891-95 black chalk 190 x 300 mm

Thematically related to the drawing of *Man with Umbrella,* this lonely female figure is derived from Munch's earlier painting *Evening: Loneliness* of 1888 (Sigval Bergessan d.y. collection, Oslo). Identical motifs appear in a number of Munch's drawings, prints, and paintings between 1891 and 1895. The figure, as part of the conception of the *Frieze of Life,* is also in the painting *Two Human Beings — the Lonely Ones.* Loneliness and rejection as part of the love cycle were experiences drawn from Munch's own life. In the 1880s, he led a bohemian life, which his father had condemned. He belonged to the Kristiania Boheme, a radical group of young artists and writers who followed the theories of Norwegian anarchist writer

Hans Jaeger in advocating free love and openly attacking society for its Christianity, morality, and old legal code. Influenced by Jaeger's autobiographical novels such as *Perverted Love* and *Prison and Despair,* his own observations of the behaviour in the Kristiania Boheme group, and more poignantly, his doomed six-year affair with the wife of a naval medical officer in the 1880s, Munch could not help but draw such pessimistic conclusions about love.

Woman by the Gate

1893 conté crayon 140 x 100 mm
inscription: signed *E. Munch*

A study for the painting *Moonlight* of 1893 (National Gallery, Oslo), also connected with the *Frieze of Life,* this drawing is one of a group of evening studies Munch did in the early 1890s. The model for the figure is Munch's sister, Inger. The motionless and expressionless female dressed in black and standing by the gate under the moonlight is Munch's allegory of awakened sexuality, mingled with despondent loneliness, fear of contact, and the inevitability of death. In pose and mood, the figure bears an affinity with the figure of Inger in the painting of *Death in the Sickroom:* the largest work in the *Frieze of Life,* it is an analysis of the incommunicability of an individual's existential response to a psychologically dramatic experience. Munch was well acquainted with the writings of Hans Jaeger, Strindberg, Ibsen, and Kierkegaard, which helped both to clarify and to further his introspective self-examination.

Portrait of Nietzsche

1905 conté crayon 160 x 110 mm

This sheet belongs to a group of preparatory drawings for a portrait of the German philosopher Friedrich Nietzsche (different versions are in the Thielsche Galerie, Stockholm, and the Munch Museum, Oslo). They were all based on a postcard photograph Munch received from Frau Förster-Nietzsche, which is still preserved in the Munch Museum in Oslo. Munch never met Nietzsche, but learned about him indirectly through the Polish writer Stanislaw Przybyszewski; Munch himself collected Nietzsche's aphorisms. His introduction to Nietzsche's philosophy probably began soon after his scandalous exhibition in Berlin in 1892, when he became part of the literary circle around Strindberg at the Zum Schwarzen Ferkel café; the group's interests included Nietzsche, symbolism, erotic themes, and death fantasies. No doubt Nietzsche's great concern for the individual's loneliness, anguish, doubt, and passion, and his uncompromising attitude towards Christianity, must have struck a deep chord in Munch's profoundly pessimistic character.

Man with Umbrella

1891 graphite

345 x 260 mm

inscription:

signed *E. Munch*

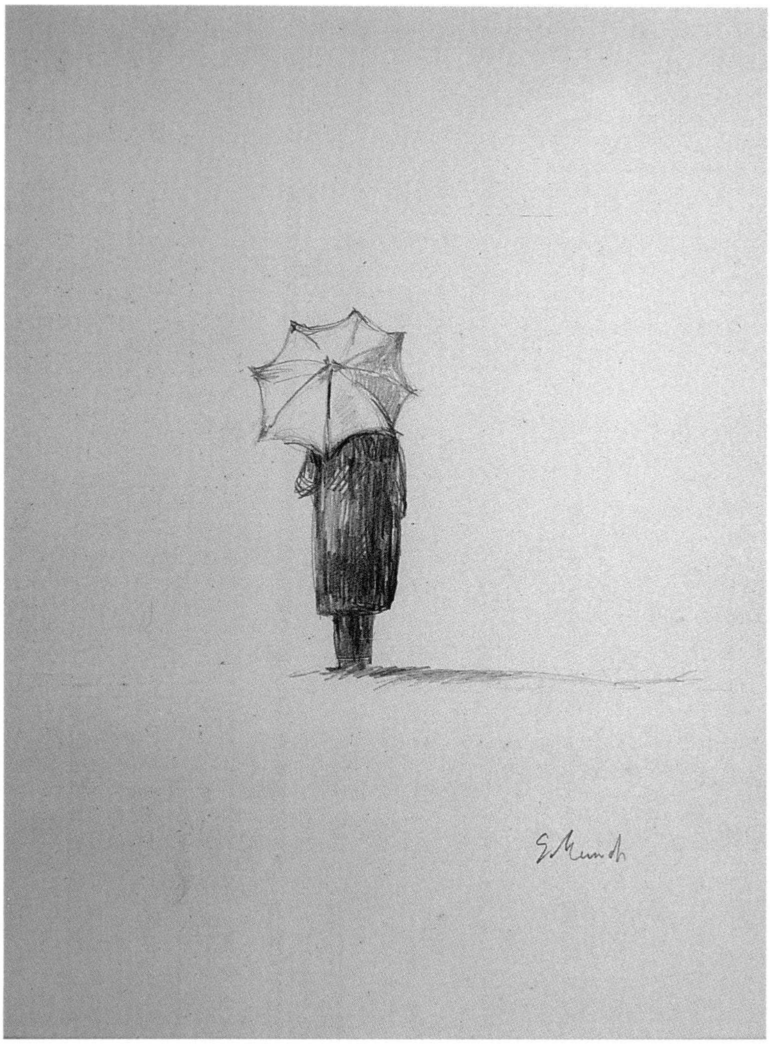

Jean Marc Nattier

1685 – 1766 | French

Study for a Female Portrait

circa 1745
pen and brown ink
with gray wash and
red chalk over graphite
240 x 200 mm

Three great portraitists marked the first half of the eighteenth century in France: Hyacinthe Rigaud, Nicolas de Largillierre, and Jean Marc Nattier. Of the three, it was Nattier who created the quintessential Rococo portraits fostered by the court of Louis XV and Madame de Pompadour. Nattier came from a family of portraitists, and in his early years he copied Rubens' Medici cycle in the Luxembourg Palace for Picart's engravings of 1707. It was another of his copies — this time a drawing after Rigaud's portrait of Louis XIV — that attracted the attention of Mansart, who introduced him to the aging king in 1712. Louis XIV said to Nattier: "Monsieur, continuez à travailler ainsi et vous deviendrez un grand homme." Although Nattier worked briefly for Peter the Great in Holland, he was the sensation of Paris. In the Salon of 1737, the *Mercure* proclaimed him to be "l'élève des Grâces." Nattier's gift lay in his ability to record a likeness speedily, at the same time endowing his relaxed sitters, predominantly women, with beauty, grace, and charm unmatched by any other portraitist. From time to time he also ennobled the genre of portraiture with his talent as a history painter by transforming his sitters into mythological figures, muses, or goddesses. In fact, he was admitted to the French Royal Academy in 1718 as a history painter, the reception piece being *Persée, assisté par Minerva, pétrifie Phinée et ses compagnons en leur présentant la tête de Medusa* (Musée des Beaux-Arts, Tours). As Michael Levey pointed out, while Nattier often portrayed his sitters "as goddesses, as the seasons, as the elements, he also portrayed them in a sort of stately intimacy, mingling such Baroque devices as pillars and looped-up curtains with modern truth to nature." Nattier's vogue, therefore, stemmed from his invention of these semi-imaginary, flattering portraits in which he playfully balanced the sitters' respectability with their libertine attitudes. He seamlessly wove together likeness and invention, reality and artifice, propriety and sensuality. His dazzling exercises thus fully embodied the craving for the wittily decorative, the delicately beautiful, and the coyly suggestive in the fashion-conscious age of Louis XV.

The appealing quality that accounts for his popularity in the French court is even reflected in this quick sketch for a female portrait with its graceful Rococo S-curve and informal pose.

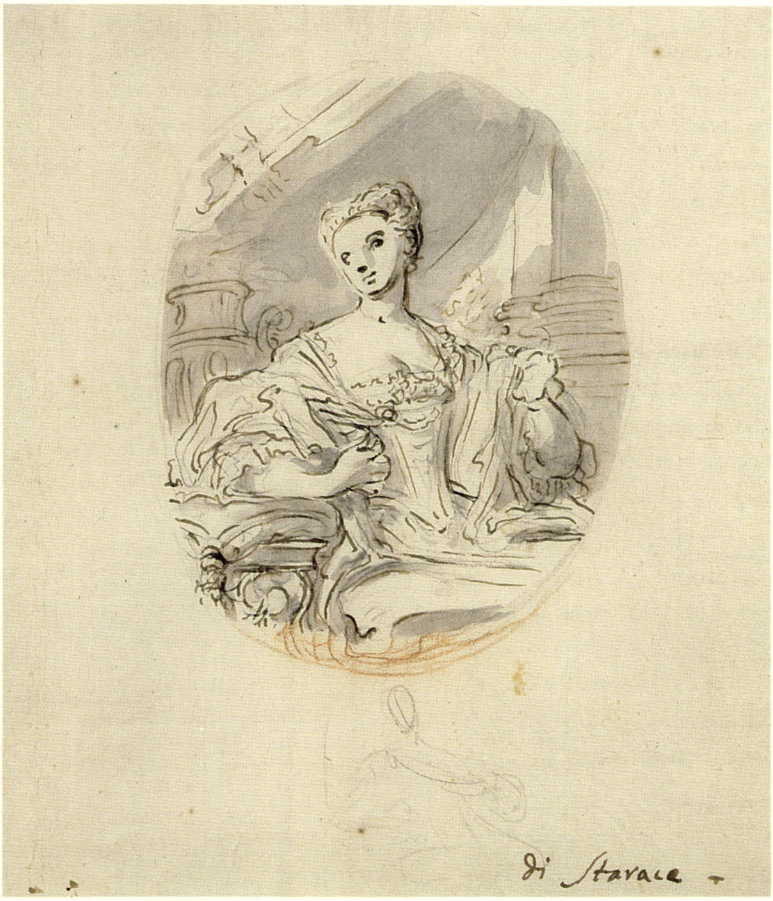

Study for a Female Portrait

circa 1745

pen and brown ink

with gray wash and

red chalk over graphite

240 x 200 mm

Giovanni Battista Piazzetta

1683 – 1754 | Italian

Studies of Female Heads

circa 1745

red chalk

350 x 455 mm

inscription:

Piazzetta

Born in Venice, Piazzetta was the son of a woodcarver. His art training began in the studio of Antonio Molinari. In 1703, he went to Bologna and completed his studies with Giuseppe Maria Crespi. About 1705, he returned to Venice and settled there permanently. He was listed in the *Fraglia dei Pittoria* in 1711 and was admitted to the Clementina academy of Bologna in 1727. His early works consist of a number of religious commissions: *St. John the Baptist* for the choir of S. Giovanni at Bassano in 1713-1717 *St. James' Martyrdom* for S. Stae in 1722, *St. Philip Neri* for S.Maria della Fava in 1725-27, and *Glory of St. Dominic* in SS. Giovanni e Paolo in 1725-27. During the 1730s and 1740s, under the influence of Lys and Strozzi, he en tered a Rococo phase in which his works lightened and began to show a pastoral mood. In this period he ran a large art academy; appropriately, when the Venetian academy was established in 1750, he became its first director. Many of his late works were carried out with the assistance of his students. He was a great influence on the young Giovanni Battista Tiepolo.

Beginning in the mid-1720s, Piazzetta painted heads and half-figures, which were very popular with the public. He also produced book illustrations and many independent finished drawings for collectors. One of the great patrons of his genre heads was the elector of Cologne, Clemens August, who had also commissioned from him altarpieces for German churches. Another foreign patron was Marshal Schulenburg, who had been purchasing his drawings since 1731. It was for Schulenburg that he painted, in the 1740s, a large pair of unique genre subjects, the *Pastorale* (Art Institute of Chicago and the Wallraf-Richartz Museum, Cologne), to which this sheet of head studies is related. The two *Pastorale* represent a fantasy, a *capriccio,* on a genre theme. Their precise meaning remains unclear, but their mystery, and picturesque charm would seem to convey the impermanence of youth, beauty, and love.

This drawing and the other head studies for the two *Pastorale* paintings (in the Art Institute of Chicago, the Cleveland Museum of Art, and other private collections) appear to have been modelled on Piazzetta's own family. While his son, Giacomo, posed for the male figures, the female heads, as found in this sheet, probably represent his daughter, Barbara Augiola, and his wife, Rosa Muzioli. Piazzetta married Rosa in 1724; their son, Giacomo, was born in 1725, and their eldest daughter, Barbara, in 1729. At the time of the *Pastorale* paintings, Rosa was about thirty-five and Barbara, sixteen.

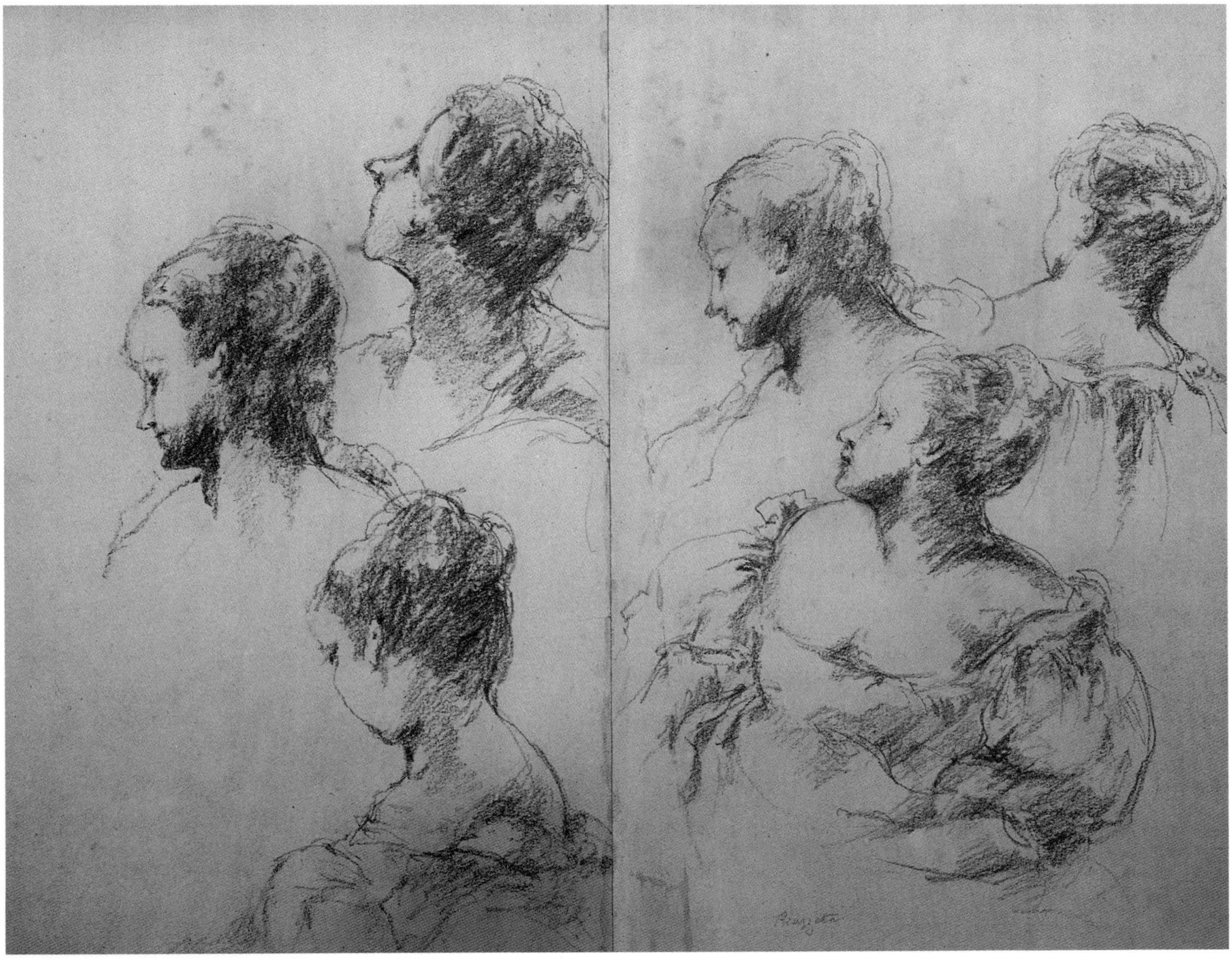

Studies of Female Heads

circa 1745

red chalk

350 x 455 mm

inscription:

Piazzetta

Pablo Ruiz y Picasso

1881 – 1973 | Spanish

Study After a Plaster Cast "Antinous"

1893-94 black chalk and graphite 512 x 362 mm

inscription: signed *Picasso*

Study After a Plaster Cast "Antinous"

1893-94 black chalk and graphite 702 x 457 mm

inscription: *93-94 Coruña* signed *P. Ruiz*

Study After a Plaster Cast Myron's "Discobolus"

1893-94 black chalk 538 x 347 mm

inscription: signed *P. Ruiz*

Study After a Plaster Cast "Discobolus"

1893-94 black chalk and graphite 622 x 405 mm

inscription: signed *P. Ruiz*

Study After a Plaster Cast "Dionysos"

1893-94 black chalk and graphite 694 x 482 mm

inscription: *93-94 Coruña* signed *P. Ruiz*

Study After a Plaster Cast

1893-94 black chalk 190 x 130 mm

Born in Málaga, Picasso was the son of José Ruiz Blasco and Maria Picasso Lopez. His father, an art teacher, provided him with his first art lessons. In the academies of La Coruña (1892-94), Barcelona (1895), and Madrid (1897), his student works already showed extraordinary accomplishment. In Barcelona, his circle of friends included young artists and intellectuals, who introduced him to the Symbolist and Art Nouveau works of the Catalan School. During his first visit to Paris in 1900, he was impressed by the works of Toulouse-Lautrec, Gauguin, and van Gogh. Between 1901 and 1904, he lived alternately in Paris and Barcelona. His subjects in this, his Blue Period were the social outcasts in the bars of Montmartre or the streets of Barcelona. In 1904 he settled in Paris and became the centre of an avant-garde circle of writers and artists, including the critic and poet, Guillaume Apollinaire. His first patrons were the American writer Gertrude Stein and her brother Leo, Wilhelm Uhde, and the Russian, S. Shchukin. During his Rose Period, his works were dominated by saltimbanques and circus performers; he also began experimenting with sculpture, under the influence of the Iberian sculptures in the Louvre. In 1906, he met Matisse, and through the dealer Ambroise Vollard, who gave him his first Paris exhibition in 1901, was introduced to the works of Cézanne. Increasingly, he became interested in primitive art, especially African sculpture, and his painting, *Les Demoiselles d'Avignon* (1907; Museum of Modern Art, New York), marked the beginning of the Negro Period — the move towards simplification and distortion. Together with Braque, he started to clarify and systematize new intellectual, artistic visions — Analytical Cubism in 1910-12 and then Synthetic Cubism in 1912-16; the latter introduced collage. In 1917, he went to Rome with Jean Cocteau to design scenery and costumes for the ballet *Parade*. His contact with Italy and antique art, as well as his reaction against the chaos of world war, led to a phase of classicism. This was followed by a metamorphic phase in the 1920s when he was in close association with André Breton, the founder of Surrealism. His series of nudes and bullfights in the late 1920s and 1930s culminated in *Guernica* in 1937 (Prado, Madrid), prompted by the Spanish Civil War. In 1944, the Paris Salon de Libération honoured his works in a large exhibition. In 1946, his move to the Mediterranean coast introduced a more idyllic tone with fauns and centaurs. He also produced painted ceramics and did variations on Old Masters: Poussin, Cranach, El Greco, Velázquez, Rembrandt, Courbet, and Delacroix. In 1957-58, he was commissioned by UNESCO to decorate its Paris headquarters. During the 1960s, he concentrated largely on his graphic production and on sheet-metal sculptures. By then, countless retrospectives and tributes were occurring around the world; in 1964, for example, he travelled to Montréal and Japan. Although he refused the French Legion of Honour in 1967, an exhibition of his selected works was placed in the Grande Galerie of the Louvre on his ninetieth birthday in 1971.

Picasso began to draw at an early age. In 1891 his art-teacher father moved his family from Málaga to Coruña, where Picasso trained as an artist. In the classes of the painter and sculptor Isidoro Modeste Brocos he made black chalk drawings after plaster casts of classical sculptures. The majority of these drawings, including these six, were done during his second school year (1893-94), when he was only twelve or thirteen. Although he later boasted that "at the age of twelve I drew like Raphael," these works — then signed P. Ruiz" — do show that Picasso was educated in the nineteenth-century academic tradition and reveal a level of competence precocious for his age. Many of these academic studies are now in the collections of his heirs and in the Museo Picasso, Barcelona.

Two Studies of Mother and Child and a Bird

1902 pen and brown ink 120 x 92 mm and 70 x 90 mm

inscription: *1902*

Of these two fragments — from either the same sheet or the same sketchbook — the smaller sketch is related to some of the drawings in Picasso's sketchbook, the *Carnet Catalan,* now in the Berggruen collection; the larger, of the mother and child, is similar to *The Death of the Torero,* a black chalk drawing in the Musée Picasso, Paris. These drawings were done in Barcelona during his Blue Period, when his subjects were chiefly the downtrodden. They show especially well Picasso's sympathy for the anguished women of Spain — victims of the country's past and its contemporary industrial and agricultural changes.

Self-portrait

circa 1904 graphite 130 x 190 mm

inscription: signed *Picasso*

In 1904, aged twenty-three, Picasso settled in Paris after repeated visits. His prospects at the beginning were poor. He lived in constant fear of the authorities suspecting him of anarchist associations. But, he had a new mistress, a model named Madeleine, who posed for some of his lesbian compositions. This *Self-portrait* was probably done about the same time in 1904 as a profile portrait drawing of Madeleine in the Musée Picasso, Paris, which seems to echo it in reverse. Another graphite profile self-portrait drawing from 1904, showing Picasso smoking a pipe and inscribed "à Max Jacob," is in the National Museum of Stockholm.

Head of a Boy

1921 black chalk and graphite 155 x 195 mm

inscription: signed and dated *5.4.21. Picasso*

Picasso's neoclassical phase, between 1917 and 1925, was one of the most fertile and complex periods in his artistic evolution. It was not necessarily a rejection of his Cubist revolution. Rather, it conformed to his post-war ideology and circumstances; for in the aftermath of the First World War, a return to the timeless classical order heralded a new beginning. Picasso was not alone; Cocteau's *Antigone,* Stravinsky's *Oedipus Rex,* and Valéry's *Jeune Parque* are other examples of this period's neoclassicism. The immediate stimulation also comes from Picasso's current social relations with members of the bourgeoisie, his Roman visit in 1917, and his fascination with the works of Ingres. This drawing is probably connected with the painting, *Two Boys Reading a Letter,* also from 1921 (Musée Picasso, Paris).

Mother with Dead Child on a Ladder

1937 graphite 321 x 245 mm

inscription: dated *10 mai 37*

From the outbreak of the Spanish Civil War, Picasso followed the tragic events closely. In early 1937, he was asked by the Spanish government to create a mural for the Spanish pavilion at the Paris World's Fair, to be opened on 24 May 1937. He decided on the subject of the mural and began sketching on 1 May, shortly after the German bombing of the small Basque town, Guernica, on 28 April. His early conception of *Guernica* was based on the figures of the bull and the agonized horse. But on 8 May, he introduced the motif of a screaming mother with a dead child, probably derived directly from newspaper photographs and reports of the shocked and suffering refugee women and children. The next day, 9 May, he placed the figure group on a ladder, obviously alluding to Christ's crucifixion. He continued to explore and repeat this motif on 10 May in a number of sketches, including this one, which is closest to two drawings: one in graphite, dated 9 May, and the other in graphite and crayon, dated 10 May (both are in the Museo Nacional Centro de Arte Reina Sofía, Madrid). Soon this screaming mother would be the main source for three of the female figures in the final composition. The enormous *Guernica* (345 x 770 cm) was finally completed in June 1937, the mother and dead child were set on the far left, leading into the entire composition in a powerful display of the brutality and monstrosity of war.

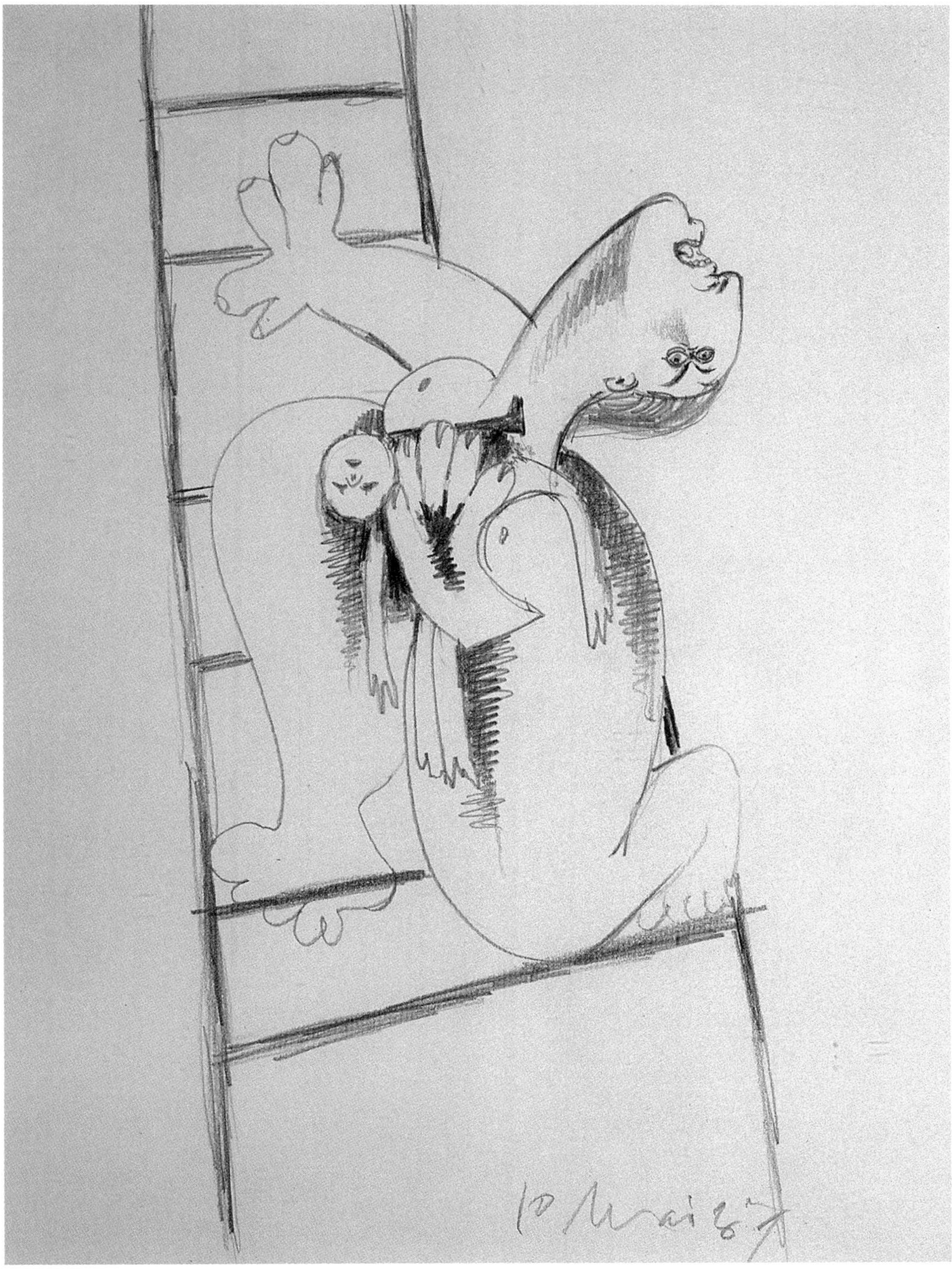

Mother
with Dead Child
on a Ladder

1937 graphite

321 x 245 mm

inscription:

dated *10 mai 37*

Giovanni Battista Piranesi

1720 – 1778 | Italian

Architectural Fantasy: Design for a Stage Set (?)

circa 1740

pen and brown ink over graphite

230 x 325 mm

Piranesi played an important role in the promotion of antiquarianism and early Neoclassicism in the eighteenth century. His earliest training was in Palladian architecture near the end of the Golden Age of the Venetian Republic, which produced Goldoni, Vivaldi, Albinoni, Canaletto, the Guardis, and the Tiepolos. He also received formal education in Baroque stage design from the Valeriani brothers and was very much influenced by the stage designs of Giuseppa Galli Bibiena and the imaginative architecture of Filippo Juvarra. Furthermore, the *veduta* works of Marco Ricci, Francesco Guardi, Giovanni Battista Tiepolo, and Antonio Canaletto equally made decisive impacts on him. In 1740, Piranesi went to Rome in the retinue of Marco Foscarini, the Venetian ambassador. There he studied printmaking and Roman monuments, publishing in 1743 the *Prima Parte di Architettura e Prospettive,* his first Roman views. His reputation was firmly established with the publication of two extensive series of large prints, *Le Antichita Romane* in 1756 and *Della Magnificenza ed Architettura de'Romani* in 1761. These two works contributed much to the contemporary Graeco-Roman debate by extolling the achievement of Rome and opposing Winckelmann's claim of Greek superiority. In the early 1760s, Piranesi reissued a fully reworked version of his earlier etched series, the *Carceri* — fourteen plates of such explicit drama in their exaggerated perspectives that they are indicative of artistic emancipation; they inspired Thomas de Quincey to describe them in the *Confessions of an English Opium-Eater* (1821) as "expressions of huge power put forth, and resistance overcome." Indeed, Piranesi's enormous output — more than 1,000 large, etched plates and a sizable collection of drawings — represents the passionate melodrama of the late Baroque; his is a richly sensuous, vital, and emotional oeuvre.

Piranesi's preference for the hard grandeur and boldness of Roman architecture, prompted in part by his fascination with a dignified national past, is found even in his early works of architectural fantasy such as this sheet. Here the unorthodox mixture of classical motifs, the manipulation of gigantic scale and the organization of powerfully receding perspective clearly represent a reinterpretation of Roman monuments. Drawn as a creative release and an exercise in skill, the composition shows motifs that often recur in Piranesi's later works: the triumphal arch approached by steps in a palace complex, the columnar hall or atrium with receding flights of steps, and the gigantic chained statues with trophies. This work is almost certainly connected with his involvement in stage design during his Venetian and early Roman years. It also suggests his familiarity with the influential stage design principles of *scena per angolo,* in Ferdinando Bibiena's *Architettura Civile* (1711) — a revolutionary concept in which the conventional viewpoint in theatre sets was replaced by diagonally receding vistas to produce a spatial structure of the utmost complexity.

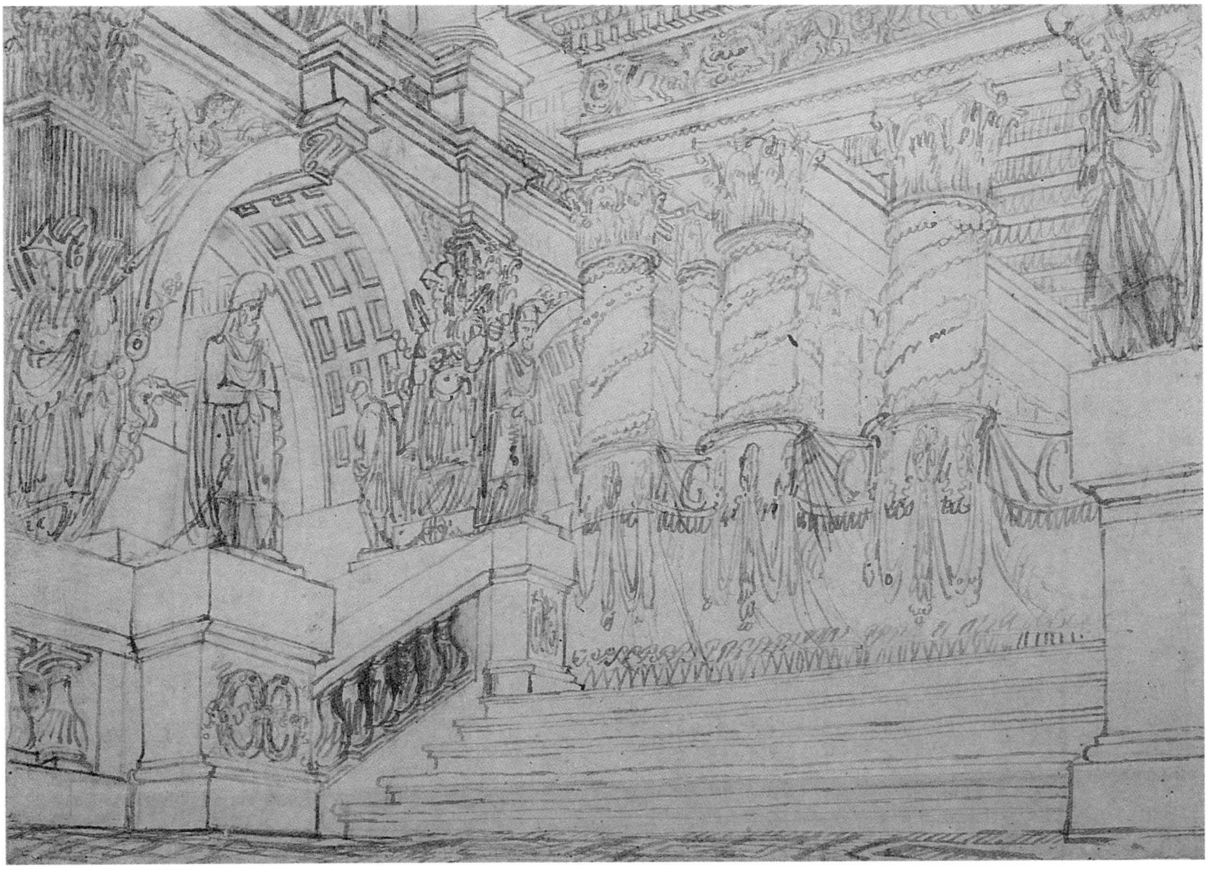

Architectural Fantasy: Design for a Stage Set (?)

circa 1740

pen and brown ink over graphite

230 x 325 mm

Nicolas Poussin

1594 – 1665 | French

Three Profiled Heads

circa 1625-30

pen and brown ink

93 x 72 mm

A native of Normandy, Poussin arrived in Paris about 1612 and worked briefly with the Flemish portraitist, Ferdinant Elle, and the history painter, George Lallemand. He then started to work with Philippe de Champaigne for the queen's mother, Marie de' Medici, in the Luxembourg. Introduced by Alexandre Courtois, he studied prints after Raphael and Giulio Romano, ancient sculptures, and Roman and Venetian paintings in the royal collection. In 1624 he went to Rome. With the recommendation of his early Parisian patron, the courtier Giovanni Battista Marino, he was presented to Cardinal Francesco Barberini, nephew of Pope Urban VIII. In the Barberini library, he completed his studies in optics, geometry, and perspective. During those Roman years, he was also working in the studio of Domenichino, producing many smaller works for upper-class patrons. Increasingly, he turned from religious to classical subjects, to mythology and to Tasso. For his dramatic compositions, he used the device of a miniature stage with small draped wax models to experiment with effects of gesture, grouping, and lighting. In 1640, after two years of persuasion from the powerful Cardinal Richelieu and Louis XIII, he returned to Paris and was commissioned to decorate the Grande Galerie of the Louvre and to provide works for the Royal Press and Richelieu. These commissions, however, brought him into rivalry with other court artists, of whose work he was decidedly critical. So, in 1642, after only eighteen months, he returned to Rome forever.

From his Parisian years in the 1630s, Poussin kept a circle of friends, later also his best patrons, who were small bankers, merchants, and minor civil servants, all members of the bourgeoisie. These men were highly educated, intellectual, and pious. It was for them that Poussin produced, in the ten years after his return to Rome, the paintings that were considered in his own time as his best. They are now recognized as the full embodiment of French Classicism. The classical themes that Poussin chose for these works were the heroic and stoical stories of Roman moral victory and sacrifice paralleling the tragedies of Corneille, or psychologically dramatic biblical subjects from the Old and New Testaments. Presented with clarity and rationality, these mature works are exercises in solid geometry and the logical expression of his theories: a painting must contain the maximum intellectual content, with pleasing patterns and vigorous colour, to provide the unity of vision.

For each of his projects, Poussin carefully produced many studies and sketches. The present drawing is datable to his early Roman period, when the influence of Giulio Romano, whose works he had studied in Paris, remained strong.

Rape of the Sabine Women

circa 1630-35 pen and wash in brown ink 115 x 198 mm

This sheet is related to the two versions of the *Rape of the Sabine Women* which Poussin painted in the 1630s. The Louvre version is dated 1631-32 and the Metropolitan Museum version, painted for Cardinal Omodei, is from about 1635. The subject, described in Livy and Plutarch, is the abduction of the Sabine women by Roman soldiers: to ensure the creation of a new community and guarantee the future of the nation, Romulus devised the scheme of inviting the neighbouring Sabines to a celebration and subsequently seizing their women. Since the Sabine women eventually married their Roman abductors, the subject had often been used to decorate wedding chests since the fifteenth-century.

Poussin's figurative motifs, especially in the depiction of women struggling against masculine brutality, were inspired by Hellenistic sculpture such as the *Gaul Killing Himself and His Wife* (Terme Museum, Rome) and by Gian Bologna's 1583 sculptural group of the *Rape of the Sabine Woman* in the Loggia dei Lanzi on the Piazza della Signoria in Florence.

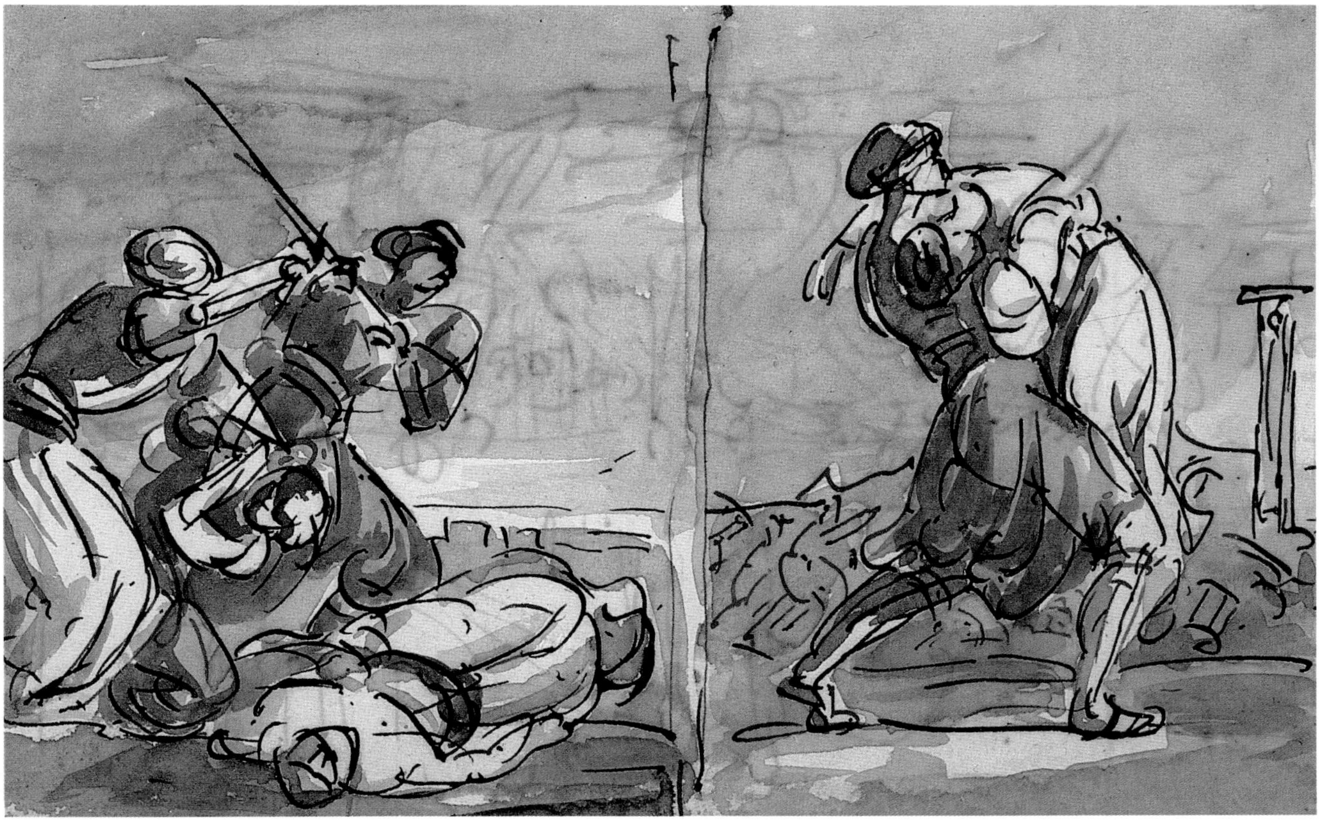

Rape of the Sabine Women

circa 1630-35

pen and wash

in brown ink

115 x 198 mm

Pierre Puvis de Chavannes

1824 – 1898 | French

Male Nude

circa 1859
graphite and
black chalk
248 x 180 mm

One of the great decorative painters of the late nineteenth century, Puvis was born in Lyon. His first trip to Italy in 1847 had a decisive impact on his artistic career. He became determined to create the style and effect of monumental Italian frescoes in his huge decorative canvases. Returning to France, he began studying with Henri Scheffer, brother of the Romantic painter Ary Scheffer. He also spent some time in the studio of Delacroix and Thomas Couture. The paramount influence, however, came from Théodore Chassériau. Although official rejection plagued him in the early 1850s, he began exhibiting regularly in the Salon after 1859. His success came in the 1860s; by 1866, he was no longer required to be judged by the Salon jury to exhibit. In 1867 he was made a chevalier of the Legion of Honour, and an officer in 1877. It was also in the 1860s that he began his major decorative projects: paintings for the museum at Amiens in 1861-65, the museum at Marseilles in 1869, the town hall at Poitiers in 1872-75, and the Panthéon in 1874-78. In 1872, while serving on the Salon jury, he defended the Realist Courbet, whose works were rejected on political grounds; he resigned — yet the Realist critics attacked him for his painting ideas. However, in the 1880s, he became a hero to the younger Symbolist artists and writers. He admired the works of Manet, Monet, Hodler, and even Matisse; in turn he was revered by Zola, Roger Marx, Antonin Proust, Mirabeau, Gauguin, Degas, Seurat, Monet, Renoir, Signac, Boudin, Carrière, and Rodin. In his last years he continued to carry out large-scale mural paintings on canvas for various decorative schemes: the Palais des Arts in Lyon (1883-86), the Sorbonne (1887-89), the Musée des Beaux-Arts at Rouen (1891), the Paris Hôtel de Ville (1891-94), the Boston public library (1894), and the Panthéon (1896-98). Many of these works were exhibited in the Salon before installation in their destined locations. In 1890, together with Rodin and Meisonnier, he formed the Société Nationale des Beaux-Arts, which ran the Salon du Champ-de-Mars, and later became its president. Throughout the 1890s, Durand-Ruel held major shows of his works in Paris and New York. Fifteen of his works were exhibited posthumously in the 1913 Armory Show in New York.

For the Symbolists, Puvis' works, in their monumental scale, subdued colour harmonies, relative flatness, simplified dramatic patterns, and linear rhythm, conform perfectly to fin-de-siècle aesthetics. His art, projecting a noble, poetical dream of a harmonious society, inspired a whole generation of artists in search of utopian visions.

The drawing *Male Nude,* perhaps a life-study, might be related to one of the figures in Puvis' early painting, *Un Retour de Chasse,* a quasi-classical, Poussin-inspired work exhibited in the Salon of 1859 (Musée des Beaux-Arts, Marseilles; a reduced version in the Nelson Gallery of Art-Atkins Museum, Kansas City).

Study of a Boatman

circa 1876 graphite 195 x 255 mm
inscription: signed *P. Puvis de Chavannes*

In 1874, Philippe de Chennevières, director of fine arts in France, handed out commissions for the decoration of the Panthéon, stating: "The decoration of the Panthéon should be a vast poem of painting and sculpture to the glory of St. Geneviève, who will remain the most ideal figure of the earlier days of our race, a poem in which the legend of the patron saint of Paris should be combined with the whole history of the origin of Christianity in France." Puvis was one of the artists invited to participate. His commission comprised four panels representing the childhood of St. Geneviève, in which religion is united with patriotism. This drawing of a boatman is a study for the left panel in the mural *The Meeting of St. Geneviève and St. Germaine in A.D. 429.* Puvis exhibited cartoons for this mural in the Salon of 1876, completing the work in 1878. Related oil sketches and drawings are now in the National Museum of Wales, Cardiff; the Louvre; the Rijksmuseum Kröller-Müller, Otterlo; and other private collections.

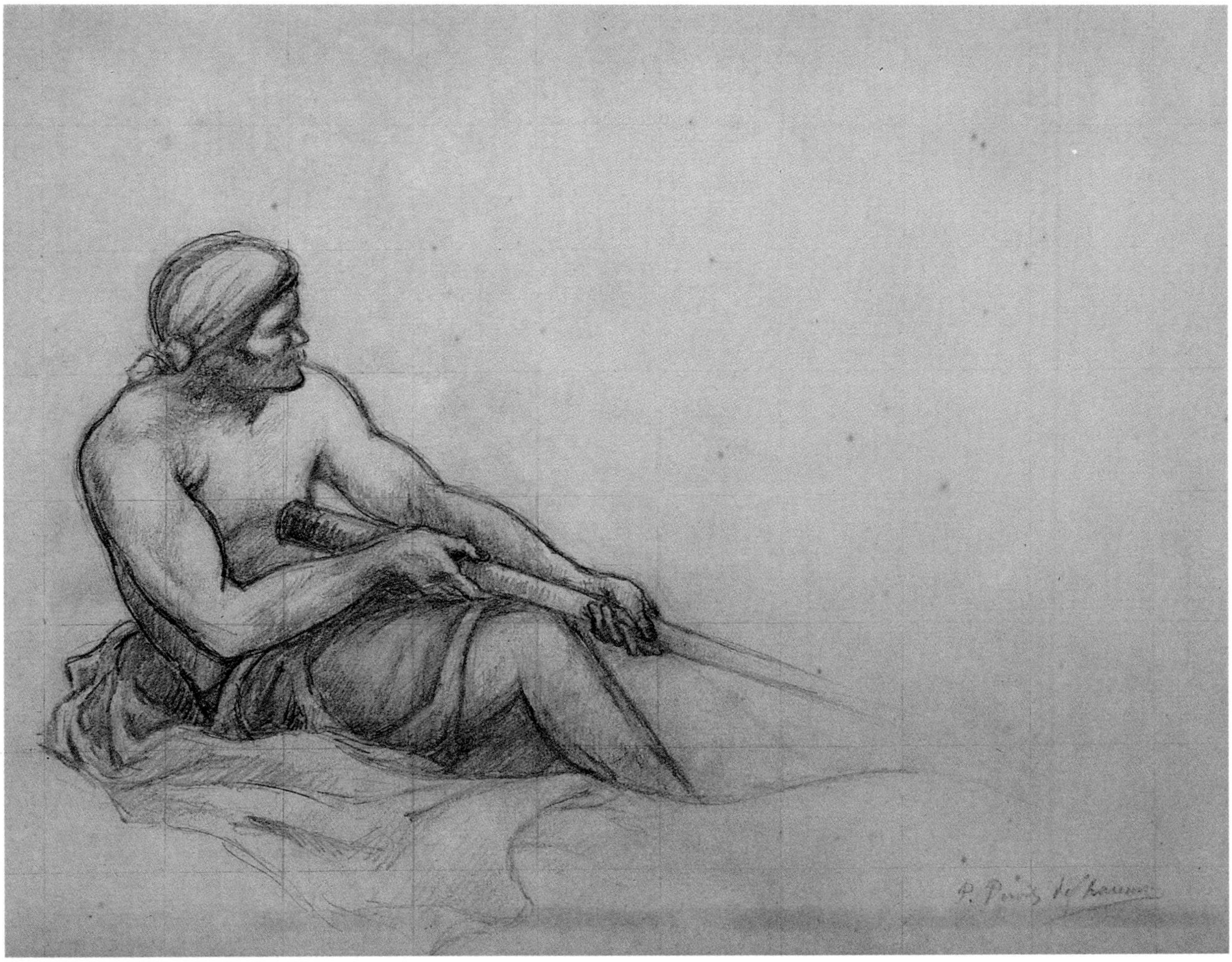

Study of a Boatman

circa 1876

graphite

195 x 255 mm

inscription: signed

P. Puvis de Chavannes

Odilon Redon

1840 – 1916 | French

Tree Study

circa 1880-85

graphite

300 x 240 mm

inscription:

signed *Od.R.*

Tree Study

circa 1880-85

graphite

290 x 220 mm

inscription:

signed *Od.R.*

Born in Bordeaux, Redon spent most of his childhood at Peyrelebade, the family estate in the Médoc. In 1859, he entered the studio of Jean-Léon Gérome, for a brief, but disastrous, stay. Returning to Bordeaux, he met the botanist Armand Clavad, who introduced him to philosophy, Hindu poetry, contemporary literature, and science. There he also learned etching and engraving from Rodolphe Bresdin. In the 1860s and 1870s he concentrated on charcoal drawings, his "noirs." After the Franco-Prussian War in 1870, he lived in Paris. He underwent a profound spiritual crisis. Turning to lithography, with some assistance from Fantin-Latour, he produced his first lithographic album, *Dans le rêve,* in 1879; later came *À Edgar Poe* (1882), *Les Origines* (1883), *Homage à Goya* (1885), *La Nuit* (1886), *Le Juré* (1887), *Le Tentation de St. Antoine* (1888) and *À Gustave Flaubert* (1889). Huysmans praised Redon in *A Rebours* (1884). Regarded as the Symbolist par excellence, he was asked to preside over the new Société des Independants in 1884 and to participate in the eighth Impressionist exhibition in 1886. In the 1890s he began using pastels. From this period onwards, he had important exhibitions at Durand-Ruel's and Vollard's galleries and in the Salon d'Automne, Amsterdam, and the 1913 Armory Show in New York.

Throughout his life, Redon was haunted by the arid landscape around his family estate at Peyrelebade, its sparse trees and strange inhabitants, and he continued to return nearly every summer until the sale of the property in 1897. He wrote in his journal, *À Soi-même,* these contacts with nature were a crucial means for renewing himself and his art. Since childhood, he had been fascinated by the intricate forms of tree branches. For him trees represented the secrets of nature's regenerative power, at once tangible and mysterious, real and symbolic. Between 1870 and 1900, he produced numerous drawings of trees, usually in graphite or charcoal, both from observation and from memory. This group of works, to which these two drawings belong, is now divided among various private and public collections; most, however, are in the Louvre.

Closed Eyes

1890 graphite 207 x 125 mm

inscription: signed *Odilon Redon*

One of his favourite subjects, Redon repeated the image of closed eyes in lithographs, paintings, pastels, many from 1890. The idea derives from Michelangelo's *Slave* (Louvre): in March 1888 Redon wrote that he had meditated before "the closed eyes of the *Slave*. . . . He sleeps, and the worried dream that crosses the brow of this marble lifts our dreams into a pensive and moving world." Although Redon's wife, Camille, posed for the picture, Redon acknowledged that the figure is "androgynous." For the Symbolists, androgyny was the ideal human state. The figure is at once a portrait and an allusion to both the Virgin Mary and Christ; and half immersed in water, it may be related to Baudelaire's "Semper Eadem" and "Fountain," which describes the illusion of two beings united as one. In 1890, Redon was illustrating Baudelaire's *Les Fleurs du Mal.* That year was also his tenth wedding anniversary. In this context, the aqueous element in this picture, symbolizing fertility, death, and healing power, may suggest Redon's reflection on recent personal events: in those years: the drowning of his friend Emile Hennequin in 1888, the deaths of his first son, Jean, in 1886 and of Armand Clavard in 1890, and the birth of his second son Arï, in 1889. *Closed Eyes* is Redon's baptism of a new self, the icon for the sacrament of life and death.

Portrait of Arï Redon

circa 1895 graphite 240 x 190 mm

inscription: signed *Odilon Redon*

The birth of his second son, Arï, in 1889 gave great joy to Redon, who recorded the growth of the child from 1890 onwards in numerous drawings, lithographs, and pastels (Art Institute of Chicago, the Louvre, and other collections).

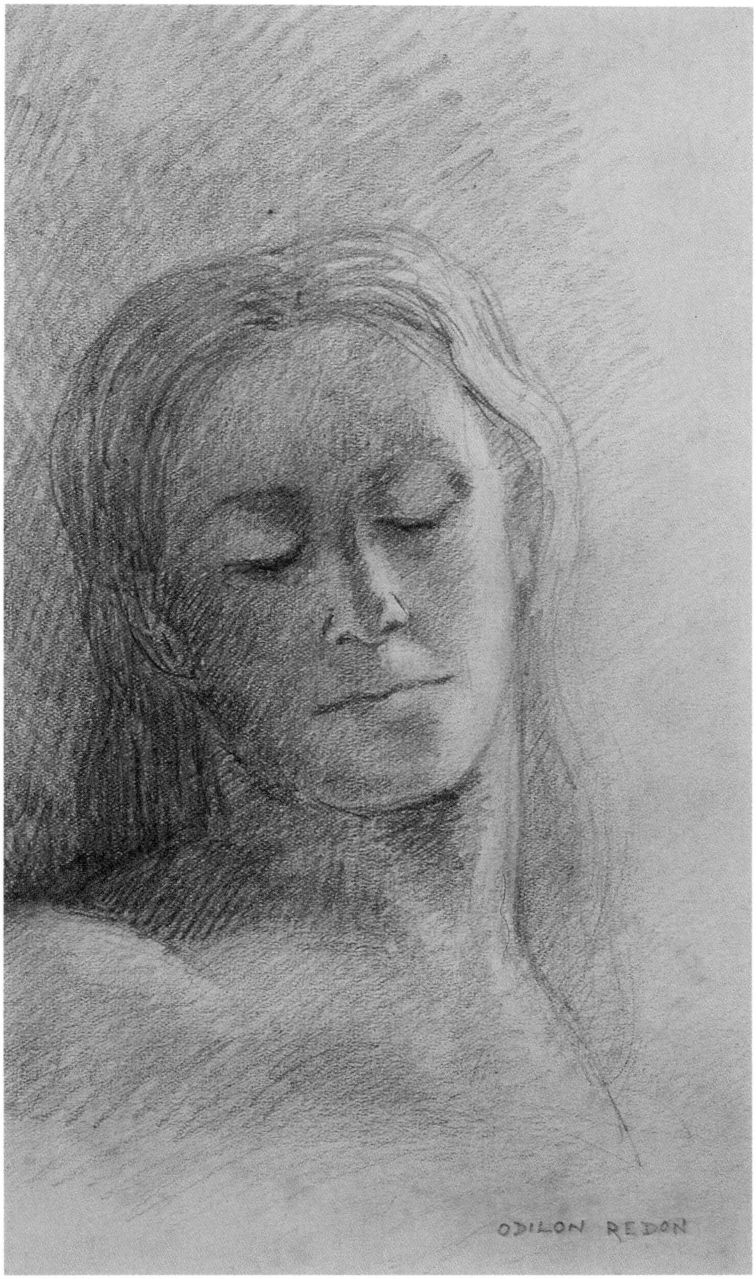

Closed Eyes

1890 graphite

207 x 125 mm

inscription:

signed *Odilon Redon*

attributed to Rembrandt van Rijn

1606 – 1669 | Dutch

Lucretia
circa 1666
pen and wash
in brown ink
114 x 118 mm

Born in the Dutch university town of Leyden, Rembrandt spent a short time at the university, preparing for a scholarly career. His art studies began in 1620 with a local artist, Jacob van Swanenbrugh. In 1624, he was the pupil of the Amsterdam history painter Pieter Lastman, who conveyed to him the influence of Caravaggio and Elsheimer. Lastman also fostered in him a love of oriental costumes, passionate gestures, vivid chiaroscuro, and the generally theatrical mode of presentation that characterized Rembrandt's early historical compositions. Returning to Leyden in 1625, he established an independent practice with Jan Lievens and produced a variety of subjects from ancient history and the Old and New Testaments. In addition to painting, he also began to make etchings. During the Leyden period, his works attracted the attention of connoisseurs, especially Constantin Huygens, who assisted him in obtaining many commissions. With great confidence he moved permanently to Amsterdam in 1632. Here he came into contact with contemporary High Baroque art and admired the works of Rubens. Very quickly he became a successful portraitist, painting works such as *The Anatomy Lesson of Dr. Tulp* in 1632, a group portrait of the Amsterdam Guild of Surgeons; and *The Civic Militia Company of Captain Frans Banning Cocq* in 1642, better known as *The Night Watch*. In 1633, through Huygens, he received a prestigious commission from the prince of Orange to paint a series of Passion pictures for the Noordeinde Palace at The Hague. With a steady income, he collected paintings, prints, costumes, and curiosities of natural history. But after 1642, his business declined — the result of changing taste among the Dutch buying public who wanted meticulously smooth, anecdotal paintings with pretty colours. In the 1650s and 1660s he developed serious personal and financial problems. His son Titus and his companion Hendrickje Stoffels managed to form a business partnership as art dealers in 1660 by making Rembrandt their employee, in order to protect him from his creditors. During these years, his art acquired greater spiritual presence and psychological insight. His works are filled with sensitivity, nobility, philosophic resignation, and majestic resolve. The historical paintings of his mature and last Amsterdam period, especially those with biblical subjects, with their evocation of the solemn pathos in human life — derived from his own experience and his deepened sense of reality — represent his greatest contribution to Protestant iconography.

Throughout his career, Rembrandt searched among various sources — history, the Bible, mythology — for the moral ties that bind humanity through history. Particularly in his last years, he preferred to depict moments of impending doom, tragic upheaval, and humanity's courageous confrontation with imminent but fearful destiny. Such is the subject of *Lucretia*. Drawn from Livy's *Histories* (I.57-58), it relates the story of the virtuous Lucretia, wife of Collatinus, who was raped by Sextus, son of the last king of Rome, Tarquin the Proud. After the assault, Lucretia called together her father and husband, who came with Publius Valerius and Brutus, and stabbed herself in their presence to expiate the stain. The action of Lucretia therefore belongs to the time-honoured theme of heroic suicide. Rembrandt painted two versions of *Lucretia* in the 1660s. The earlier version, dated 1664 (National Gallery, Washington D.C.), shows Lucretia before her suicide, addressing her chosen weapon. The later version, dated 1666 (Minneapolis Institute of Art), to which this drawing is related, represents the moment after Lucretia has given herself the fatal wound. It has been suggested that the cord of the curtain to the right might be a stage prop and that the figure could have been inspired by a stage performance. The 1666 version of *Lucretia* deliberately suppressed the outward action in favour of the heroine's inner conflict. The figure's solemn grandeur and outward calm is characteristic of Rembrandt's very late works.

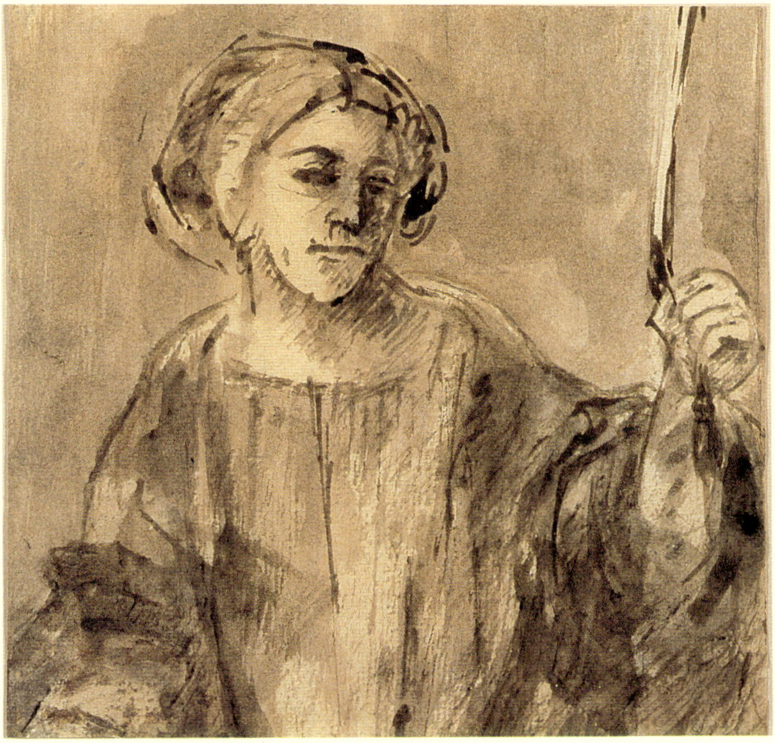

Lucretia

circa 1666

pen and wash

in brown ink

114 x 118 mm

Pierre Auguste Renoir

1841 – 1919 | French

Bathers

1884-87

graphite

256 x 366 mm

inscription:

signed *Renoir*

Bathers

1884-87

pastel

237 x 327 mm

inscription:

signed *Renoir*

A core member of the French Impressionists, Renoir was born in Limoges and settled in Paris with his family in 1845. He showed an early talent in music and studied with Charles Gounod. In the 1850s he trained as a porcelain painter in the Sèvres factory. In 1861 he entered the studio of Charles Gleyre, where he met Bazille, Pisarro, Sisley, Monet, and Cézanne. While he was impressed by the works of Delacroix, Courbet, Manet, and the Barbizon painters, he was also interested in the Rococo paintings of Watteau, Boucher, and Fragonard that he had studied in the Louvre. By the late 1860s, he was increasingly drawn into Monet's orbit, the two often working together along the Seine. Increasingly, Renoir painted outdoors in lighter, brighter colours. In the 1870s and 1880s, he participated in four of the Impressionist exhibitions. At the same time, he exhibited some of his elegant portraits in the official Salon, undoubtedly motivated by market considerations. Beginning in the late 1870s, he travelled extensively — visiting North Africa in 1879 and 1882 and Guernsey in 1880, and making several trips to Italy, London, Holland, Spain, and Germany, to study the Old Masters, especially Raphael, Velázquez, and Rubens, in museums. But the early 1880s was a period of uncertainty for Renoir, as for his Impressionist colleagues, because of profound differences of opinion, both artistic and political, among them. Renoir gradually renounced his vibrant, spontaneous Impressionist techniques and effects in favour of firmer modelling and more elaborate preparation; as he put it: "Il faut meubler la toile." In 1906, he settled in Cagnes in southern France. Crippled with arthritis, he continued to paint and to sculpt, with the help of an assistant. In his last years he was in regular contact with Matisse, who lived nearby, and was sympathetic to the ideas of Fauvism.

The two *Bathers* drawings form part of a group of nearly two dozen compositional sketches Renoir did for the large painting, *Bathers* (1887), now in the Philadelphia Museum of Art. (The sketches are in the Fogg Art Museum, the Wadsworth Atheneum, the Louvre, the Budapest Museum, and private collections.) These studies, executed between 1884 and 1887, suggest that Renoir was experimenting, and at times struggling, with technique, form, posture, and composition; the aesthetic problems are not resolved in the final painting, which remains partly classical and partly impressionistic. The Bathers, first exhibited in the fashionable international exhibition of painting and sculpture at the Galerie Georges Petit in Paris, is Renoir's first group scene of nudes. It evolved from a series of nude bathers of the 1860s and 1870s. In contrast to the earlier soft, sensuous figures bathed in fugitive, shimmering light, the 1887 *Bathers* insists on great firmness and permanent qualities. The aesthetic shift indicates that Renoir's art was in transition during the 1880s when he was suffering from a lowered income and isolation from the Impressionist group. Moreover, his divergence from naturalism towards a new classicism was also stimulated by literary friends such as Mallarmé, the anti-natural cult of Wagnerian music, and even Cézanne's *Bathers.* Certainly Renoir's renewed interest in the traditional masters during his Italian trip of 1881-82 left its mark: his *Bathers* shows more than traces of influence from Raphael's *Galatea,* Girardon's *Bathing Nymphs,* Boucher's *Diana at the Bath,* and Ingres' *Odalisques* and *Bathers.* For Renoir in the 1880s, tradition was not just a means of sustaining the classical ideal, it could also provide an opportunistic formula for official and commercial success, as illustrated by the popular Salon nudes of Adolph-William Bouguereau. Unfortunately, *Bathers* did not achieve the financial success Renoir had hoped for, but received much negative response, especially from his Impressionist colleagues.

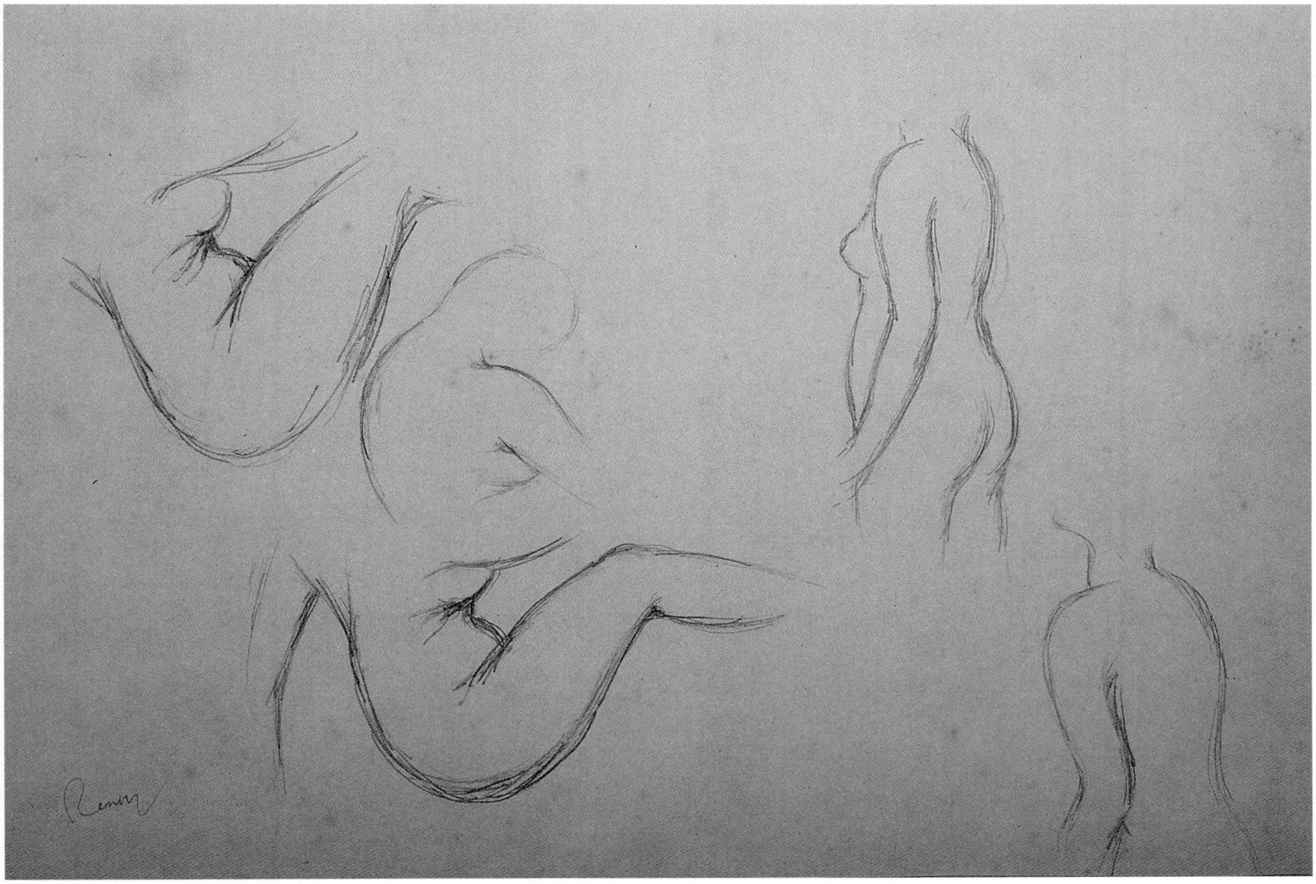

Bathers

1884-87

graphite

256 x 366 mm

inscription:

signed *Renoir*

Hubert Robert

1733 – 1806 | French

Landscape with Obelisk

circa 1797-98

red chalk

165 x 115 mm

Robert was the student of the sculptor Michelangelo Slodtz. His father was the valet to the marquis de Stainville, who later, as duc de Choiseul, became Louis XV's powerful prime minister. When Stainville was appointed French ambassador to Rome in 1754, Robert was in the ambassadorial suite and was able to obtain quarters at the Académie française in Rome. Here he came under the spell of antiquarianism, then in its first great vogue. He savored fully the melancholy and grandeur of Roman ruins and was much influenced by those Italian artists who had specialized in the picturesque depiction of real or imaginary ruins. One of these was Giovanni Panini, who taught perspective in the Académie. Another was the notable architect and engraver of Roman ruins, Giovanni Piranesi, with whom Robert formed a close friendship. At the same time, the two essential early Neoclassical essays Robert admired — Johann Winckelmann's *Thoughts on the Imitation of Greek Works in Painting and Sculpture* (1755) and *The History of Ancient Art* (1764) — had created a fashion for a particular type of landscape painting enriched with "significant" antique ruins and architecture. With his fellow students in Rome, including Clerisseau, La Traverse, Cherpitel, and Peyre, Robert helped to spread the antique mode in France after his return in 1765. It was also in Rome that Robert met Watelet, the creator of the romantic *jardin anglais-chinois,* who directed his attention to landscape gardening. Back in France, he concentrated on painting ruins and designing gardens; the latter amounted to a translation into physical reality of the picturesque painted compositions. In 1766, he was admitted into the Académie as a "painter of ruins" and in 1778, named "the designer of the king's gardens." He also became keeper of Louis XVI's pictures. It was these royal connections that, during the French Revolution, netted him years of imprisonment. He narrowly missed execution. After Robespierre fell in 1794, however, he became a member of the commission in charge of the new Central Museum and was appointed, together with his friend Honoré Fragonard, the first curators of the Louvre.

Robert belonged to the early proto-Romantic phase of Neoclassicism, concerned with the poetic evocation of antiquity. He humanized the Neoclassical vision of monumental grandeur. His works, combining the influence of the late Baroque stage design of the Bibiena family and the archaeological antiquarianism of Piranesi, had a direct link with the utopian architectural fantasies of Ledoux and Boullee.

The present drawing, dating from the late 1790s, belongs to a group of representations that include pyramids and obelisks; such imagery was inspired by the mounting excitement in France at the beginning of Napoleon's Egyptian campaign. (A painting, *Young Girls Dancing Around an Obelisk,* in the Musée des Beaux-Arts, Montréal, is dated 1798.) Here the imaginary combination of exotic Egyptian ruins and lush landscape poetically evokes the themes of history and nature.

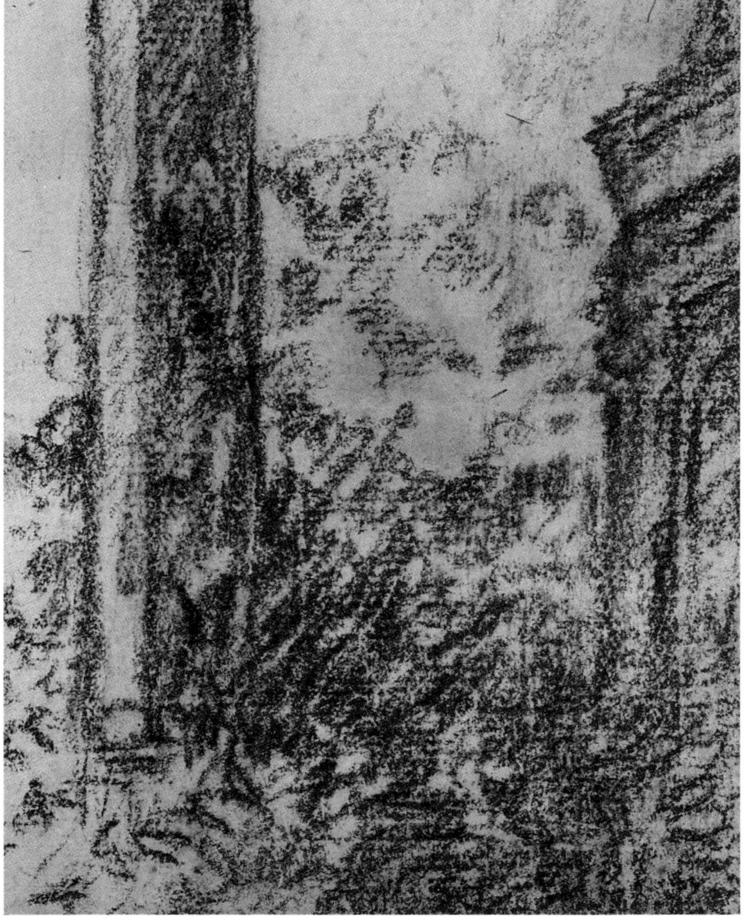

Landscape
with Obelisk

circa 1797-98

red chalk

165 x 115 mm

François-Auguste-René Rodin

1840 – 1917 | French

Torso of Adèle

circa 1882

graphite

272 x 196 mm

inscription:

signed *A.R.*

Born in Paris, Rodin attended the École Impériale Spéciale de Dessin et de Mathématiques in 1854-57. He also studied in the Louvre and the print room of the Bibliothèque Impériale and developed an interest in Dante. In the following years he failed three times to enter the École des Beaux-Arts. In 1862, after a religious crisis, he briefly joined the Order of the Fathers of the Holy Sacrament. In 1864, he worked for the fashionable sculptor, Albert-Ernst Carrier-Belleuse. During the early 1870s, he was in Brussels working with Joseph van Rasbourg on various public monuments and decorative projects. Moved by Michelangelo and Donatello during a visit to Italy in 1875-76, he began working on *The Age of Bronze* and *The Walking Man*. But when *The Age of Bronze* was exhibited in Brussels and the Paris Salon in 1877, he was accused of using casts from life. Between 1879 and 1882, he again worked for Carrier-Belleuse. During a visit to London in 1881-82, he learned drypoint technique from Alphonse Legros, head of London's Slade school. In 1880 he received a state commission to design an entrance portal to the new museum of decorative arts — *The Gates of Hell.* Its various related figures and groups, such as *The Thinker* and *The Kiss,* occupied him for the rest of his life. Other public and government commissions soon followed: *The Burghers of Calais* (1884-85), *Monument to Victor Hugo* (1889), *Monument to Balzac* (1891-98), and *Monument to Labour* (1894-97). He also carried out numerous portrait commissions and illustrated Baudelaire's *Les Fleurs du Mal* (1898). He became a chévalier of the Legion of Honour in 1888, and an officer in 1910; and president of the sculpture section of the Société Nationale des Beaux-Arts in 1893. The Paris World's Fair of 1900 gave him enormous international exposure through a large retrospective. In 1902 and 1903, he made triumphal visits to London and succeeded Whistler as president of the International Society of Sculptors, Painters and Gravers. Shortly before his death in 1916, after a long dispute, the French government formally accepted his offer of all his works and copyright as a gift in exchange for permission to stay at the Hôtel Biron, where Rodin had lived and worked since 1908. The Hôtel Biron was to become the Musée Rodin.

This drawing of a female torso, after the studio model Adèle, is related to an earlier sculptural version Rodin used as a caryatid for the Villa Neptune, Nice, in 1878. In about 1882 Rodin had made a separate study of the *Torso of Adèle* and incorporated it in the top left corner of the tympanum of the *Gates of Hell.* His conception of humanity's frustrated passion in the *Gates of Hell* might originally have been inspired by Dante's *Inferno* and Baudelaire's *Les Fleurs du Mal.* But his romantic involvement with the young sculptor Camille Claudel in the early 1880s also heightened the erotic element in the Gates. The project was substantially completed in 1884, but the prohibitive cost of bronze casting deterred further progress. Rodin continued to make changes throughout his life, and strictly speaking, the *Gates* was never finished; the first bronze casting was made in the 1920s. Most of the drawings for the *Gates of Hell* are in the Musée Rodin in Paris.

Head of Pierre de Wiessant

circa 1889 graphite 233 x 176 mm

inscription: signed *A.Rodin*

In 1884, Rodin was commissioned by the city of Calais to make a monument to commemorate the patriotic self-sacrifice of Eustache de St. Pierre. According to Froissart's fourteenth-century *Chronicles,* during 1346-47, after laying siege to Calais for nearly a year, the English king, Edward III, demanded that the city present six hostages in exchange for its freedom. Eustache de St. Pierre, a wealthy Calais citizen, volunteered; he was joined by Jean d'Aire, Pierre and Jacques de Wiessant, Jean de Fiennes, and Andrieu d'Andres. Expecting death, the six burghers were, however, spared by King Edward. As Rodin proposed to the mayor of Calais: "The subject imposes a heroic conception, and the ensemble of these six self-sacrificing figures has a communicative expression and emotion." Rodin devoted considerable time to developing each figure's character and psychology, modelling all of them with a powerful realism and endowing them with symbolic significance. The spiritually anguished head of Pierre de Wiessant, as this drawing and other studies show, was derived from Gothic sculptures of Christ as Man of Sorrows, which Rodin had studied in the Louvre. *The Burghers of Calais* was Rodin's first successfully completed public monument. It was unveiled in the Place de Richelieu in Calais in 1885. The British government purchased a second cast from Rodin and placed it next to the Houses of Parliament in 1913.

Study for "Monument to Balzac"

circa 1891-92 graphite 190 x 147 mm

inscription: signed *A.R.*

In 1883, the Société des Gens de Lettres, through Emile Zola, invited Rodin to erect a monument to commemorate its first president, the novelist Honoré Balzac. For the project, Rodin researched Balzac's own works and read books about him; he also collected photographs and engravings, and visited Balzac's home town, Tours. He explored different possibilities in poses and finally decided, in about 1896, to portray Balzac dramatically tilted in a large dressing gown, both the writer's and Rodin's favourite attire. Rodin exhibited a plaster version of the forceful and nearly phallic *Balzac* in the 1898 Salon, to mostly hostile reviews. The committee of the Sociéte broke its contract with him, claiming the work unfinished. Rodin considered it his most important work, "the sum of my whole life, result of a whole lifetime of effort, the mainspring of my aesthetic theory. From the day of its conception, I was a changed man." The present drawing is closely related to a group of small early graphite sketches showing Balzac either robed or naked, which are in the Philadelphia Museum of Art.

Study for Dance Movement D

1911 graphite 230 x 160 mm

inscription: *A.R.*

After 1900, Rodin concentrated on smaller sculptures, one notable group being dancing figures (1910-12). Like Degas, Rodin was fascinated by the dance — an extension of their interest in body movements. But unlike Degas, he was not interested in the classical ballet, but the uninhibited "free" dance of Loïe Fuller and Isadora Duncan, and the exotic dance of companies from Java and Cambodia that visited Paris in 1900 and 1906. Rodin wrote in *Le Matin* in 1912: "During the last twenty years, dancing seems to have set for itself the task of making us love the beauty of the body, movement and gesture. First there came Loïe Fuller. . . . Then came Isadora Duncan . . . and today we see Nijinsky. . . ." The article was written in defence of Nijinsky, accused of indecency in his performance of *L'après-midi d'un faune* in the Théâtre de Châtelet in 1912.

This drawing is identical to the plaster version of *Dance Movement D* of 1911 (cast in bronze only after Rodin's death). Its "impressionist" quality suggests that it could be a traced drawing, for Rodin made tracings of his favourite drawings, preserving only the essentials.

Study for Dance Movement D

1911 graphite

230 x 160 mm

inscription:

signed *A.R.*

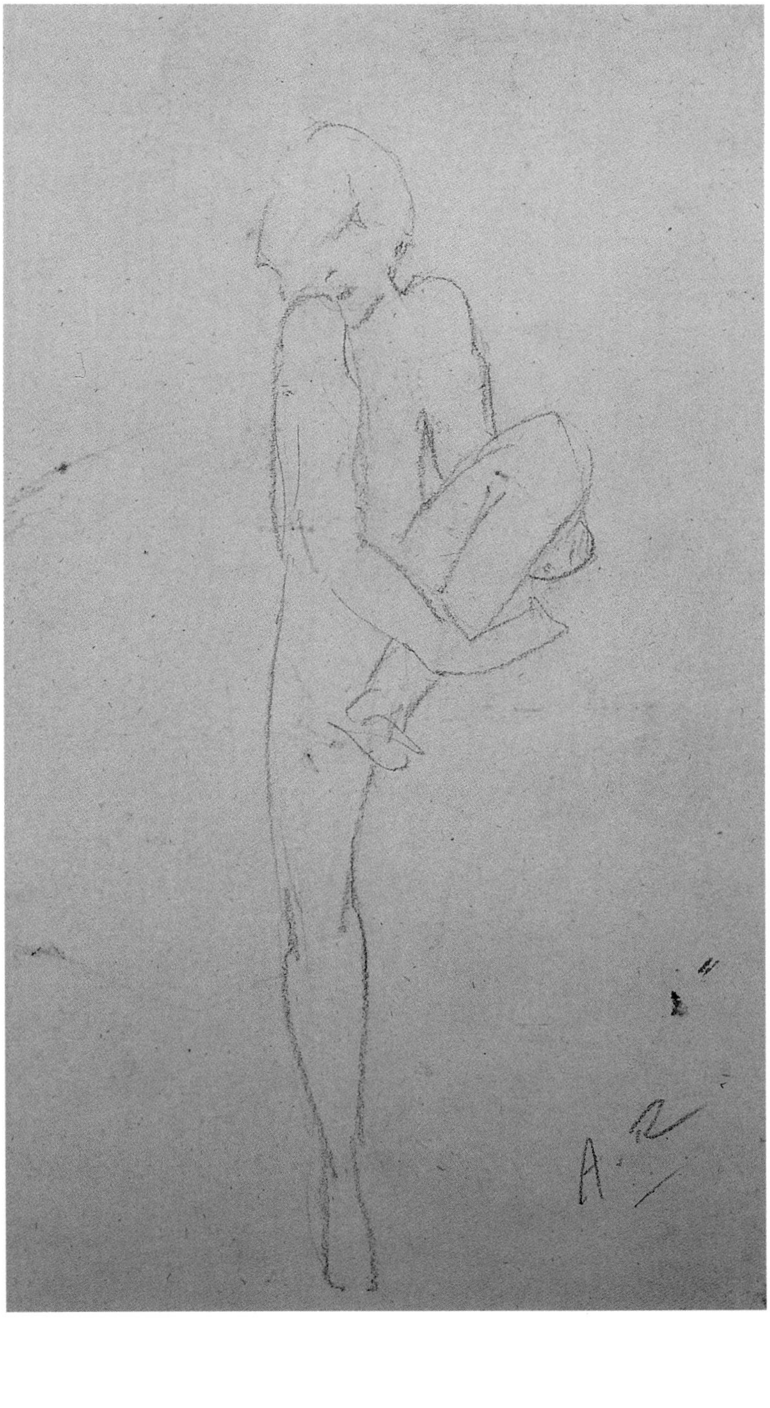

George Romney

1734 – 1802 | British

Three Sheets of Female Figure Studies

circa 1775-80

pen and brown ink

80 x 145 mm each

Romney, Reynolds, and Gainsborough were the most important fashionable English portraitists of the eighteenth century prior to Thomas Lawrence. Romney, born in Lancashire, studied with portraitist Christopher Steele (1755-57), moving to London in 1762. While complaining about the drudgery of portraiture, he was glad of his financial security, and continued in the genre for the rest of his career — during which he produced over 5,000 drawings, some one-third of them portrait studies. These three sketchbook sheets form a sequence, apparently related to several similar studies for the *Portrait of Joanna, Lady Rumbold* of 1777. Like the best of Romney's pen drawings — most successful when least planned — these were done with great speed and little detail. They often appear fevered, obsessive, impulsive, and compulsive. Comparable drawings can be found in the Hampstead Public Library and the Victoria and Albert Museum, London.

Count Langorysky's Death

circa 1790-95 graphite 106 x 167 mm

inscription: *Count Langorysky Death*

From 1777, when they met, the poet William Hayley had given Romney ideas for historical compositions, from classical dramas to contemporary subjects. While the source remains obscure, the subject of this drawing may be inspired by a forgotten literary work recommended by Hayley.

Banquo's Ghost in the Banquet Scene from "Macbeth"

circa 1794 graphite 167 x 230 mm

Romney's interest in Shakespeare was longstanding, stimulated in the 1770s by Hayley and George Stevens, editor of John Boydell's Shakespearean library, and by two famous Shakespearean actors of his aquaintance, Sheridan and Henderson. In 1792 Hayley recorded Romney's desire to paint the banquet scene from *Macbeth* (III, iv) for Boydell's Shakespeare Gallery. Numerous similar sketchbook studies are in the Fitzwilliam Museum, Cambridge; Yale University's Mellon Centre; and the Folger Shakespeare Library, Washington D.C.

John Howard Visiting Prisoners

circa 1794 graphite 111 x 171 mm

Among Romney's drawings based on contemporary social events, the most outstanding is the large group of drawings (over 500) representing the subject of John Howard. Romney's admiration for Howard was shared by many. Howard was a modern hero who had no prototype; he made himself known and respected through his many perilous visits to prisons in England and abroad, his publications on the subject, and his proposals to Parliament for penal reform. Before his untimely death in 1790, Howard had travelled 42,000 miles and spent £30,000 of his own money during seventeen years of prison survey. Hayley first wrote *Ode to Howard* in 1780, and Romney provided a frontispiece. Immediately following Howard's death, Hayley encouraged Romney to renew his project of developing the deeds of Howard into a historical composition. Although Romney never painted a Howard picture, he was very much preoccupied with the subject in the early 1790s, not so much as a historical event, but rather as a state of mind. Throughout the *Howard* drawings, he particularly emphasized the prisoners' misery and helplessness. These scenes are lamentations, rather than protests about prison conditions — the prisoners and Howard seem momentarily arrested in a Dante-esque stillness and despair. There is an irony in the difference between Romney's hero, Howard, and Romney himself — Romney went to classical and other art sources to imagine what Howard had the courage to experience in life.

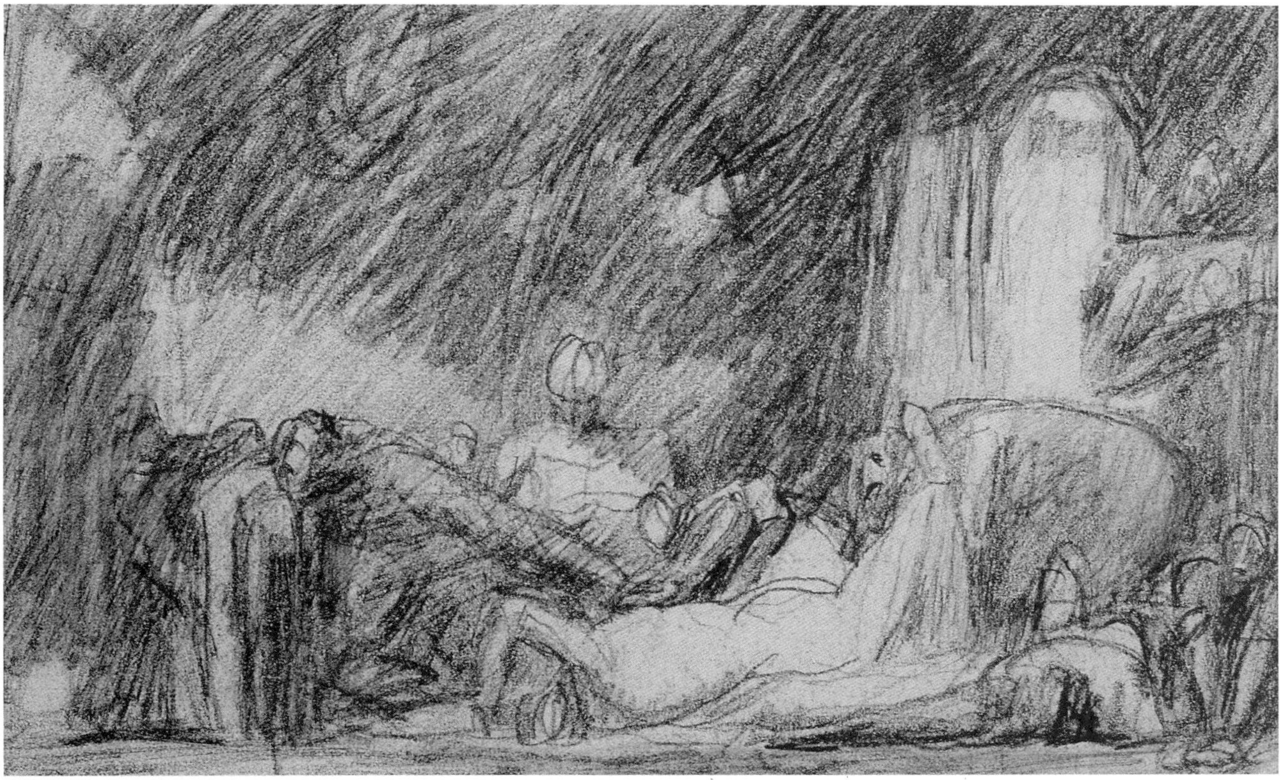

John Howard
Visiting Prisoners

circa 1794

graphite

111 x 171 mm

Dante Gabriel Rossetti

1828 – 1882 | British

Mary Magdalene

1876 graphite

190 x 150 mm

inscription:

signed in monogram

and dated *DGR 1876*

Rossetti's father was a well-known Italian revolutionary poet who arrived in London in 1824 as a political refugee and became a professor of literature at King's College. Rossetti thus grew up with Italian literature, especially Dante, whose work was the focus of his father's research and later a continual source of inspiration for the artist. At thirteen, Rossetti left school to study in the Bloomsbury art school. In 1848 he enrolled in the Royal Academy, associating himself with the poets William Bell Scott and Leigh Hunt. Upon leaving the Royal Academy, he became a pupil of Ford Madox Brown and William Holman Hunt. Towards the end of 1848, Rossetti, with Hunt, Millais, William Michael Rossetti, Thomas Woolner, Frederick George Stephens, and William Collinson, formed the Pre-Raphaelite Brotherhood. A Pre-Raphaelite journal, *The Germ,* was published, though it lasted only four issues. Their works, when exhibited in the Royal Academy, were bitterly attacked by critics, but defended by the influential John Ruskin. In 1850, Rossetti met his muse, Elizabeth Siddal, who modelled for the Pre-Raphaelites and became Rossetti's wife in 1860. During the 1850s, Rossetti's work was mostly watercolours and drawings. He illustrated Dante, Shakespeare, Browning, Tennyson and Malory's King Arthur. By 1856-57, he became the inspirational force for a younger group of artists such as Burne-Jones and William Morris, then undergraduates at Oxford. In 1857, he convinced the architect Benjamin Woodward to provide him, with the assistance of Burne-Jones, William Morris, and others, with the project of a series of medieval murals for the Debating Society Hall in the new Oxford Union. In Oxford, the second phase of Pre-Raphaelitism took shape. It was in Oxford, too, that Rossetti discovered and fell in love with Jane Burden, later William Morris's wife. In 1862, Elizabeth Siddal committed suicide. Her death greatly affected Rossetti's physical and mental health. Living as a recluse, he collected blue-and-white china, mirrors, rich fabrics, jewels, and other curiosities. In 1864, he completed *Beata Beatrix* (Tate Gallery, London), a painted homage and memorial to his wife. Increasingly fearing public criticism, he refused to exhibit. With deteriorating health, he turned more seriously to poetry and other literary activities. He also began a romantic affair with Jane Morris, then the Pre-Raphaelite ideal. For her he wrote a collection of poetry, *The House of Life.* The publication of *Poems by D.G. Rossetti* in 1871 established his reputation as a prominent poet-painter. His last book, *Ballads and Sonnets,* was published in 1881, the year before his death.

The present drawing is a study for the 1877 painting *Mary Magdalene,* now in the Wilmington Society of Fine Arts, Delaware. The sitter is probably Alexa Wilding, who, between 1866 and 1877, was Rossetti's favourite model, together with Jane Morris. Rossetti first met Wilding in the street in 1864, and paid a retaining fee to keep her exclusively in his service. The subject of Mary Magdalene fascinated Rossetti. He had been exploring it since the 1850s. For Rossetti, as well as for the Pre-Raphaelites and the Symbolists, Mary Magdalene represented the beautiful but fallen woman, the *femme fatale.* Clearly the prostitute in *Found* (begun in 1854), and the women in *Bocca Baciata* (1859), *Lucrezia Borgia* (1860-61), *Fair Rosamund* (1861), and *Lady Lilith* (1868) were conceived by Rossetti in this light. Thus the flowers in the painting of *Mary Magdalene* — black hellebore and white Christmas roses — are sexual symbols. So is the figure's long flowing hair, which adorns all of Rossetti's female figures. As suggested in his own sonnets, hair is a sexual net to capture the hearts and lives of men.

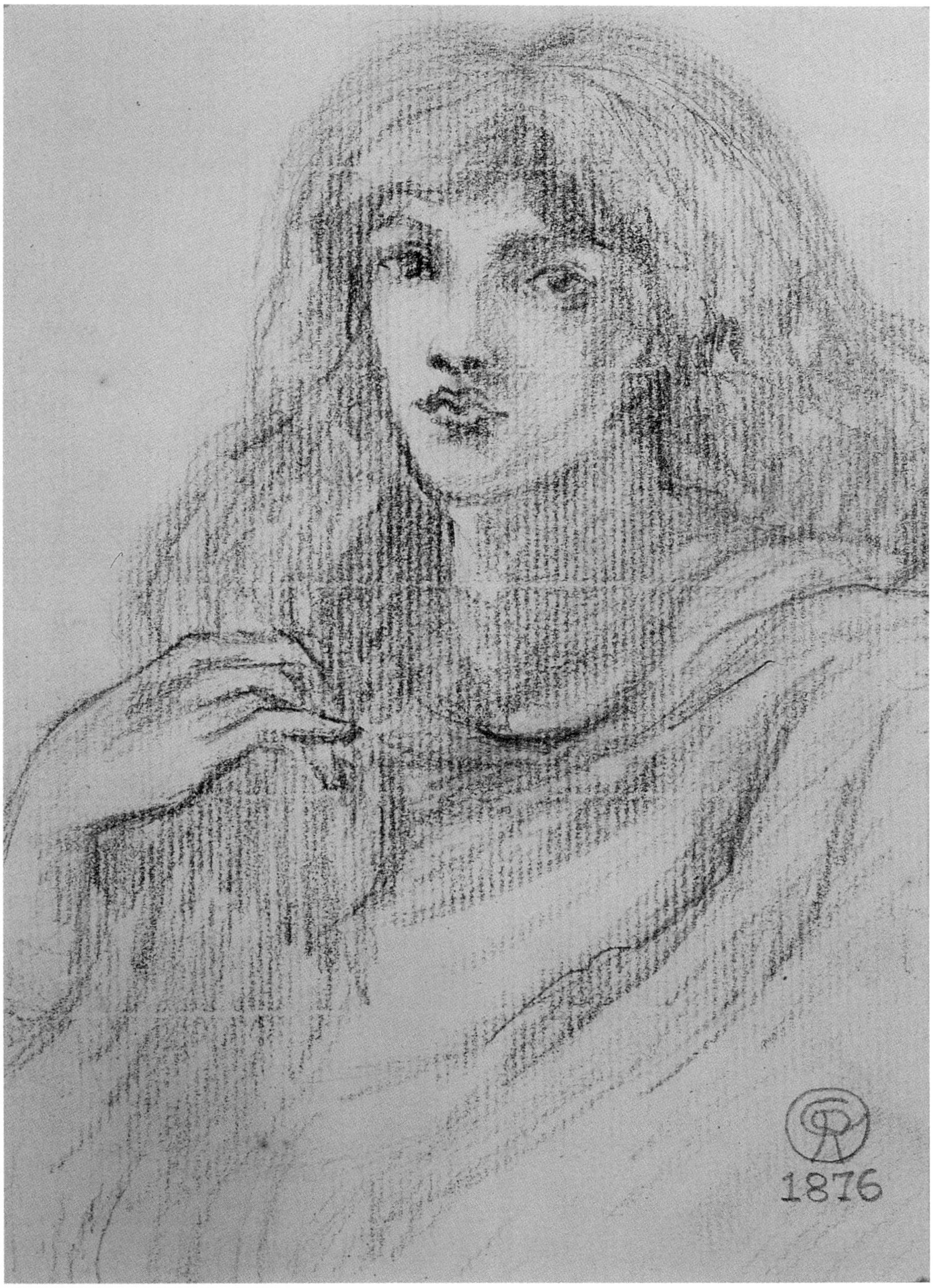

Mary Magdalene

1876 graphite

190 x 150 mm

inscription:

signed in monogram

and dated *DGR 1876*

Peter Paul Rubens

1577 – 1640 | Flemish

Head of Pan

circa 1608-20

red chalk

117 x 110 mm

Study of an Arm

circa 1608-20

red chalk

124 x 110 mm

Born in Leigen, Westphalia, Rubens was the son of Johannes, legal advisor to Anne of Saxony, second wife of William of Orange. He began his training as a painter under several Antwerp masters — most notably Otto van Veen. Between 1600 and 1608, he was in Italy, serving as court painter to the duke of Mantua. Returning to Antwerp in 1608, he was appointed court painter to Albert and Isabella, vice regents in the Spanish Netherlands. For the remainder of his life, he lived in Antwerp, where he created a highly successful practice with a large corps of collaborators and assistants including the young van Dyck, Jordaens, and Snyders. In 1628, Rubens was at the Spanish court for a briefing in connection with a diplomatic mission to the English court. There he studied the works of Titian in the Spanish royal collection and became friends with the court painter, Diego Velázquez. In 1629, he travelled to England to represent the Spanish government in peace negotiations. While in England he became a favourite among the English aristocracy; Charles I knighted him in Cambridge. His principal English commission involved a series of huge canvases for the ceiling of the Banquet Hall at Whitehall in London. In the last ten years of his life, he lived in a country estate near Antwerp, the Château Steen, and continued to carry out ambitious commissions.

Rubens not only possessed great classical literary knowledge, he was also familiar with descriptions and engravings of classical sculptures even before his Italian journey in 1600-08. He came into more extensive contact with antique art when he was in the court of the duke of Mantua and during his travels in Tuscany, Venice, and Rome. Especially in Rome, in the collections of the Palazzo Farnese, Villa Borghese, the Palazzo dei Conservatori, the Vatican Belvedere, Ciriaco Mattei, and Fulvio Orsini, he made numerous copies after the antique — full figures and heads, marble reliefs, as well as coins, cameos, and gems. His indefatigable draughtsmanship in recording and assembling these images of antiquity was not merely for his own education and future reference, but was also intended for the instruction of his students in Antwerp. He carefully preserved these drawings; in his will, he specified that they were to stay in his family for future painters.

The antique models for these two drawings were probably based on the figures on a Roman marble sarcophagus relief (now in the castle of Wörlitz, Anhalt), which Rubens studied in his last Roman years (1606-08). There are three existing drawings related to the *Head of Pan:* one in a London private collection, one in the possession of Kurt Meissner, Zurich, and one in the Museum Boymans-van Beuningen. Throughout the late 1610s and 1620s, Rubens incorporated Pan-like motifs in many of his paintings of satyrs, Silenus, and scenes of bacchanal.

Head of an Old Man

circa 1608-20 red chalk 115 x 184 mm

inscription: *P.P. Rubens fec.*

Woman Carrying a Charger

circa 1608-20 red chalk 114 x 180 mm

With paper type and coloured chalk similar to the two previous drawings, all four fragments might once have belonged to a sketchbook Rubens kept. *The Head of an Old Man* is most likely a study for a panel now in the Metropolitan Museum, New York. *Woman Carrying a Charger* is perhaps connected to a group of paintings depicting rural life that Rubens executed in the late 1610s and 1620s.

A Crouching Young Woman

circa 1620-25 red chalk and traces of graphite

253 x 193 mm

The drawing is a study for one of the cow-girls in the painting *Polder Landscape with Herd of Cows* (circa 1620-25) now in the Munich Ältere Pinakothek. A similar drawing, in black chalk heightened with white, is in the Albertina, Vienna.

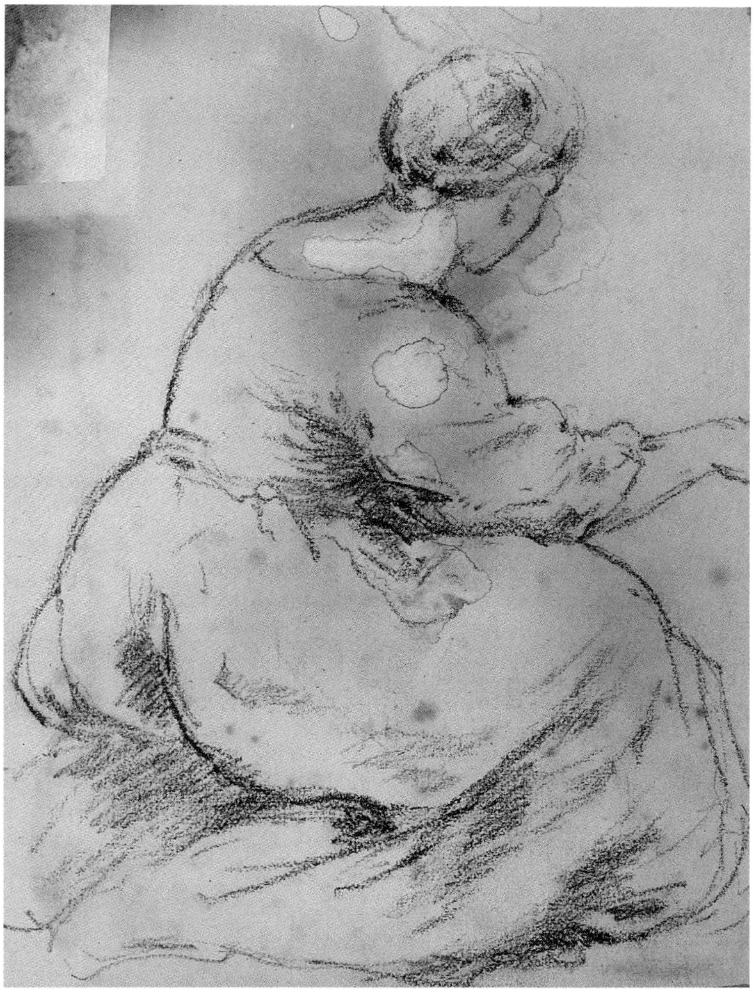

A Crouching Young Woman

circa 1620-25

red chalk and traces of graphite

253 x 193 mm

Egon Schiele

1890 – 1918 | Austrian

Self-portrait

1910 graphite

330 x 230 mm

inscription:

signed and dated

S. 1910

Schiele was born in Tulln, on the Danube. He began studying art in the Vienna academy in 1906. In 1907, he met Gustav Klimt and became part of the Museum Café circle in Vienna. Klimt encouraged him and introduced him to potential patrons. Through Klimt he also began working for the Wiener Werkstätte, an art business originating from the Secession and founded in 1903 by the architect Hoffmann, the painter Moser, and the banker Wärndorber. In 1909, a decisive year for Schiele, he left the academy and exhibited in Klimt's important Kunstschau. He also participated in the Neukünstler exhibition at Gustave Pisko's gallery. His works attracted the influential Arthur Roessler, art critic of the Vienna *Arbeiter Zeitung,* who later wrote five books about Schiele between 1912 and 1923. Roessler also introduced him to important Viennese patrons such as Carl Reininghaus and Oskar Reichel. In 1910, with fellow Neukünstler Erwin Osen, he went to Krumau, in southern Bohemia. Inspired by Osen's bizarre and often sexually suggestive theatrical performances, Schiele produced a series of unconventional self-portraits, portrait paintings, and drawings. He also did a group of erotic drawings of young female models engaged in highly provocative sexual acts. Returning to Vienna in 1911, he lived in the nearby town of Neulengbach and began painting dying towns and destitute landscapes. More importantly, he started to explore the popular German literary theme of the *Doppelgänger* (a person's exact double). When, in 1912, Neulengbach's inhabitants complained to the police about his scandalous behaviour, especially with their children, many of his erotic drawings were confiscated as pornography, and he was briefly imprisoned. Fortunately, the Neulengbach affair had no negative effects on his career. In 1912, he was invited to participate in Vienna's Hagenbund and Cologne's Sonderbund exhibitions. The important Munich dealer, Hans Goltz, represented him, and his international reputation grew. In 1914, he experimented with etching and photography. At the end of that year, the leading Viennese gallery, Arnot, presented a successful exhibition of his works, with a catalogue by Otto Benesch. In 1916, the important Expressionist periodical, *Die Aktion,* published a special Egon Schiele issue. In 1917, he was invited to participate in a government-sponsored exhibition in Stockholm and Copenhagen. Shortly before his death in 1918, he was a major contributor to the Vienna Secession exhibition and also received numerous commissions for portraits and murals for the Burgtheater.

Schiele's short and tormented life, his preoccupation with anxiety, disease, and death within the milieu of a decadent and disintegrating Viennese society, is perhaps best reflected in his many self-portraits. Like other Expressionists — Oskar Kokoschka and Richard Gerstl, for example — Schiele used his self-portraits to explore the human psyche as spectacle. They are voyeurist and exhibitionist, filled with tense pathos and impending doom. Most of all, they reveal an acute awareness of the self. Especially in the self-portraits before 1914, such as this one, the representations offer a penetrating concern with his own being that goes far beyond a contemporary description of him: "a thin young man of more than average height and with an erect, unaffected posture. A pale but not sickly small face, great dark eyes and luxuriant dark brown hair which stood up from his head in uncontrolled long strands" (Heinrich Benesch). Such revelation shows a direct parallel to the new science of Freudian psychology. It also echoes the existentially conceived and self-contained, bony figures of George Minne, which Schiele greatly admired at the International Kunstschau in 1909.

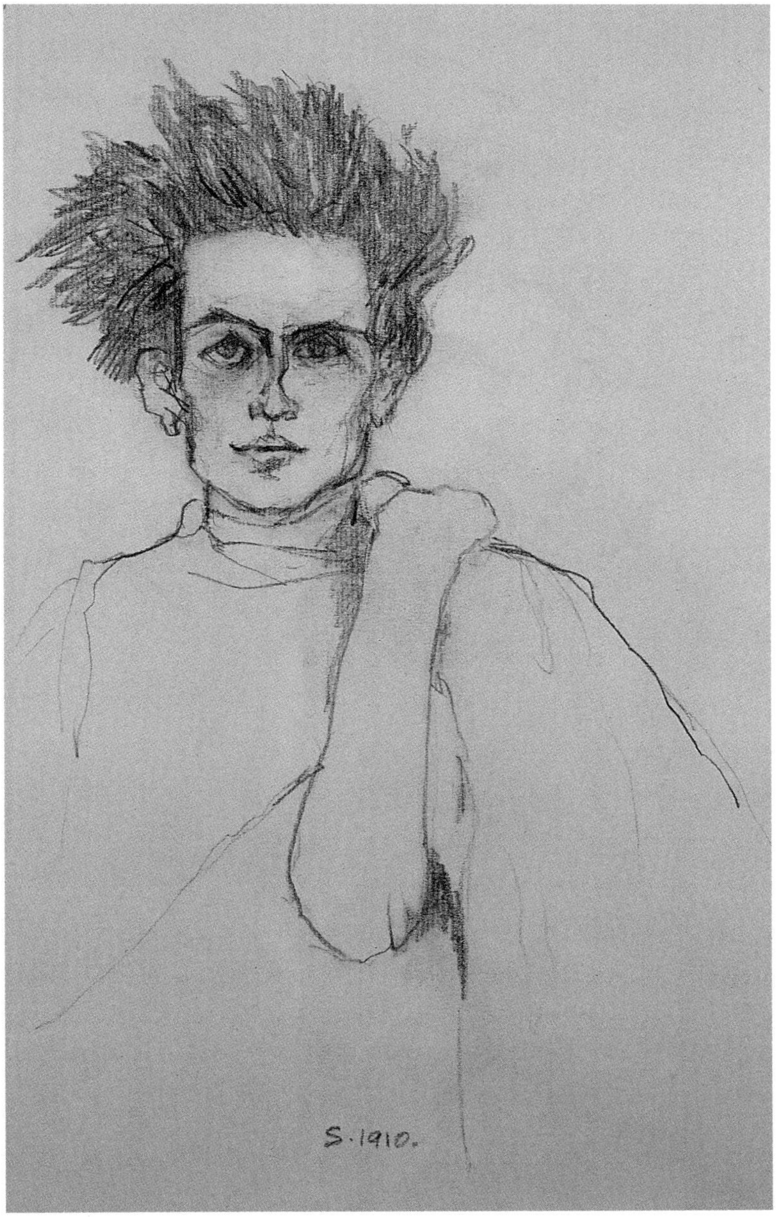

Self-portrait

1910 graphite

330 x 230 mm

inscription:

signed and dated

S. 1910

Georges Seurat

1859 – 1891 | French

Athena

circa 1878-79
black chalk
625 x 488 mm
inscription: signed on verso *G. Seurat*

Niobe

circa 1878-79
black chalk
535 x 452 mm
inscription: signed on verso *G. Seurat*

Born of bourgeois parents in Paris, Seurat first enrolled in the local municipal drawing school in 1875. In 1878-79, he was at the École des Beaux-Arts studying with Ingres' pupil Henri Lehmann, and reading Charles Blanc's *Grammaire es arts du dessin* (1867). After serving briefly in the military, he returned to Paris in 1880 and shared a studio with Aman-Jean. For the next three years he experimented vigorously and devoted himself almost exclusively to drawing. By 1882, inspired by the blurred prints of Rembrandt and the drawings of Daumier, Fantin-Latour, Millet, and Redon, he used conté crayon on highly textured Michallet paper to develop a distinctive tonal style of drawing in the tenebrist tradition. While advancing his draughtsmanship, he also acquainted himself with scientific theories of colour and light, including Chevreul's law of the simultaneous contrast of colours and Rood's *Modern Chromatics.* The majority of his early landscapes are small sketches on cigar-box lids, stylistically influenced by the Impressionist works of Monet and Pissarro. Thematically, these suburban subjects were inspired by the social and political dislocation of the working class in the outer suburbs of Paris, also found in the naturalistic novels of the Goncourt brothers, Zola, and J.K. Huysmans as well as the paintings of Jean-François Raffäelli. In 1884, his painting *Une Baignade, Asnières* (National Gallery, London) was rejected by the Salon, but exhibited in the newly constituted Société des Artists Indépendants. With the Indépendants, Seurat joined an exciting circle of poets, painters, journalists, art critics, and novelists. Between 1884 and 1886, he worked on his painting, *La Grande Jatte* (Art Institute of Chicago), shown in the eighth and last Impressionist exhibition in 1886. In *La Grande Jatte,* he adapted scientific findings about colour, light, and experimental psychology by using complementary colour dots and simplified forms. The work put him in the front rank of the Neo-Impressionist avant-garde. In the later 1880s, he worked alternately between the Channel coast in the summer and Paris in winter, where he completed large-scale figurative works such as *Les Poseuses* (1887-88; Barnes Foundation), *La Parade de Cirque* (1887-88; Metropolitan Museum, New York), *Le Chahut* (1889-90; Kröller-Müller Museum, Otterlo), and his last major painting, *Le Cirque* (1890-91; Louvre).

Between 1875 and 1879, when he was an art student in the Paris municipal drawing school and the École des Beaux-Arts, Seurat made many drawings after Old Masters and antique sculptures. While most of his drawings after antique sculptures were done at Lequien's school in 1875-76, these two large drawings, *Athena* and *Niobe,* were more likely made at the École des Beaux-Arts (1878-79). For Lehmann, the study of antique sculpture was an essential part of the conservative academic training that served to prepare students for the Prix de Rome competition, which often selected classical subjects. Not surprisingly, during those years Seurat also did a number of drawings inspired by Flaxman's Homeric outline engravings.

The Echo: Study for "Une Baignade, Asnières"

1883 conté crayon 202 x 162 mm

Shown in the Salon of the newly founded Société des Artists Indépendants in 1884, *Une Baignade* exemplifies the modern suburban subjects Seurat had been exploring in the early 1880s. Related to the social realism of Millet, Raffäelli, the Goncourt brothers, Zola, and Huysmans, it is Seurat's social, and ultimately political, commentary on the irony of the fleeting pleasures of the working class from Asnières.

In preparation for this painting, Seurat produced many small oil sketch panels in the open air. But the drawings, including this one, were all executed in the studio. This drawing is an example of the evocative, personal style of conté drawing he began developing in 1882. A comparable but larger drawing of *The Echo* is in the Yale University Art Gallery, New Haven.

Woman with an Umbrella

1885 conté crayon 210 x 150 mm

This drawing is probably a study for the small 1885 oil panel depicting a suburban riverside subject, *The Seine at Courbevoie* (private collection, Paris), exhibited along with *La Grande Jatte* in the eighth Impressionist exhibition in 1886. In the late nineteenth century, Courbevoie was an outer suburb of Paris just upstream from Asnières, noted for the large trees and smart houses lining the river banks.

Girl Holding an Umbrella: Study for "La Grande Jatte"

1884-85 conté crayon 205 x 125 mm

inscription: signed *Seurat*

Girl Holding an Umbrella: Study for "La Grande Jatte"

1884-85 conté crayon 207 x 138 mm

Its new technique, large scale, simplified forms, colour structure and luminosity undoubtedly made *La Grande Jatte* the shocking centrepiece of the eighth and last Impressionist exhibition, in 1886. A contemporary art critic, Maurice Hermel, referred to it in *La France Libre* as a *tableau-manifeste* ("manifesto painting"). Others, such as Alfred Paulet of Paris, even recognized the meaning of the picture — *La Grande Jatte* is a painting about a place of intense social neutrality: the meeting of different social classes from different suburbs on a Sunday afternoon in a public park. In Seurat's conception of the politics of aesthetic harmony, the painting may underline a connection to the late nineteenth-century French anarchist hope of a decentralized, non-authoritarian socio-economic order, advocated by his friend Felix Fénéon.

Throughout *La Grande Jatte,* Seurat used fashion to distinguish and to blur classes and roles. The figure of the girl with the umbrella, depicted in these two drawings, is a case in point. One writer stated in 1883: A "Today there is not a lady or a working-class girl who does not have her umbrella, . . . the indispensable complement to any *toilette de promenade*." Another wrote in the same year: "First and foremost, the umbrella is the symbol of equality."

Theatre Scene

circa 1887-88 conté crayon 205 x 121 mm

Datable to the same period when Seurat painted *Le Parade de Cirque,* this theatre scene is related to a larger drawing showing two figures on stage (Louvre). These theatre scenes were probably inspired by performances in Antoine's Théatre Libre, which opened in the Passage de l'Elysée des Beaux-Arts in 1887. Seurat was an *habitué* of the theatre and had some of his works exhibited there. Seurat's depiction of nocturnal performances is in line with Symbolist theory, suggesting the alienation of the performer from the audience and the failure of these popular performances to conceal the divisions of society.

The Echo:
Study for
"Une Baignade,
Asnières"

1883 conté crayon

202 x 162 mm

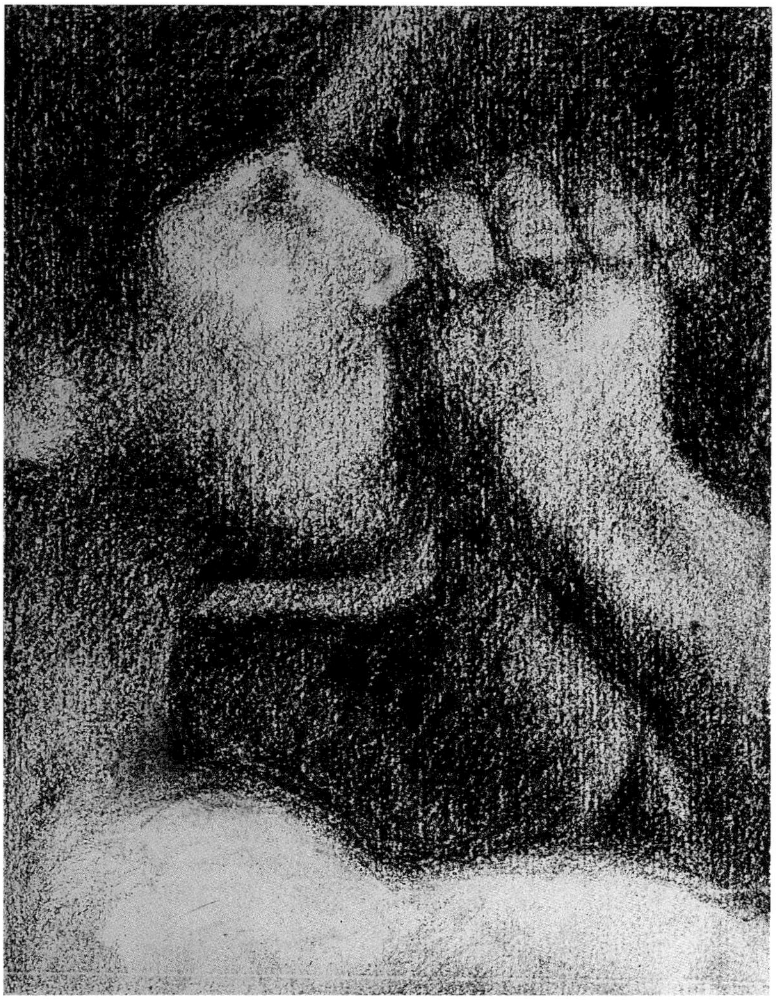

Giovanni Battista Tiepolo

1696 – 1770 | Italian

Flying Female Figure

circa 1745
pen and wash
in brown ink
300 x 210 mm

Venetian himself, Tiepolo apprenticed to Venetian painter Gregorio Lazzarini about 1710, and was influenced by masters of the grand Venetian tradition, Veronese especially, and by contemporaries Piazetta and Sebastian Ricci. In 1719, he married Cecilia Guardi, sister of the famous Venetian *veduta* painter, Francesco Guardi. Of their nine children, Giandomenico and Lorenzo were to become Tiepolo's chief assistants. Among his earliest commissions was the decoration of the Palazzo Sandi in Venice in 1725, followed by those for Udine's archbishop's palace in 1726. His fame grew rapidly in the following years, and succeeding commissions were numerous in Italy. In 1732, Count de Tessin negotiated with him the decoration of the royal palace in Stockholm, and Count Algarotti commissioned work for the court of Saxony during the 1740s. Tiepolo also provided frescoes for the church of the Gesnati in Venice in 1737-39; the Scalzi church, Venice, in 1743-44; and the Palazzo Labia in 1745. Between 1750 and 1753, he worked in the Residenz of the Prince-Archbishop Carl Philipp von Greiffenklau in Würzburg. Back in Venice, he was elected first president of the newly founded Venetian academy of painting (1756-58). In the late 1750s, before leaving Italy, he also decorated the Villa Valmarana near Vicenza, the Palazzo Rezzonico in Venice, and the Villa Pisani at Stra, near Padua. In 1762, he was invited by Carlos III of Spain to Madrid. For the next two years he decorated the newly built royal palace: the ceilings of the hall of the halbardiers, the antechamber, and the throne room, in which he personified the world paying homage to Spain. Before his death in Madrid, he painted many altarpieces in Spain, but he was hindered by the disapproval of the king's father confessor and, perhaps, by the competition of the young German Neoclassicist, A.R. Mengs.

Throughout his career, Tiepolo produced hundreds of casual, simple, but airy and graceful figure drawings in his favourite medium of pen and wash. They are not life-studies from models; rather, they are artistic impressions to devise types and rehearse motifs. This drawing, with a nearly identical sheet in the University of California Art Museum, Berkeley, might have been connected with the mural of *Bellerophon on Pegasus* in the Palazzo Labia, painted about 1745.

Head of a Boy

circa 1750 red chalk 120 x 190 mm
inscript on: *J.B. Tiepolo*

Unrelated to any particular painting or mural composition, this drawing was produced around the time when Tiepolo was decorating the Residenz of the Prince-Archbishop Carl Philipp von Greiffenklau in Würzburg in the years 1750 to 1753.

A Bearded Oriental

circa 1757 pen and wash in brown ink 245 x 170 mm

Orientals, so much part of Venetian cultural and economic history, began to appear frequently in Tiepolo's compositions in the 1750s, beginning with the frescoes in the Würzburg Residenz, in its *Homage to the Emperor* and in the scenes on its staircase representing the four continents. Similar oriental figures are found in the four panels showing *Scenes from Gerusalemme Liberata* (circa 1755; National Gallery, London) and in *Sacrifice of Iphigenia* in the Villa Valmarana, Venice, completed in 1757.

Study of the Figure of Agamemnon

circa 1757 pen and wash in brown ink 235 x 195 mm

About 1757, Tiepolo was commissioned by Count Giustino Valmarana to decorate four rooms in his palazina near Vicenza with scenes from Homer's *Iliad,* Virgil's *Aeneid,* Tasso's *Gerusalemme Liberata,* and Ariosto's *Orlando Furioso* to create an ancient and modern poetic and pictorial *paragone.* This sheet is a study of the figure of Agamemnon for the fresco of *Eurybates and Talthybius Conducting Briseis from the Tent of Achilles to Agamemnon* in the Iliad room.

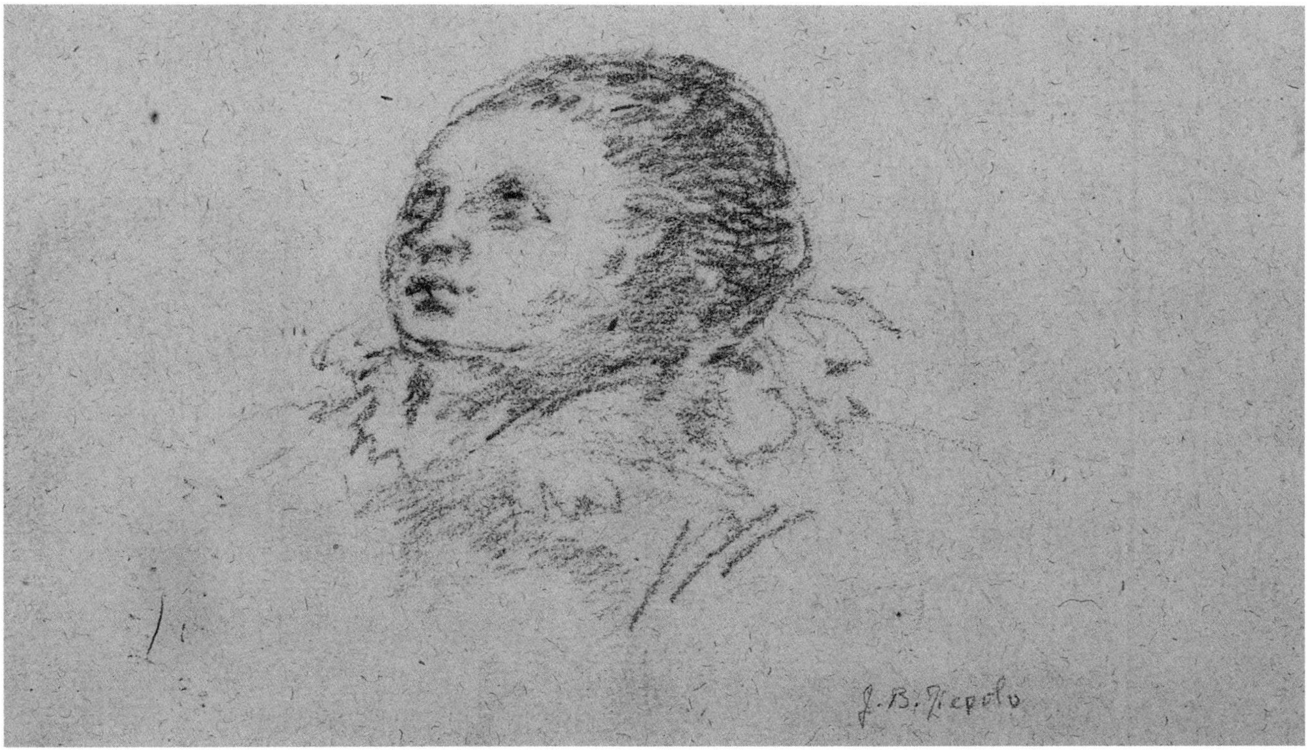

Head of a Boy

circa 1750

red chalk

120 x 190 mm

inscription: *J.B. Tiepolo*

Henri de Toulouse-Lautrec

1864 – 1901 | French

Figures and a Horse-drawn Wagon

circa 1883

graphite

106 x 172 mm

inscription:

Toulouse-Lautrec

Toulouse-Lautrec was born in Albi. A frail child, he fractured his left femur in 1878 and broke his other leg the following year, resulting in the termination of his leg growth in childhood. About the time of the accidents, he had begun studies with the sporting artist René Princeteau. In 1882, he entered the Paris studio of the academic painter Léon Bonnat and later that of Fernand Cormon. In Cormon's studio he met Emile Bernard and Vincent van Gogh. Soon he rented a studio in Montmartre and began frequenting dance halls and cabarets such as the Chat Noir and Elysée-Montmartre, where the *chahut* (can-can) was performed. From 1885 onwards, some of his works were exhibited in the Cabaret Mirleton, whose owner, the singer Aristide Bruant, also commissioned him to produce designs and illustrations for the cabaret songs. In 1888, he was invited to exhibit with Les XX in Brussels. At the beginning of the 1890s, he produced his first poster for the Moulin Rouge and colour lithographs of entertainers Yvette Guilbert and Jane Avril. In this period he also began visiting and working in brothels, even residing briefly in a famous brothel, the Rue de Moulins, near the Opéra. Following his first exhibition in the Goupil gallery in 1893, he travelled to Brussels in 1894 and to London, Spain, and Holland in 1895. Although he was very active in the mid-1890s, he was already an alcoholic. In 1901, he died shortly after suffering from a paralytic stroke, caused by either alcoholism or syphilis.

Toulouse-Lautrec's early works centred around equestrian subjects, inspired by the activities in his family circle. His father, Count Alphonse, and his uncles were ardent sportsmen and amateur sporting artists; and their depictions of horses and the hunt filled their residences. At the château in Albi where Toulouse-Lautrec was born, the library contained numerous illustrated publications of sporting and equestrian subjects. Moreover, his first art teacher was René Princeteau, a notable sporting artist and a family friend. In the nineteenth century, sporting art was very popular among those French aristocrats who emulated the English way of country life. In addition, Toulouse-Lautrec would certainly be aware of Géricault's and Vernet's equestrian works from the beginning of the century, and those of Manet and Degas after mid-century.

The present drawing, probably executed while he was studying with Fernand Cormon between 1882 and 1885, still shows some of the remnants of his early equestrian interests. But now, under Cormon's influence, it reveals a more sober style and subject, in line with mid-century realism.

Seated Female Clown (Cha-u-ka-o)

1896 graphite 312 x 228 mm

inscription: signed with monogram *T-L* and *T-Lautrec*

For his whole adult life, Toulouse-Lautrec, an aristocrat, lived and worked on the margins of society. He began frequenting brothels in the early 1890s, taking up residence in the Rue de Moulins in 1894. By 1896, he also visited lesbian bars. It was in 1896 that he produced the daring *Elles* series — consisting of a lithographic cover, a frontispiece, and ten colour lithographs — representing the private world of prostitutes in brothels. This drawing is a study for one of the plates in the series. The figure is Cha-u-ka-o, the female clown and acrobat who was a regular performer at the Moulin Rouge and the Nouveau Cirque. Her name is an orientalization of *chahut-chaos,* the dance can-can. Lautrec was fascinated by her, much as he was with La Goulue and Jane Avril, especially her lesbianism. In this depiction of the lonely seated clown in her costume ball dress at the Moulin Rouge, Lautrec has subtly expressed his sympathy with those nocturnal outcasts in real life and in the fiction of Huysmans, the Goncourts, Zola, Maupassant, and Halévy, as well as in the works of Degas. His sharp and penetrating observation is a challenge to conventional morality and an indictment of organized prostitution.

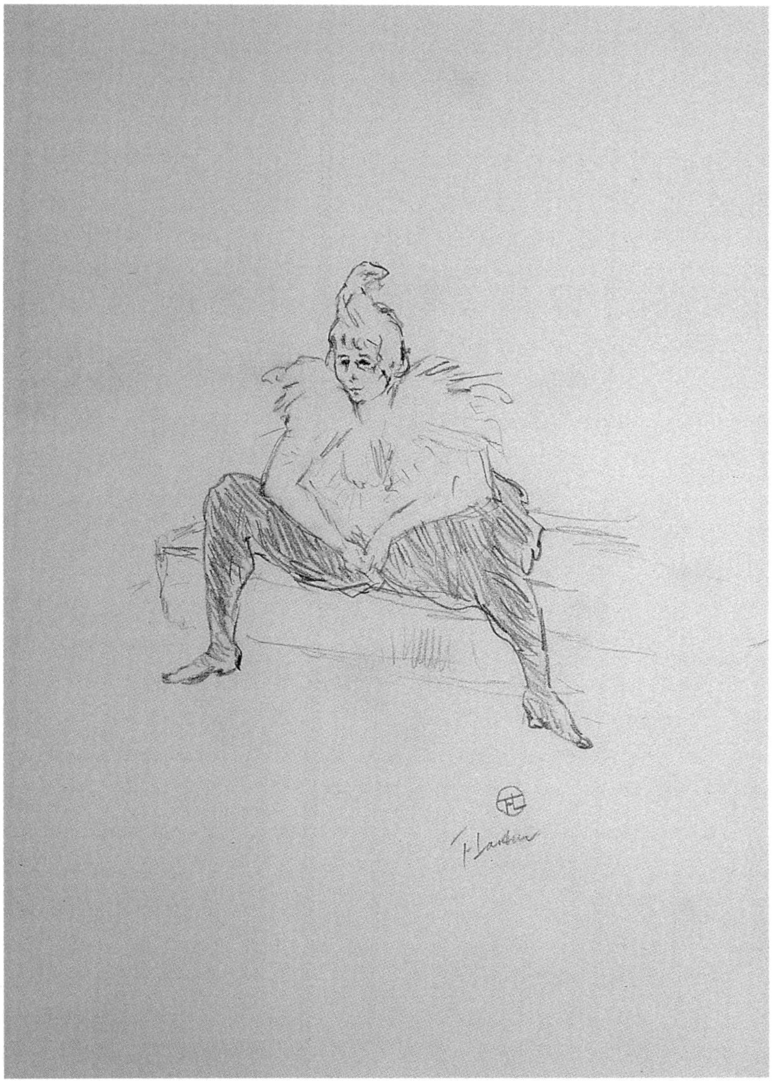

Seated
Female Clown
(Cha-u-ka-o)

1896 graphite

312 x 228 mm

inscription:

signed with monogram

T-L and *T-Lautrec*

Vincent van Gogh

1853 – 1890 | Dutch

Worn Out. At Eternity's Gate

1890 pen and gray-black ink
116 x 94 mm
inscription: signed on verso *Vincent*

Born into a family of Dutch Reformed ministers in Zundert, North Brant, van Gogh was first employed in the art firm Goupil & Co. of The Hague in 1869. In 1873 he was alternately stationed in the London and Paris branches. Dismissed from Goupil in 1876, he became a teacher in England. By 1878, he was admitted to an evangelical school in Brussels. Unable to obtain a minister's post he became a missionary in the coal-mining district of the Borinage in Belgium, but his excessive zeal led to his dismissal by the church council committee. Between 1880 and 1886, he lived variously at Brussels, Etten, The Hague, Drenthe, Nuenen, and Antwerp, teaching himself to draw and paint, with occasional lessons from his cousin Antoine Mauve and at the Antwerp academy. He also read profusely and collected English newspaper illustrations and Japanese prints. In 1886, he went to live with his brother Theo in Paris. In February 1888, he left for Arles in Provence, where he rented the Yellow House on the Place Lamartine. During that autumn he decorated a room with the *Sunflower* paintings and waited for Gauguin, who finally arrived in October. Unknown to van Gogh, Gauguin's stay with him was due to pragmatic reasons: Theo had promised to pay for his trip and expenses in Arles in exchange for paintings. Originally, Gauguin planned to stay for a year, but he left in December, as arguments between the two artists turned into explosive confrontations. Gauguin spoke of an "incompatibility of temper" with van Gogh, and he wrote to Emile Bernard: "Vincent and I generally agree very little, especially about painting." On December 23, van Gogh mutilated his left ear and gave it to a prostitute named Rachel. After Gauguin's departure, van Gogh, exhausted but recovering, remained in Arles. In May 1889, he voluntarily entered the asylum at nearby St. Rémy. The next year, while under the supervision of Dr. Paul Gachet at Auvers-sur-Oise, he shot himself.

The initial idea of depicting a worn-out seated figure dates to September 1881 when van Gogh was living in Etten and made two nearly identical drawings, one he gave to his friend van Rappard and the other to Theo, with this description in the accompanying letter: "an old, sick farmer sitting on a chair near the hearth, his head in his hands and his elbow on his knees." Two years later, a female version of the same motif appeared in the chalk and wash drawing of *A Seated Crying Woman,* posed by his then live-in companion Clasina ("Sien") Maria Hoornik. Whether the present drawing dates before or after the lithograph and the painting of *Worn Out. At Eternity's Gate* (Kröller-Müller Museum, Otterlo) is unknown. Certainly, these three works were produced about the same time in 1890 when van Gogh was at the asylum in St. Rémy, just months before his suicide. The last year and a half of his life were especially difficult. The departure of Gauguin from Arles shattered his utopian dream of establishing a new artistic community and also resulted in his exclusion from Gauguin's Café Volpini exhibition at the Paris World's Fair in 1889. Eighty-one residents of Arles sent a petition to their mayor demanding his expulsion. His illness and his life in the St. Rémy asylum among other mental patients must have been a struggle. In contrast to the buoyant, sunny works of the early Arles period, he now painted desolate landscapes, wide fields, twisted olive trees, and gloomy cypresses; he copied Delacroix's *Pietà* and Rembrandt's *Good Samaritan* and *Resurrection of Lazarus.* He spoke of "suffer[ing] without complaint" and said "I no longer see any possibility of having courage or hope." In a long letter to Theo from St. Rémy, dated 25 May 1889, he wrote: "At present this *horror of life* is less strong already and the melancholy less acute. But I have no *will,* hardly any wish for anything belonging to ordinary life, for instance almost no desire to see my friends, although I keep thinking about them. That is why I have not yet reached the point where I ought to think of leaving here; I should have this depression anywhere."

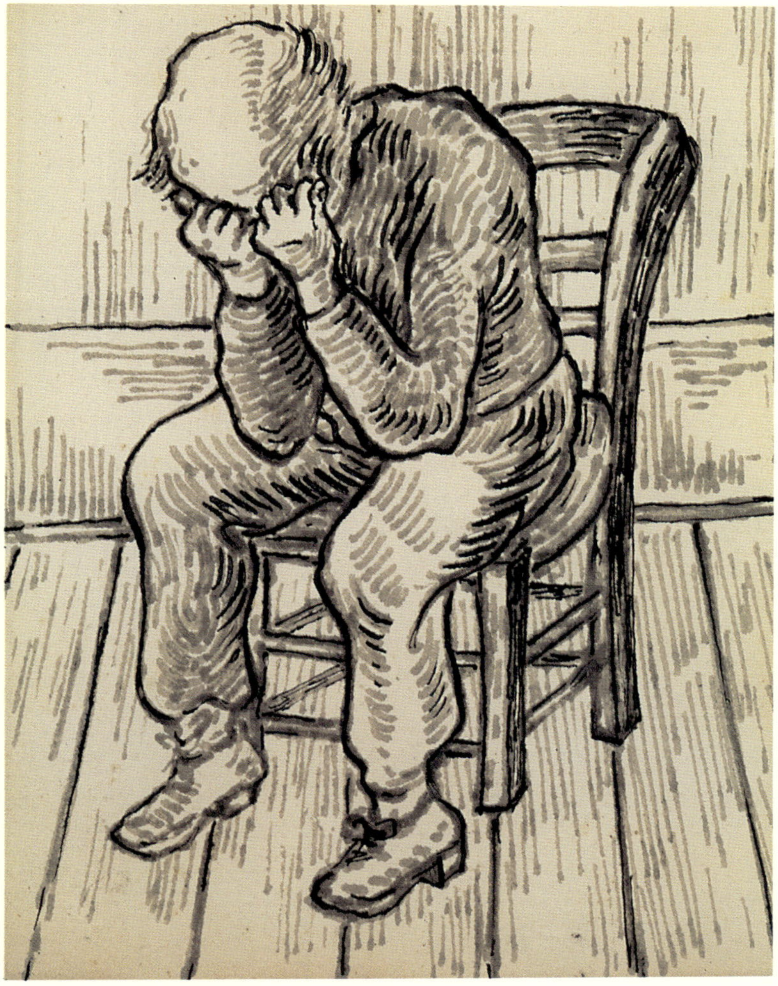

Worn Out. At Eternity's Gate

1890 pen and gray-black ink

116 x 94 mm

inscription: signed on verso

Vincent

Jean Antoine Watteau

1684 – 1721 | French

Cassandre

circa 1721

red chalk

180 x 195 mm

inscription:

Watteau

Watteau came from Valenciennes, a southern Flemish town that had only become part of France in 1678. At an early age he was apprenticed to a local painter, Jacques Albert Gérin. In 1702, he moved to Paris, where he worked for the picture dealer Metayer in the mass production of small religious canvases. In Paris he met the cultivated dealers, editors, and art collectors, Pierre and Jean Mariette; and through them became acquainted with the master works of Italian art. About 1703, he was employed by the theatre painter Claude Gillot, who introduced him to the world of French comedy and the *commedia dell'arte.* By 1708, he was working for Claude III Audran, then the keeper of the Luxembourg palace; thus he was able to study Rubens' *Marie de' Medici* cycle. Watteau's works at this time were of military subjects, inspired by impressions of Valenciennes in the midst of the War of the Spanish Succession. Gradually he developed and evolved the concept of the *fête galante,* a special category of pictures in which he depicted elegant society at play, surrounded by music, song, dance, and love in park settings; but in the bliss of the Arcadian world, he also conveyed the sense of the transience and frailty of human happiness. The Académie française honoured him for this invention by admitting him in 1712; his reception piece, *The Pilgrimage to the Island of Cythera* (Louvre), was completed in 1717. In 1715, Watteau was introduced by Audran to Crown treasurer Pierre Crozat, an immensely wealthy and cultivated man commissioned by the regent of France to purchase the art collection of Queen Christina of Sweden. Under Crozat's patronage, he studied Crozat's own great art collection and was admitted into fashionable and cosmopolitan society. He now worked for important dealers and private patrons, mostly members of the class of financiers and moneyed bourgeoisie. Watteau's career was cut short by his premature death in 1721. But following his death, from 1726 to 1739, *Oeuvre d'Antoine Watteau grave après ses tableaux et dessins* in four volumes was published by Jean de Jullienne, with some plates engraved by François Boucher. The publication is responsible for disseminating Watteau's style and imagery throughout Europe and shaping the taste of the Rococo generation and beyond.

The *Cassandre* drawing belongs to the last year of Watteau's career and is a figure study for the famous painting *Gilles/Pierrot* (circa 1721; Louvre). *Gilles/Pierrot* may have been a shop sign that Watteau painted for the café named Au Caffé Comique, opened by the retired actor Bellori in about 1718. The central figure may represent Bellori, whose most appreciated role was Gilles/Pierrot; in the painting he is accompanied by other players who had worked with him. Perhaps merely coincidentally, there seemed to be a special bond between Bellori and Watteau: both artists were about the same age; Bellori's retirement from theatre was due to a mortal illness that struck at about the same time as Watteau's tuberculosis; and they both died in 1721. Thus the painting could have been a poignant gift from Watteau to Bellori — it depicts the end of a performance, Gilles/Pierrot having stepped forward to take his final bow.

The *Cassandre* drawing was engraved (in reverse) in Jullienne's publication. There are two versions of this study, the present drawing and another in a London private collection.

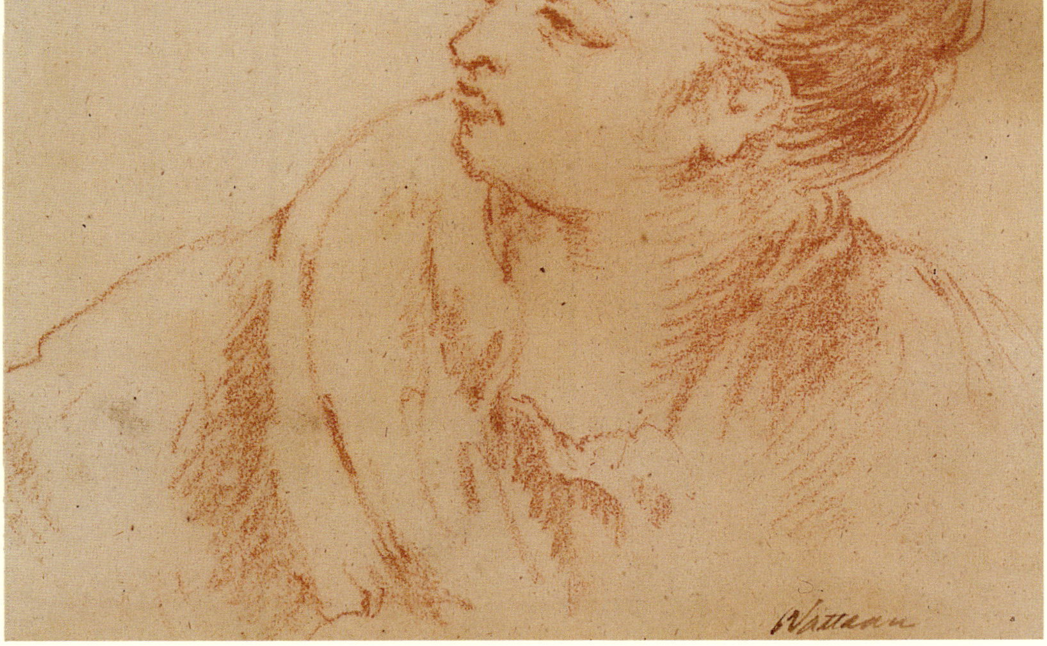

Cassandre

circa 1721

red chalk

180 x 195 mm

inscription:

Watteau

Benjamin West

1738 – 1820 | American-British

Eve

circa 1801-1804

graphite

220 x 125 mm

Born near Springfield, Pennsylvania, West was the son of Quaker parents. On a journey to Philadelphia in 1756, he met the American artist William Williams, who advised and assisted him to pursue a career in history painting. In 1760 he travelled to Rome. Benefiting from the prestige of novelty — American painters were unknown — he was introduced to the German Neoclassicist Anton Raphael Mengs and to Johann Winckelmann's patron, Cardinal Albani. In northern Italy he became a member of the academies of Parma, Florence, and Bologna. West produced few works in Italy, although he did draw after the antique in a sketchbook. His artistic transformation in Italy, similar to Joshua Reynolds' a decade earlier, was the intellectual conception of the principles of classical art. His assimilative style was moulded by classical relief sculpture and the painting of Raphael and Poussin, as well as Mengs and Gavin Hamilton. He settled in London in 1763 as a portrait painter. His first patrons were mostly Anglican clergy: James Johnson, bishop of Worcester; Thomas Newton, bishop of Bristol; and Robert Drummond, archbishop of York. Drummond introduced him to George III, who commissioned *The Departure of Regulus* (Royal Collection, Kensington Palace), shown in the first Royal Academy exhibition in 1769. The date marked the beginning of a long and highly profitable association with George III. West was a founder-member of the Royal Academy in 1768. Following the success of his *Death of Wolfe* (Academy exhibition, 1771; versions in National Gallery of Canada and Kensington Palace), a turning point in modern British history painting, West was appointed historical painter to George III in 1772. Until 1811, when his stipend and title were rescinded, he produced numerous portraits and historical works for the royal family. In 1792, he succeeded Reynolds as the president of the Royal Academy, but refused a knighthood because of his Quaker principles.

Considering his American origins, West's phenomenal success as a major public history painter is unparalleled. Just as unusual is the large number of religious works he produced throughout his career, comprising nearly half of his prodigious output. Undoubtedly his Quaker outlook and personal religious orientation enhanced his extensive Anglican patronage. During the late eighteenth century, the Anglican bishops and George III were determined to reintroduce art into the church, a religious and political move to alter public opinion concerning the English Reformation since Henry VIII; traditionally art was associated with Catholicism, and Henry VIII had destroyed much church art. Nevertheless, George III's enthusiasm was also motivated by his religious piety and his artistic interests. Believing in creating a new spirit of art and religion, George III conceived, in 1780, the idea of a private chapel at Windsor representing the history of revealed religion. In West's 1801 scheme, the chapel would contain thirty-five paintings distributed among four dispensations. While West completed most of the paintings, the chapel was never finished, owing partly to the king's successive illnesses and partly to political and artistic reasons.

The drawing *Eve* is probably related to this project. In the final scheme of the chapel, however, only one subject representing Eve was included: *The Expulsion of Adam and Eve from Paradise.* (An oil sketch for it is in the George F. Harding Museum in Chicago.)

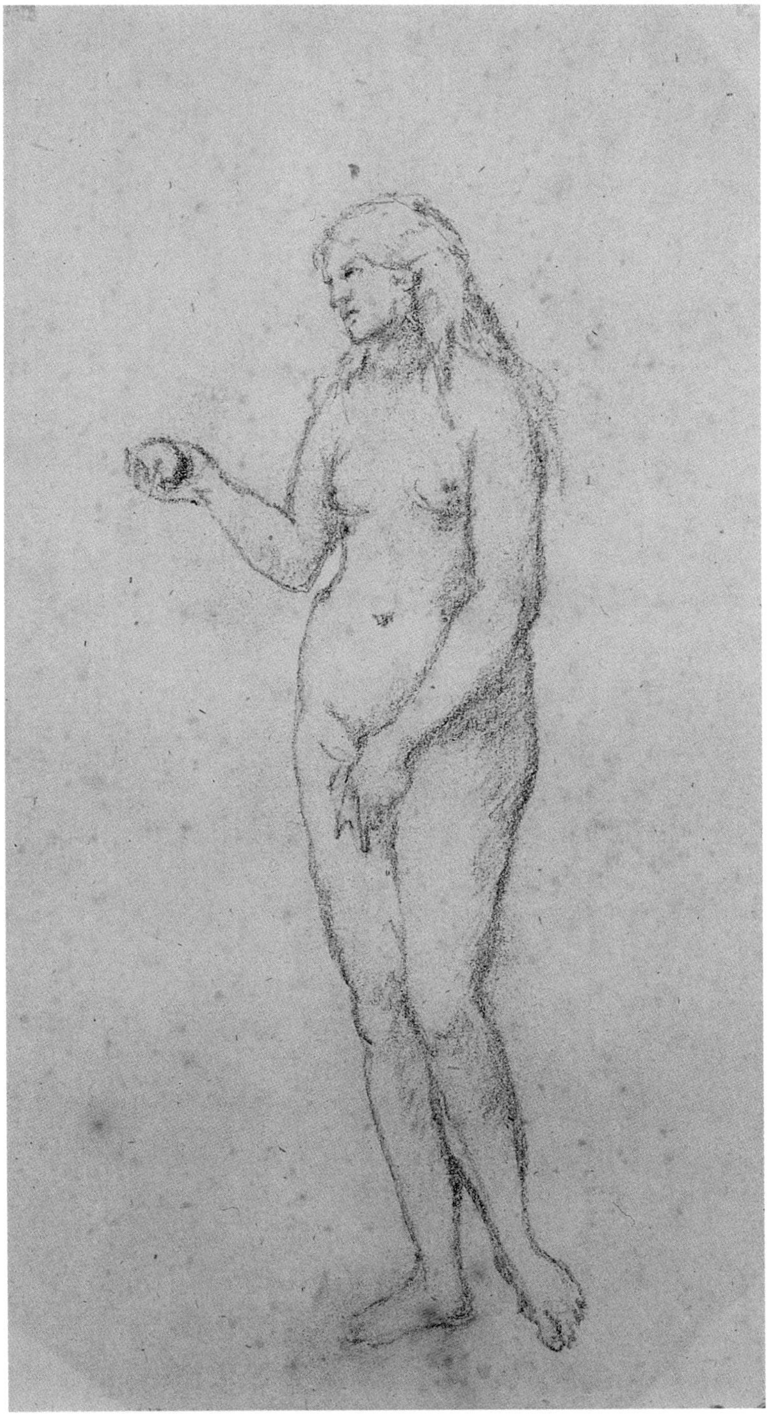

Eve

circa 1801-1804

graphite

220 x 125 mm

Further Reading

Ast, Balthasar van der 1593/4 – 1657 | Dutch

Bergström, I. | *Dutch Still-Life Painting in the Seventeenth Century*, London, 1956.

Bol, Laurens J. | *The Bosschaert Dynasty*, Leigh-on-Sea, (1960), 1980.

Segal, Sam | *A Prosperous Past: The Sumptuous Still Life in the Netherlands 1600-1700*, The Hague, 1988.

Braque, Georges 1882 – 1963 | French

Cooper, Douglas | *Braque: The Great Years*, Chicago, 1972.

Mangin, N. (ed.) | *Catalogue complet de l'oeuvre de Georges Braque*, 5 volumes, Paris, 1959-68.

Museum of Modern Art | *Picasso and Braque: Pioneering Cubism*, New York, 1989.

Burne-Jones, Sir Edward 1833 – 1898 | British

Harrison, Martin and Bill Waters | *Burne-Jones*, London, 1973.

Hayward Gallery | *Burne-Jones: The Paintings, Graphic and Decorative Work of Sir Edward Burne-Jones*, London, 1975.

Löcher, Kurt | *Der Perseus-Zyklus von Edward Burne-Jones*, Stuttgart, 1973.

Caillebotte, Gustave 1848 – 1894 | French

Berhaut, Marie | *Caillebotte, sa vie et son oeuvre*, Paris, 1978.

Sutton, Denys | *Gustave Caillebotte 1848-1894*, London, 1966.

Varnedoe, Kirk | *Gustave Caillebotte*, New Haven and London, 1987.

Callot, Jacques 1592/3 – 1635 | French

Knab, Eckhart | *Jacques Callot und sein Kreis*, Vienna, 1968.

Meanme, E. | *Recherches sur la vie et les oeuvrages de Jacques Callot*, 2 volumes, Paris, 1860.

Russell, H. Diane | *Jacques Callot — Prints and Related Drawings*, Washington D.C., 1975.

Canal, G.A. (Canaletto) 1697 – 1768 | Italian

Baetjer, Katherine and J.G. Links | *Canaletto*, New York, 1989.

Bettagno, Alessandro, et al. | *Canaletto: Disegni, Dipinti, Incisioni*, Venice, 1982.

Parker, K.T. | *The Drawings of Antonio Canaletto in the Collection of His Majesty the King at Windsor Castle*, Oxford and London, 1948.

Carracci, Ludovico 1555 – 1619 | Italian

Bodmer, H. | *Lodovico Carracci*, Burg, 1939.

Mahon, Denis | *Mostra dei Carracci. Disegni*, Bologna, 1956.

Wittkower, Rudolf | *The Drawings of the Carracci at Windsor Castle*, London, 1952.

Cézanne, Paul 1839 – 1906 | French

Andersen, Wayne | *Cézanne's Portrait Drawings*, Cambridge, Massachusetts, 1970.

Chappins, Adrien | *The Drawings of Paul Cézanne: A Catalogue Raisonné*, 2 volumes, Greenwich, Connecticut, 1973.

Venturi, L. | *Cézanne, son art, son oeuvre*, 2 volumes, Paris, 1936.

Chardin, J. B. S. 1699 – 1779 | French

Pascal, A., H. de Rothschild and R. Gaucheron | *Documents sur la vie et l'oeuvre de Chardin*, Paris, 1931.

Rosenberg, Pierre | *Chardin 1699-1779*, Cleveland, 1979.

Wildenstein, George | *Chardin*, Zurich, 1963.

Constable, John 1776 – 1837 | British

Cormack, Malcolm | *Constable*, Oxford, 1986.

Fleming-Williams, Ian | *Constable and His Drawings*, London, 1990.

Rosenthal, Michael | *Constable: The Painter and His Landscape*, London, New Haven, Connecticut, 1982.

Courbet, Gustave 1819 – 1877 | French

Arts Council of Great Britain | *Gustave Courbet 1819-1877*, London, 1978.

Linsay, Jack | *Gustave Courbet, His Life and Art*, Somerset, 1973.

Nochlin, Linda | *Gustave Courbet: a Study of Style and Society*, New York, 1976.

Dance, Nathaniel 1734 – 1811 | British or
Dance, George 1741 – 1825 | British

George, M.D. | *Social Change and Graphic Satire from Hogarth to Cruikshank*, London, 1967.

Sabin Gallery | *The Sublime and Beautiful: Portraits and Other Drawings by Nathaniel Dance R.A. and George Dance R.A.*, London, 1973.

Victoria and Albert Museum | *English Caricature 1620 to the Present*, London, 1984.

Daumier, Honoré 1808 – 1879 | French

Adhémar, Jean | *Honoré Daumier*, Paris, 1954.

Larkin, Oliver | *Daumier: Man of His Time*, London, 1967.

Maison, K.E. | *Honoré Daumier: Catalogue Raisonné of the Paintings, Watercolours and Drawings*, 2 volumes, London, 1968.

David, Jacques-Louis 1748 – 1825 | French

Brookner, Anita | *Jacques-Louis David*, London, 1980.

Delecluze, Etienne | *Louis David, son école et son temps*, Paris, 1855.

Wildenstein, D. and G. | *Documents complémentaires au Catalogue de l'oeuvre de Louis David*, Paris, 1973.

Degas, Edgar 1834 – 1917 | French

Lemoisne, P.A. | *Degas et son oeuvre*, 4 volumes, Paris, 1946.

Thomson, Richard | *The Private Degas*, London, 1987.

Villa Medici | *Degas e l'Italia*, Rome, 1984-85.

Delacroix, Eugène 1798 – 1863 | French

Escholier, Raymond | *Delacroix, peintre, graveur, écrivain*, 3 volumes, Paris, 1926-29.

Johnson, Lee | *The Paintings of Eugene Delacroix: A Critical Catalogue 1816-1831*, 2 volumes, Oxford, 1981.

Trapp, Frank A. | *The Attainment of Delacroix*, Baltimore and London, 1970.

Ensor, James 1860 – 1949 | Belgian

Fierens, Paul | *Les Dessins d'Ensor*, Brussels and Paris, 1944.

Gindertael, Roger van | *James Ensor*, New York, 1975.

Haesaerts, Paul | *James Ensor*, Brussels, 1973.

Flaxman, John 1755 – 1826 | British

Colvin, Sidney | *The Drawings of Flaxman in the Gallery of the University College, London*, London, 1876.

Irwin, David | *John Flaxman 1755-1826. Sculptor, Illustrator, Designer*, London, 1979.

Royal Academy of Arts | *John Flaxman R.A.*, edited by David Bindman, London, 1979.

Fragonard, Jean Honoré 1732 – 1806 | French

Cuzin, Jean-Pierre | *Jean-Honoré Fragonard: Life and Work. Complete Catalogue of the Oil Paintings*, New York, 1988.

Léveque, J.J. | *Fragonard*, Paris, 1983.

Wildenstein, George | *Fragonard*, New York and Oxford, 1960.

Friedrich, Caspar David 1774 – 1840 | German

Einem H.v. | *Caspar David Friedrich*, Berlin, 1938.

Sumowski, W. | *Caspar David Friedrich — Studien*, Schweinfurt, 1970.

Tate Gallery | *Caspar David Friedrich 1774-1840: Romantic Landscape Painting in Dresden*, London, 1972.

Füssli, J.H. (Fuseli) 1741– 1825 | Anglo-Swiss

Forster-Hahn, Françoise | *Old Master Drawings from the Collection of Kurt Meissner, Zürich*, Stanford, 1969.

Schiff, Gert | *Johann Heinrich Füssli 1741-1825*, 2 volumes, Zurich and Munich, 1973.

Tate Gallery | *Henry Fuseli 1741-1825*, London, 1975.

Gauguin, Paul 1848 – 1903 | French

Andersen, Wayne | *Gauguin's Paradise Lost*, New York and London, 1971.

Gray, Christopher | *Sculpture and Ceramics of Paul Gauguin*, Baltimore, 1963.

Stuckey, Charles and Richard Brettell | *Paul Gauguin*, Washington D.C., 1988.

Géricault, Theodore 1791 – 1824 | French

Eitner, Lorenz | *Géricault's Raft of the Medusa*, London, 1972.

—— | *Géricault: His Life and Work*, London, 1983.

Laverssière, Sylvain and Régis Michel | *Géricault*, Paris, 1991.

Girodet de Roucey-Trioson, A.L. 1767 – 1824 | French

Bernier, Georges | *Anne-Louis Girodet*, Paris and Brussels, 1975.

Levitine, George | *Girodet-Trioson: An Iconographical Study*, New York, 1978.

Musée de Montargis | *Girodet. 1767-1824*, Montargis, 1967.

Goya y Lucientes, Francisco 1746 – 1828 | Spanish

Gassier, Pierre and Juliet Wilson | *Goya: His Life and Work*, London, 1971.

—— | *The Drawings of Goya: The Complete Albums*, London, 1973.

Williams, Gwyn A. | *Goya and the Impossible Revolution*, Harmondsworth, 1976.

Greuze, Jean Baptiste 1725 – 1805 | French

Brookner, Anita | *Greuze: The Rise and Fall of an Eighteenth Century Phenomenon*, London, 1972.

Mauclair, C. | *Greuze et son temps*, Paris, 1926.

Munhall, Edgar | *Jean-Baptiste Greuze: 1725-1805*, Hartford, Connecticut, 1976.

Guys, Constantin 1802 – 1892 | French

Baudelaire, Charles | *Selected Writings on Art and Artists, translated and with an introduction by P.E. Charvet*, Harmondsworth, 1972.

Hall, C. | *Constantin Guys*, London, n.d.

Palazzo Braschi | *Constantin Guys: Le pittore della vita moderna*, Rome, 1980.

Hugo, Victor 1802 – 1885 | French

Bory, Jean-François | *Victor Hugo: dessins*, Paris, 1980.

Cornaille, Roger and Georges Herschen | *Victor Hugo dessinateur*, Paris, 1963.

Géorgel, Pierre | *Drawings by Victor Hugo*, London, 1974.

Ingres, Jean-Dominique 1780 – 1867 | French

Hattis, Phyllis | *Ingres' Sculptural Style: A Group of Unknown Drawings*, Cambridge, Massachusetts, 1973.

Pansu, Evelyne | *Ingres dessins*, Paris, 1977.

Wildenstein, George | *Ingres*, Oxford, New York, 1954.

Khnopff, Fernand 1858 – 1921 | Belgian

Delevoy, R., C. de Croës, and G. Ollinger-Zinque | *Fernand Khnopff: catalogue de l'oeuvre*, Brussels, 1979.

Howe, Jeffery | *The Symbolist Art of Fernand Khnopff*, Ann Arbor, Michigan, 1982.

Musée des Arts Décoratifs | *Fernand Khnopff: 1858-1921*, Paris, 1979.

Klee, Paul 1879 – 1940 | Swiss

Grohmann, Jürgen | *Paul Klee Handzeichnungen*, 3 volumes, Berne, 1973-1979.

Verdi, Richard | *Klee and Nature*, New York, 1984.

Werckmeister, O.K. | *Paul Klee, Leben und Werk*, Stuttgart, 1987.

Klimt, Gustav 1862 – 1918 | Austrian

Hofmann, Werner | *Gustav Klimt,* New York, 1971.

Nebehay, Christian | *Gustav Klimt: Documentation,* Vienna, 1969.

Strobl, Alice | *Gustav Klimt: Drawings and Paintings,* Salzburg, 1962.

Kollwitz, Käthe 1867 – 1945 | German

Bittner, Herbert | *Käthe Kollwitz Drawings,* New York and London, 1959.

Klipstein, August | *The Graphic Works of Käthe Kollwitz,* New York, 1955.

Kollwitz, Käthe | *The Diary and Letters of Käthe Kollwitz,* edited by Hans Kollwitz, translated by Richard and Clara Winston, Chicago, 1955.

Lancret, Nicolas 1690 – 1743 | French

Holmes, Mary | *Nicolas Lancret 1690-1743,* New York, 1991.

Kalnier, Wend Graf and Michael Levey | *Art and Architecture of the Eighteenth Century in France,* Harmondsworth, 1972.

Wildenstein, G. | *Lancret,* Paris, 1924.

Manet, Edouard 1832 – 1883 | French

Hanson, Ann Coffin | *Manet and the Modern Tradition,* New Haven, Connecticut, and London, 1977.

de Leiris, A. | *The Drawings of Edouard Manet,* Berkeley, 1969.

Metropolitan Museum of Art | *Manet 1832-1883,* New York, 1983.

Maratta, Carlo 1625 – 1713 | Italian

Bellori, G.P. | *Vita di Guido Reni, Andrea Sacchi e Carlo Maratti* (edited by M. Piacentini), Rome, 1942.

Raffaele, E. | *Notizie della familia de pittore Carlo Maratti,* Monza, 1943.

Wittkower, Rudolf | *Art and Architecture in Italy 1600-1750,* Baltimore, 1958.

Matisse, Henri 1869 – 1954 | French

Barr, Alfred | *Matisse: His Art and His Public,* New York, 1951.

Elderfield, John | *The Drawings of Henri Matisse,* London, 1984.

Gowing, Lawrence | *Henri Matisse,* New York and Toronto, 1979.

Millet, Jean François 1814 – 1875 | French

Fermigier, André | *Jean-François Millet,* New York, 1972.

Herbert, Robert | *Jean-François Millet,* London, 1976.

Murphy, Alexandra R. | *Jean-François Millet,* Boston, 1984.

Modigliani, Amedeo 1884 – 1920 | Italian

Lauthemann, Jacques | *Catalogue raisonné de l'oeuvre de Modigliani,* Barcelona, 1970.

Lipchitz, Jacques | *Modigliani,* London, 1953.

Mann, Carol | *Modigliani,* London, 1980.

Mondrian, Piet 1872– 1944 | Dutch

Milner, John | *Mondrian,* London, 1992.

Seuphor, Michel | *Piet Mondrian: Life and Work,* New York, 1956.

Welsh, Robert | *Piet Mondrian's Early Career: The "Naturalistic" Periods,* New York and London, 1977.

Monet, Claude 1840 – 1926 | French

House, John | *Claude Monet,* London, 1978.

Isaacson, Joel | *Observation and Reflection: Monet,* Oxford, 1978.

Seitz, William | *Claude Monet,* New York, London, 1961.

Moreau, Gustave 1826 – 1898 | French

Kaplan, Julius | *Gustave Moreau,* Los Angeles, 1974.

Paladilhe, Jean | *Gustave Moreau,* Paris, 1971.

von Holten, Ragnar | *Gustave Moreau, Symbolist,* Stockholm, 1965.

Munch, Edvard 1863 – 1944 | Norwegian

Messer, Thomas | *Edvard Munch*, New York, London, 1972.

National Gallery of Art | *Edvard Munch: Symbols and Images*, Washington D.C., 1978.

Svenaens, Gösta | *Edvard Munch. Im Männlichen Gehirn*, 2 volumes, Lund, 1972.

Nattier, Jean Marc 1685 – 1766 | French

Dimier, Louis | *Les peintres français du XVIIIème siècle*, Paris and Brussels, 1930.

Nolhac, P. de | *Nattier, peintre de la cour de Louis XV*, Paris, 1905.

—— | *Nattier*, Paris, 1925.

Piazzetta, Giovanni Battista 1683 – 1754 | Italian

Jones, Leslie | *The Paintings of Giovanni Battista Piazzetta*, Ann Arbor, 1981.

Mariuz, Adriano | *Opera completa del Piazzetta*, Milan, 1982.

Ruggeri, Ugo | *Disegni Piazzetteschi*, Bergamo, 1973.

Picasso, Pablo Ruiz y 1881 – 1973 | Spanish

Barr, A. | *Picasso: Fifty Years of His Art*, New York, 1946.

Richardson, John | *A Life of Picasso: Vol. I. 1881-1906*, New York, 1991.

Zervos, Christian | *Pablo Picasso*, 33 volumes, Paris, 1932-1978.

Piranesi, Giovanni Battista 1720 – 1778 | Italian

Scholz, Janos | *Baroque and Romantic Stage Design*, New York, 1949.

Thomas, Hilton | *The Drawings of Giovanni Battista Piranesi*, London, 1954.

Wilton-Ely, John | *The Mind and Art of Giovanni Battista Piranesi*, London, 1978.

Poussin, Nicolas 1594 – 1665 | French

Blunt, Anthony | *The Paintings of Nicolas Poussin: a Critical Catalogue*, London, 1966.

—— | *The Drawings of Nicolas Poussin*, 4 volumes, London, 1953.

Mérot, Alain | *Nicolas Poussin*, New York, 1990.

Puvis de Chavannes, Pierre 1824 – 1898 | French

Arts Council of Great Britain | *French Symbolist Painters: Moreau, Puvis de Chavannes, Redon and Their Followers*, London and Liverpool, 1972.

d'Argencourt, Louise, et al. | *Puvis de Chavannes 1824-1898*, Ottawa, 1977.

Wattenmaker, Richard | *Puvis de Chavannes and the Modern Tradition*, Toronto, 1975.

Redon, Odilon 1840 – 1916 | French

Bacou, Roseline | *Musée du Louvre: La donation Arï et Suzanne Redon*, Paris, 1984.

Druick, Douglas et al. | *Odilon Redon: Prince of Dreams 1840-1916*, Chicago, 1994.

Hobbs, Richard | *Odilon Redon*, London, 1977.

Rembrandt van Rijn 1606 – 1669 | Dutch

Benesch, Otto | *The Drawings of Rembrandt: A Critical Chronological Catalogue*, 6 volumes, London, 1954-57.

Gerson, Horst | *Rembrandt Paintings*, Amsterdam, 1968.

Rosenberg, J. | *Rembrandt*, 2 volumes, London, 1964.

Renoir, Pierre Auguste 1841 – 1919 | French

Fosca, François | *Renoir: His Life and Works*, London, 1961.

Perruchot, H. | *La vie de Renoir*, Paris, 1964.

Rewald, John | *Renoir Drawings*, New York, 1946.

Robert, Hubert 1733 – 1806 | French

Beau, M. | *Dessins d'Hubert Robert au Musée de Valance*, Lyon, 1968.

Berda, H. | *Die Ruine in den Bildern Hubert Robert*, Munich, 1967.

de Nolhac, P. | *Hubert Robert*, Paris, 1910.

Rodin, F. Auguste R. 1840 – 1917 | French

Arts Council of Great Britain | *Rodin: Sculpture and Drawings*, London, 1970.

Elsen, Albert | *Rodin*, New York, 1963.

Giessbuhler, Elizabeth | *Rodin: Late Drawings*, London, 1963.

Romney, George 1734 – 1802 | British

Chan, Victor | *Leader of My Angels: William Hayley and His Circle*, Edmonton, 1982.

Jaffé, Patricia | *Drawings by George Romney from the Fitzwilliam Museum, Cambridge*, Cambridge, 1977.

Rump, Gerhard C. | *George Romney (1734-1802) Zur Bildform der Bürgerlichen Mitte in der Englischen Neoklassik*, 2 volumes. Hildesheim, New York, 1974.

Rossetti, Dante Gabriel 1828 – 1882 | British

Doughty, Oswald | *A Victorian Romantic: Dante Gabriel Rossetti*, London, 1960.

Royal Academy of Arts | *Dante Gabriel Rossetti: Painter and Poet*, London, 1973.

Surtees, Virginia | *The Paintings and Drawings of Dante Gabriel Rossetti (1828-1882): A Catalogue Raisonné*, 2 volumes, Oxford, 1971.

Rubens, Peter Paul 1577 – 1640 | Flemish

Burchard, L. and R.A. d'Hulst | *Rubens Drawings*, 2 volumes, Brussels, 1963.

Jaffé, Michael | *Rubens and Italy*, New York, 1977.

Rooses, M. | *L'Oeuvre de P.P. Rubens*, 5 volumes, Antwerp, 1886-1892.

Schiele, Egon 1890 – 1918 | Austrian

Comini, Alessandra | *Egon Schiele's Portraits*, Berkeley, Los Angeles, and London, 1974.

Leopold, Rudolf | *Egon Schiele, Gemälde, Aquarelle, Zeichnungen*, Salzburg, 1973.

Mitsch, Erwin | *Egon Schiele*, Salzburg and Vienna, 1974.

Seurat, Georges 1859 – 1891 | French

Herbert, Robert | *Seurat's Drawings*, New York, 1962.

Thompson, Richard | *Seurat*, Oxford, 1985.

Zimmermann, Michael F. | *Seurat and the Art Theory of His Time*, Antwerp, 1991.

Toulouse-Lautrec, Henri de 1864 – 1901 | French

Adriani, G. | *Toulouse-Lautrec und das Paris um 1900*, Cologne, 1978.

Dortu, M.G. | *Toulouse-Lautrec et son oeuvre . . .*, 6 volumes, New York, 1971.

Murray, Gale B. | *Toulouse-Lautrec: The Formative Years 1878-1891*, Oxford, 1991.

van Gogh, Vincent 1853 – 1890 | Dutch

de la Faille, J.B. | *The Works of Vincent van Gogh: His Paintings and Drawings*, Amsterdam and London, 1970.

Hulsker, J. | *The Complete van Gogh Paintings, Drawings and Sketches*, New York, 1980.

van Gogh, Vincent | *The Complete Letters of Vincent van Gogh*, 3 volumes, Greenwich, Connecticut, London, 1958.

Watteau, Jean Antoine 1684 – 1721 | French

Parker, K.T. and J. Mathey | *Antoine Watteau: Catalogue complet de son oeuvre dessiné*, Paris, 1957.

Posner, Donald | *Antoine Watteau*, London, 1984.

Rosenberg, Pierre and M. Morgan-Grasselli | *Watteau*, Washington, D.C., Paris, and Berlin, 1984-85.

West, Benjamin 1738 – 1820 | American-British

Dillenberger, John | *Benjamin West: The Context of His Life and Work, with Particular Attention to Paintings with Religious Subject Matter*, San Antonio, 1977.

Evans, Grose | *Benjamin West and the Taste of His Times*, Carbondale, Illinois, 1959.

Kraemer, Ruth | *Drawings by Benjamin West and His Son Raphael Lamar West*, New York, 1975.